Litlinks:
Activities for Connected Learning in Elementary Classrooms

Dena G. Beeghly
West Chester University

Catherine M. Prudhoe
West Chester University

Boston   Burr Ridge, IL   Dubuque, IA   Madison, WI   New York   San Francisco   St. Louis
Bangkok   Bogotá   Caracas   Kuala Lumpur   Lisbon   London   Madrid   Mexico City
Milan   Montreal   New Delhi   Santiago   Seoul   Singapore   Sydney   Taipei   Toronto

McGraw-Hill Higher Education
*A Division of The **McGraw-Hill** Companies*

LITLINKS: ACTIVITIES FOR CONNECTED LEARNING IN ELEMENTARY CLASSROOMS
Beeghly/Prudhoe

Published by McGraw-Hill, an imprint of the McGraw-Hill Companies, Inc., 1221 Avenue of the Americas,
New York, NY 10020.

2 3 4 5 6 7 8 9 0 QPD/QPD 0 9 8 7 6 5 4 3

ISBN 0-07-251063-3

DEDICATION

To those we teach and to those who have taught us.

Contents

Appendix   National Standards for the Elementary Classroom   165

Preface

How does a book begin? From where does it come? Without knowing it, we have been "writing" this book since we began working with pre-service and in-service teachers. Our classes have always emphasized showing over telling. Therefore, demonstration lessons that provide our students with models for using children's literature across the curriculum in meaningful ways are an integral part of the courses we teach. While these experiences are very effective, only so much can be accomplished in the course of a semester. Time, in this case, was not on our side. Students were wishing for more and so were we. We began to search for an activity book that would pick up where we left off—a book that students could carry with them into their classrooms. Such a book would provide inspiration as well as models and examples. After searching, we were sorely disappointed. Many of the books simply present "make-n-take" or "cute" activities that have little to do with real learning in elementary classrooms. Others are geared for a limited audience, usually preschool or the primary grades. In this case, necessity was the mother of our invention. We decided to write an activity book that would offer appropriate and meaningful ways to infuse children's literature in pre-kindergarten through upper-elementary grade curricula. We hope this book will both guide and inspire teachers to use children's literature to enrich the personal and academic lives of students in classrooms.

LINKS TO NATIONAL STANDARDS

National professional organizations (Consortium of National Arts Education Associations, National Council of Teachers of English Language Arts, International Reading Association, National Council of Teachers of Mathematics, National Research Council, and National Council for the Social Studies) have undertaken the task of articulating education standards that recommend what children should know and be able to do in the arts, language arts/reading, mathematics, science, and social studies. These standards are part of ongoing efforts to improve the education of students in the United States. In *Litlinks: Activities for Connected Learning in Elementary Classrooms,* we discuss the national standards and present specific standards for each activity. By linking the national standards to our activities, we hope to demonstrate for teachers how they can develop and implement original, developmentally appropriate, engaging activities that are intellectually important and educationally sound.

ORGANIZATION AND CONTENT

Litlinks: Activities for Connected Learning in the Elementary Classroom is designed to be used as a supplemental text in children's literature and reading/language arts courses at the pre-service and graduate levels. The text contains seven chapters: three of which set the stage for teaching effectively with children's literature and four of which provide examples of activities using specific children's books.

The first chapter introduces the reader to the richness and power of literature for children. The second chapter presents an overview of three methods for integrating literature in the elementary classroom: one book at a time, the thematic unit approach, and the generative curriculum approach. A discussion of the National Standards for mathematics, reading and language arts, science, social studies, and the arts examines how teachers can use trade books to implement these standards in their curricula. Chapter 3 discusses effective reading and language arts strategies that teachers may use as they plan their interdisciplinary curricula. In addition to several one-book-at-a-time lessons, an example demonstrating how a teacher might use children's literature in the generative curriculum approach is included.

The next four chapters present the rationale for and examples of activities that connect literature selections with different content areas in the elementary curriculum. Chapter 4 focuses on children's books that engage the artists (dancers, singers, musicians, actors, and visual artists) in us. In this chapter, examples of using the one-book-at-a-time method in primary and intermediate grades as well as a unit on "Rock Art" for the intermediate grades are included. In Chapter 5, we explore the use of children's literature in mathematics. In addition to examples using the one-book-at-a-time method, a unit on "Measurement" for the primary grades is provided.

The final two chapters present the thematic unit approach for both primary and intermediate grade levels. The focus of Chapter 6 is to connect children's books with the excitement of science. The last chapter demonstrates the use of children's literature as an avenue to explore history and the social studies.

SPECIAL FEATURES

Good teachers always have had the desire to plan engaging activities/lessons for their students that result in meaningful learning experiences. *Litlinks: Activities for Connected Learning in the Elementary Classroom* provides special features that we believe will support teachers in their efforts. These special features illustrate the unique nature of this text.

- **Connecting to Standards** provides a listing of national standards that apply to each activity.
- An appendix includes the **National Standards for the Arts; English Language Arts/Reading; Mathematics; Science;** and **Social Studies** for the elementary grades.
- Each chapter provides a wealth of suggestions for **Children's Literature** related to the chapter.
- Suggestions for **Web sites** related to the activities in Chapters 3 through 7 are listed on *Childlit,* the McGraw-Hill children's literature Web site at *www.mhhe.com/childlit.*

ACKNOWLEDGMENTS

Writing this book has been a wonderful journey. Like most people who set off on journeys, we planned where and how we would go. Our prospectus was our map. We began our writing "trip" thinking we would present cross-curricular activity ideas to accompany read-alouds of selected children's books. Along the way we took detours that were not on our map. These detours, often inspired by our reviewers, enriched our writing and, we think, our book. Thanks are due to the many reviewers whose critical comments and thoughtful suggestions greatly improved the final manuscript:

Laura Apol, Michigan State University

Susan Bennett, Humbold State University

Christine Doyle, Central Connecticut University

Terrance Flaherty, Minnesota State University

Lynn Graham, Iowa State University

Linda LeBert, McNeese State University

Carolyn Lott, University of Montana

Susan Knell, Pittsburgh State University

Priscilla Kurchinski, Colorado Christian College

Amy S. Meekins, Salisbury State University

Sheila Most, Eastern Michigan University

Sharon O'Neal, Southwest Texas State University

Leslie Perry, Eastern Tennessee State University

Louise Stearns, Southern Illinois University

Nancy Upchurch, University of North Alabama

We are indebted to Penny McElroy, Redlands University, and Martha Drobnak, West Chester University, for their helpful suggestions. We thank, too, the many students we have taught and who have taught us what it means to be a teacher and learner.

A thousand thank yous go to Dena's father, Wood Beeghly, and Cathy's mother, Margaret Prudhoe. Their delight in us and this project has truly been a gift.

Finally, to the editors at McGraw-Hill—Beth Kaufman, who suggested our project to Cara Harvey, and especially to Cara, who graciously and patiently worked with two novices—we give our thanks and heartfelt gratitude.

CHAPTER 1

The Power of Story

"Once, oh small children round my knee, there were no stories on earth to hear."

—GAIL HALEY

In her picture book *A Story, A Story*, Gail Haley retells an African tale that explains how stories came to be a part of life on earth. According to the tale, there was a time when all the stories in the world belonged to the Sky God, Nyame. Because they were so precious to their owner, they were kept by his throne in a box made of gold. When Nyame is asked by Ananse, the spider man, to name his price for the stories, the Sky God roars with laughter. He finds it impossible to believe that one very small, weak old man will be able to pay the price he has set. As readers and listeners, so do we. How can Ananse possibly capture the "leopard of-the-terrible-teeth, the hornet who-stings-like-fire, and the fairy whom-men-never-see"? But we don't know Ananse. Our skepticism soon turns to admiration as Ananse proves himself to be clever, confident, and cunning. We cheer and howl with delight as the spider man outwits all of his opponents. As Huck, Hepler, Hickman, & Kiefer (2001) remind us, "From the time of the earliest primitive fire circle to the Middle Ages—when minnesingers and troubadours sang their ballads—to the modern age of television, people have found delight in hearing stories and poems" (p. 575).

If we stop and take a moment to consider the place stories have in our lives, we realize that we are surrounded by them. As a matter of fact, our daily lives are filled with stories. Stories are exchanged on the way to work and school. They are recounted in places of learning, worship, and business. We use them not only to entertain ourselves and others but also to remember, to share experiences, to begin conversations, or to make points in a discussion (Rosen, 1993). Janet A. Langer (1995) believes that literature, like the everyday stories we tell, provides us with opportunities to examine ourselves and the world around us, to figure out who we are and who we want to be, and to contemplate the kind of place that we would like the world to be. Think back to *A Story, A Story*. Like many folk tales, the message is clear: yes, the world is full of challenges, but take heart. If we use our wits and have confidence, we, like

Ananse, can succeed. We should never underestimate ourselves or others; for if we do, we may, like the Sky God, lose something precious. Clearly, the story has much to tell us about the world and ourselves.

THE PLACE OF CHILDREN'S LITERATURE IN TODAY'S CLASSROOMS

Celebrating Children's Individuality

As we read, each of us creates meaning for ourselves. We relate to the characters, plot, theme, and setting based on who we are and the experiences we have lived. The meanings we create as we read can and do vary from person to person. The same is true for children. While research (Zimet, 1966; Lynch-Brown, 1977; Wolfson, Manning, & Manning, 1984) suggests that age and gender affect preferences, we need to remember that individual differences exist within generalities. Summers and Lukasevich (1983) found in their study of 1,000 children living in three different communities that reading preference is highly variable and is influenced by the communities in which children live as well as by age and gender. As teachers, we might think we know how the children in our classrooms will respond to a certain story on the basis of our own reactions or the reactions of students from previous years. But we need to be cautious in our generalizations. Each child brings his unique experiences and individuality to the reading.

All we have to do is look within our classrooms during DEAR (Drop Everything And Read) or free reading time to understand that children have varied and particular interests, different purposes for reading, and different ideas about the books that are right for them. Sometimes these choices make perfect sense to us on the basis of what we know about the individual children. Janice's family is raising a guide dog, and so at the moment any book about dogs is sure to find its way into her hands. Darius, on the other hand, is trying a challenging book that is popular with many of his classmates. Two best friends, Amanda and Rosa, prefer to read together, most often rereading a book their teacher read during story time.

At other times, children surprise us. Micah reads only books about Curious George during DEAR time. He's willing to read what his teacher suggests during the rest of the day, but for free reading, his choice is always the same. Sharon, a very able reader, prefers to revisit books that she has already read. Tamika, an exceedingly quiet student, uncharacteristically takes charge of a small group that listens to her read aloud classroom favorites. Children are constantly communicating what and how they like to read. Our job is to use this information as we plan instruction and choose reading materials for our classrooms.

Acknowledging Children's Diversity

Perhaps more than at any other time in our history, children need to read and hear stories that assure them that society values them and their families, that we believe in them, and that we expect them to succeed. Today, American schools are microcosms of the world. In any given classroom, we may find children from many different ethnic, racial, and religious backgrounds from a variety of income levels, and who may or may not have identified disabilities. All of these children need to see themselves in the curriculum. When school is relevant to children's lives, they are more eager to participate, and they learn better. Furthermore, they are likely to see the value of education and to believe that they can succeed and perhaps change the world for the better. Good literature can play an important role in helping all children see themselves in the curriculum. Picture the delight of Mexican-American children as they listen to their teacher read aloud Gary Soto's *Too Many Tamales*. Think about Katie, who after listening to Sook Nyul Choi's *Halmoni and the Picnic*, chooses it during free reading for an entire week because "the little girl in the story looks like me." Or consider George who heads off to college with *Harlem* by Walter Dean Myers because the

book speaks of the rich artistic traditions of African-Americans. These books, as well as many others, help children feel valued and accepted in their schools and classrooms.

Books can help students to see within and beyond themselves. Students need to appreciate and understand cultures and viewpoints that are different from their own. Students reading *Zlata's Diary* by Zlata Filipovic; Mildred Taylor's *Roll of Thunder, Hear My Cry;* or *Sees Behind Trees* by Michael Dorris find themselves in different times or places. It is through reading and conversation that children are able to safely explore the world beyond. Moreover, books provide opportunities for children to gain multiple perspectives. Elementary school children familiar with the story of the three little pigs whoop with delight while listening to Jon Scieszka's *The True Story of the Three Little Pigs*. The book is in part appealing because it captures perfectly the innocent "not me!" tone that all of us have used at one time or another. But, more importantly, the book offers the "other side" of the story. Children now have at their disposal two versions of the same events to examine. Perhaps the truth lies somewhere in between, perhaps not. This juxtaposition of the two tales provides an opportunity for children to ask interesting questions and use their critical thinking skills. In a more serious vein, books such as *Encounter* by Jane Yolen, *Dancing with the Indians* by Angela Shelf Meaderis, and *The Butterfly* by Patricia Polacco give students a way to step outside of their everyday lives and experience events from the perspectives of others.

Older students we know who have read *Escape from Slavery: The Boyhood of Frederick Douglass in His Own Words*, edited and illustrated by Michael McCurdy, report over and over again that they find Douglass' story and words more compelling than any other "school" reading they have done. In their article in *Booklinks*, Lowe & Matthew (2000) point out that "Events in American history take on new meaning as students discover real and fictitious characters who suffered for freedoms they take for granted" (p. 27). Many of today's students simply know that slavery existed in America's distant past. They have had little opportunity to put a human face on slavery. Douglass' story allows them to experience enslavement in a very personal way. Students enter the story and offer Douglass both solace and encouragement as he faces the harsh realities of slavery. These kinds of experiences have the power to transform the learner. They engage students and create intellectual interest, which often leads to a willingness to confront issues that are uncomfortable or controversial.

Fostering Children's Love of Reading

Books are indeed wonderful. They can cause us to laugh or cry. They can help us make sense of our lives and the world in which we live. They have the power to both validate and extend our experiences and thinking. But in order to enjoy these benefits, we must want to read. The landmark publication *Becoming a Nation of Readers: The Report of the Commission on Reading* (Anderson, Hiebert, Scott, & Wilkinson, 1985) strongly recommends that America needs to increase the number of children who enjoy reading and who read widely and frequently. This recommendation gains urgency when we become aware of the fact that while 20 percent of our population is illiterate, only about 20 percent of the competent readers read regularly of their own volition (Anderson et al., 1985).

In order to create lifelong readers, teachers must do something akin to casting a spell over their students. The particular spell we have in mind transforms every student into an inveterate reader. By that we mean a person who reads as naturally as she breathes, who can't imagine a day that doesn't include some kind of self-selected reading. Such a reader reads for the sheer pleasure that comes with being lost in a book. She reads to find out about herself and the world around her. She chooses to read because she enjoys reading.

How can we help such lifelong readers to develop? We assure you that neither magic potions nor incantations are necessary. What is necessary is exposure and access to good books and the time and freedom in which to enjoy them. Book lovers have long known that nothing gets a person wanting to read more than a good book. And the Commission on Reading agrees. Two of its recommendations were that 1) children should be read to

several times a day, and 2) children should spend more time in school reading for pleasure (Anderson et al., 1985).

In terms of developing an appreciation of literature and overall reading ability, there is nothing quite like listening to an eloquent reader as he shares a quality piece of literature. A forty-something friend of ours counts fourth grade as his very best year in school because he was fortunate to have a teacher who set aside time each day to share a chapter from a book he thought the class would love. Jerry and his classmates were introduced to E. B. White's *Stuart Little* and *Charlotte's Web*, along with Roald Dahl's *James and the Giant Peach* during that wonderful year. Perhaps the rest of us can remember when we met those books for the very first time, too. We, like Jerry, may have fallen in love with books because a teacher shared favorite stories and poems with us. Many of our preservice teachers bring very worn copies of Shel Silverstein's *Where the Sidewalk Ends: Poems and Drawings* to class when we ask them to share a book they came to love in school.

Today we understand that reading aloud to students—no matter what age—serves many instructional purposes. The teacher who shared Shel Silverstein's poetry with us helped us fall in love with words, books, and reading. And even though we didn't know it, while we were giggling over "Cynthia, Sylvia Sara Stout Would Not Take the Garbage Out," our teacher was modeling how a competent and fluent reader sounds. Just as importantly, she was teaching us how a skilled reader thinks when she paused to share her thoughts about a character or what might happen next.

As we listened to Silverstein's poems or E. B. White's stories, we discovered that book language contains a lyrical quality lacking in everyday speech. We were exposed to wonderful new words and phrases like "gloomy," "cluttered," "gnarled," "spidery corner," and "shadowy silence," all found in *Kele's Secret* by Tololwa M. Mollel. We learned about characters, setting, and plot, as well as what makes for a good story. With our teacher's help, we learned how to make predictions and how to confirm or change those predictions when necessary. Our oral language, background knowledge, and writing ability all increased and became richer as we listened to stories and poems (Dressel, 1990; Feitelson, Kita, & Goldstein, 1986).

We also know that just as with any other skill, the more we read the better we read. The expression "practice makes perfect" comes to mind. Independent or recreational reading enhances comprehension, vocabulary, and fluency. We understand that it also helps increase background knowledge. Perhaps most importantly, we know it promotes reading as a lifelong activity. The question, of course, is what can classroom teachers do to encourage students to "practice"? The research on motivation and reading is clear. Just as we are more inclined to practice the piano or work on our forehand in tennis if playing the piano or tennis is enjoyable for us, we are more willing to read if the experience is pleasurable. The Commission on Reading recognized that, if children are going to become competent readers who like to read, they need to have access to a wide selection of reading materials, to be able to choose what they want to read, and to have time to read whatever they choose during the school day. How much time? The Commission recommends that by third or fourth grade children should be spending two hours a week engaged in free reading while in school (Anderson et al., 1985). Students at all grade levels also need teachers and librarians who can assist them in selecting engaging and appropriate books geared to their interests.

CONCLUSION

We began this chapter with the story of Ananse, the spider man, who successfully overcame the sky god's challenges and thus was able to share Nyame's precious stories with his village and the world. As we have seen, children's literature can speak to children's diverse interests, their heritages, and their development as lifelong readers.

Certainly reading aloud and providing children with time to read independently are essential parts of the curriculum. But we can't stop there. We believe teachers may increase the likelihood of fostering reading as a habit of the heart and the mind if children are immersed in literature throughout the school day. The purpose of this book is to share examples of how to integrate children's literature into the curriculum. We believe that connecting literature to the academic subjects and the arts enriches learning. Through books we can find the dancer, painter, cook, mathematician, or scientist within us. We hope that what we have provided sparks creative juices and demonstrates how to integrate children's literature throughout the curriculum.

Children's Literature Cited in the Chapter

Choi, S. N. (1993). *Halmoni and the Picnic.* Illustrated by K. M. Dugan. Boston: Houghton Mifflin.

Dahl, R. (1962). *James and the Giant Peach.* Illustrated by N. Burkert. New York: Alfred A. Knopf.

Dorris, M. (1996). *Sees Behind Trees.* New York: Hyperion.

Filipovic, Z. (1995). *Zlata's Diary.* New York: Penguin Books.

Haley, G. (1970). *A Story, A Story: An African Tale.* New York: Atheneum.

McCurdy, M. (Ed.). (1994). *Escape from Slavery: The Boyhood of Frederick Douglass in His Own Words.* Ilustrated by M. McCurdy. New York: Alfred A. Knopf.

Meaderis, A. S. (1991). *Dancing with the Indians.* Illustrated by S. Byrd. New York: Scholastic Inc.

Mollel, T. M. (1997). *Kele's Secret.* Illustrated by C. Stock. New York: Dutton.

Myers, W. D. (1997). *Harlem.* Illustrated by C. Myers. New York: Scholastic Press.

Polacco, P. (2000). *The Butterfly.* New York: Philomel Books.

Scieszka, J. (1989). *The True Story of the Three Little Pigs.* Illustrated by L. Smith. New York: Viking.

Silverstein, S. (1963). *Where the Sidewalk Ends: Poems and Drawings.* New York: Harper & Row.

Soto, G. (1992). *Too Many Tamales.* Illustrated by E. Martinez. New York: Putnam Books.

Taylor, M. (1976). *Roll of Thunder, Hear My Cry.* Illustrated by J. Pinkney. New York: Dial Books.

White, E. B. (1952). *Charlotte's Web.* Illustrated by G. Williams. New York: Harper & Row.

White, E. B. (1945). *Stuart Little.* Illustrated by G. Williams. New York: Harper & Row.

Yolen, J. (1992). *Encounter.* New York: Harcourt Brace.

References

Anderson, R. C., Hiebert, E. H., Scott, J. A., & Wilkinson, I. A. G. (1985). *Becoming a Nation of Readers: The Report of the Commission on Reading.* Urbana, IL: Center for the Study of Reading, University of Illinois.

Dressel, J. H. (1990). The effect of listening to and discussing different qualities of children's literature on the narrative writing of fifth graders. *Research in the Teaching of English, 24,* 397–414.

Feitelson, D., Kita, B., & Goldstein, A. (1986). Effects of listening to stories on first graders' comprehension and use of language. *Research in the Teaching of English, 20,* 339–356.

Huck, C., Hepler, S., Hickman, J., & Kiefer, B. (2001). *Children's Literature in the Elementary School.* Boston, MA: McGraw-Hill.

Langer, J. A. (1995). *Envisioning Literature: Literary Understanding and Literacy Instruction.* New York: Teachers College Press.

Lowe, J. L., & Matthew, K. I. (2000). Struggle for freedom: Slavery to Reconstruction. *Booklinks, 9*(3), 27–31.

Lynch-Brown, C. (1977). Procedures for determining children's book choices: Comparison and criticism. *Reading Horizons, 17,* 243–250.

Rosen, H. (1993). *Troublesome Boy.* London: English and Media Centre.

Summers, E. G., & Lukasevich, A. (1983). Reading preferences of intermediate-grade children in relation to sex, community, and maturation (grade level): A Canadian perspective. *Reading Research Quarterly, 18*(3), 347–360.

Wolfson, B. J., Manning, G. & Manning, M. (1984). Revisiting what children say their reading interests are. *Reading World, 24,* 4–10.

Zimet, S. F. (1966). Children's interests and story preferences. *Elementary School Journal, 67,* 122–133.

CHAPTER 2

Using Stories to Teach

In the first chapter, we described the many ways in which literature enriches the lives of the children we teach. When we move beyond the textbook and use a variety of books in our teaching, we have an opportunity to both broaden and personalize the curriculum. Through the use of trade books, we are able to provide our students with a choice of materials that matches their interests and abilities. Trade books also allow us to extend the sometimes limited information presented in a textbook and offer students a more in-depth and engaging treatment of the subject at hand. In addition, using a variety of sources enables us to expose students to multiple perspectives and up-to-date information on a given topic. Finally, quality literature allows students to experience a variety of author styles that may serve as models for their own writing. Because of all these benefits, professional associations and textbook companies are now encouraging the use of literature to teach content areas such as social studies and science as well as the language arts.

THE NATIONAL STANDARDS

All students deserve to have access to the best educational opportunities and the best educators. Professional organizations have developed stan-

dards that lay the foundation for excellence in education. Each organization—the International Reading Association (IRA), the National Council of Teachers of English (NCTE), the National Council of Teachers of Mathematics (NCTM), the National Research Council (NRC), the National Council for the Social Studies (NCSS), and the Consortium of National Arts Education Associations (CNAEA)—has charged experts in their fields (i.e., content area teachers, researchers, teacher educators, and practitioners) to develop the standards that represent the core knowledge that students should learn throughout their schooling. A listing of the standards developed for the elementary grades can be found in the Appendix. Figure 2.1 provides bibliographic information for further reading. Throughout our book, in the *Connecting to Standards* boxes, we have indicated how the suggested activities link to the National Standards for the intended grade levels. We believe this is an effective way to document accountability while creating dynamic curricula.

INTEGRATING LITERATURE INTO THE CURRICULUM

Teachers continuously search for ways to plan instruction that is purposeful and meaningful for

---

The Consortium of National Arts Education Associations. (1994). *Dance, Music, Theatre, Visual Arts: What Every Young American Should Know and Be Able to Do in the Arts. The National Standards for Arts Education.* Reston, VA: Music Educators National Conference.

The National Council of Teachers of English and The International Reading Association. (1996). *Standards for the English Language Arts.* Urbana, IL: NCTE.

The National Council of Teachers of Mathematics. (2000). *Principles and Standards for School Mathematics.* Reston, VA: NCTM Inc.

The National Research Council. (1996). *National Science Education Standards.* Washington, D. C.: National Academy Press.

The National Council for the Social Studies. (1994). *Curriculum Standards for Social Studies: Expectations of Excellence.* Washington, D. C.: NCSS.

· ⌣ Figure 2.1 ⌣ ·

National Standards of Professional Organizations

children. Good literature can and should be used to help create an integrated curriculum. In an integrated curriculum, literature can be used to teach content in an interconnected and meaningful way. Freeman & Person (1998) remind us that, like our everyday lives, the curriculum is more than the sum of its parts. They suggest that language arts and children's literature can be used to foster the fundamental connections that exist across subject areas. Three of the ways to integrate children's literature into the curriculum include 1) one book at a time, 2) thematic unit planning, and 3) the generative curriculum. Let's look at each of these in more detail.

One Book at a Time

The first and simplest way to integrate literature into the curriculum is by planning instruction around a particular title. Using the book as the catalyst, the teacher implements related activities/lessons designed to enhance student learning across the curriculum. When incorporating literature in this way, selections generally are made because the book is a quality piece that the teacher wishes to share with students. An example using Gary Soto's *Chato's Kitchen* follows.

Sample Lesson

Example: Quesadillas de Chato

Read aloud *Chato's Kitchen* written by Gary Soto and illustrated by Susan Guevara. *Chato's Kitchen* is the classic mice-cat-dog triangle tale set in the barrio. Opportunity knocks when five mice move next door to Chato, a "low-riding" kind of cat. Chato can't believe his luck; the perfect meal has been delivered to his doorstep. Of course he hasn't counted on the mice being friends with Chorizo, a sausage kind of dog. All ends well with a grand fiesta—vegetarian—but fiesta a none the less. Susan Guevara's vibrant illustrations capture the rhythm of life in the barrio.

Preparation
1. Make copies of a recipe for quesadillas. Decide on accompaniments such as salsa, guacamole, etc.
2. Gather the ingredients and equipment for making quesadillas.
3. Practice reading *Chato's Kitchen*. You will want your students to take particular note of how Soto's use of language and Guevara's illustrations convey the setting. Select a few stopping points to discuss language and/or illustrations. Your students' background knowledge will guide your choices.
4. Obtain a copy of "Comida/Food," a poem by Victor M. Valle, which can be found in Norma Panzer's *Celebrate America in Poetry and Art*.

Introduction
Your introduction will depend upon the background knowledge of your students. Tell the children that the book you're going to share takes place in the barrio. Ask if anyone knows what barrio means. Work with the children's answers. Barrio is the Spanish word for neighborhood, and so this book will take us into a Latino neighborhood. At this point, show your students the entire cover so that all can

see the front and back at the same time. Ask what they notice about the cover. Most likely they will mention characters, food, buildings, plants, cars, and trucks. What might these things tell us about the story? What can we tell about the story from the colors the illustrator chose to use? Call the children's attention to the title. Then suggest that children listen to find out why the book is called *Chato's Kitchen* and what happens to the characters on the cover.

Reading the Book

Read the story, stopping periodically to request comments and questions. When finished, solicit personal responses, perhaps the part/illustration that the children liked best. Make sure that you share your thoughts as well.

Curriculum Connections

Language Arts

Revisit the book. Ask students to listen for words that let the reader know the story takes place in the barrio. Reexamine the illustrations. Discuss how the illustrations contribute to defining the setting. Have the students review the plot without mentioning the setting or any references to Latino culture. Record the elements of the story on chart paper, overhead, or blackboard. Suggest to the students that this is a story that could take place anywhere; the author chose to have the story take place in the barrio. Ask the class to consider how the words and the pictures would be different if the story took place somewhere else. What if it took place in their neighborhood? What kind of clothes would the characters wear, what kind of food would Chato cook, what would their names be, what would the characters say? These are all things to consider when thinking about setting. Record student responses; then, either as a class or in groups, pairs, or individually, have students write their own version of this story. (**Literary Elements**.)

Interdisciplinary (Cooking and Language Arts)

Recipe: Use a recipe for quesadillas that you like or the one that follows.

QUESADILLAS
1 can refried beans
1 package 6- to 8-inch round flour tortillas
1 block monterey jack cheese, or 1 package grated "Mexican Mix" cheese.

Directions:
1. Spread 2 T of beans on 1 tortilla and sprinkle a handful of cheese on top.
2. Heat an electric skillet to medium-hot. Place the tortilla on the hot skillet and top with a second tortilla. Cook about a minute and then flip.
3. Cook about another minute on the second side. When the tortilla is golden brown on both sides, transfer to a plate.
4. Caution children to blow on the quesadilla until it is cool enough to eat. The cheese in a freshly cooked quesadilla will be very hot, so be sure students don't bite into it right away.
5. Eat and enjoy!

After enjoying the quesadillas, share the poem "Comida/Food" by Victor M. Valle. Talk with the students about the metaphors in the poem. They've tasted frijoles and tortillas in the quesadillas. They may also have tried salsa or chile. Why do they think the poet chose to describe each food the way he did? How else might the author have chosen to describe each food? You may also want to have students choose foods they like and describe them using the poem's pattern. (**Figurative Language**; **Poetic Styles**.)

Art

Share the information about the illustrator found on the inside jacket. Susan Guevara says that she considers Chorizo to be a self-portrait. Ask students to compare the photo of Guevara with the illustrations of Chorizo. Have students choose characters for self-portraits. The self-portraits can be used to illustrate the class' version(s) of the story or to create a portrait gallery. (**Media, Techniques, and Processes**.)

Depending on the interest of the students, you may want to find out more about the Mexican painter Diego Rivera. The work of Simón Silva, a Chicano painter, may also be of interest for exploring contemporary Mexican-American life. (**Visual Arts**; **History/Culture**.)

Social Studies

Chato's Kitchen may be used along with the stories the students are writing in language arts to investigate local culture or neighborhoods. The story may also lead to an exploration of Mexican and Mexican-American culture. (**Culture**; **Global Connections**.)

Connecting to Standards
Quesadillas de Chato

Language Arts #1: Students read a wide range of print and nonprint texts to build an understanding of texts, of themselves, and of the cultures of the United States and the world.

Language Arts #5: Students employ a wide range of strategies as they write and use different writing process elements appropriately to communicate with different audiences for a variety of purposes.

Language Arts #6: Students apply knowledge structure, language conventions, media techniques, figurative language, and genre to create, critique, and discuss print and nonprint texts (NCTE & IRA, 1996).

The Arts (Visual Arts): Understanding and applying media, techniques, and processes.

The Arts (Visual Arts): Understanding the visual arts in relation to history and cultures (CNAEA, 1994).

Social Studies (Culture): Students explore how cultures express themselves through the arts and oral and written language.

Social Studies (Global Connections): Students explore how exposure to the diversity found in cultural universals (cooking, dance, hospitality, etc.) may lead to global understandings or misunderstandings (NCSS, 1994).

Thematic Planning

A second way to incorporate children's literature is through thematic planning. Most of us feel a tremendous sense of responsibility; what we do and how well we do it affect the lives of the children we teach. It is important that we engage children both intellectually and emotionally. In order to do this, we need to know what topics or issues interest the students in our classrooms as well as the grade level content to be covered. The scope and sequence of the school's or school district's curriculum guides will provide the long-range planning objectives for each grade level. In most cases, how the instruction is delivered is left up to the individual teacher or the grade level team. Integrating curriculum through thematic planning provides students with the means to organize and construct their knowledge within the context of an encompassing topic or theme (Ellis & Stuen, 1998). The unit focus allows children to integrate knowledge from different content areas and different perspectives in a way that makes sense to them. Teachers plan an entire unit of activities and lessons that may last a week or longer around a chosen topic. Researchers have found that student learning is fostered when children's literature selections based on the topic theme are included throughout the unit plan. For example, Morrow, Pressley, Smith, & Smith (1997) found that when children's literature was integrated into science instruction, children learned the targeted concepts and facts better than those who used only textbooks.

The literature selections should represent the diverse nature of our world in terms of gender, race, ethnicity, age, and social class. A variety of genres should also be included. In addition, the texts should span a range of reading abilities and interests. These related literature selections add to the richness of the curriculum whether in science, social studies, or math.

Topic Selection

Thematic planning begins with the selection of the topic to be studied. In many cases, the district's curriculum guide may be a source of topics. Teachers may also choose topics that are of interest to them and the children they teach. Vivian Paley (1997) relates her kindergarten class's year-long involvement with Leo Lionni and his many books in her own book *The Girl with the Brown Crayon*. This author study of Lionni's books was triggered by the children's response to a read-aloud of *Frederick*. While it is highly unusual for units to last longer than a week or two for children in the primary grades, Paley's book illustrates the power children's literature has to hook children and hold their interest.

Webbing

Once a topic is selected, we make decisions about the concepts we plan to teach. An easy way to achieve this task is to develop a topic web. The topic web is a visual scheme that organizes the concepts and illustrates the relationships among them.

The first step in creating a topic web is to brainstorm all the possible ideas related to the theme. As with any brainstorming activity, the result will initially look very disorganized and random. Figure 2.2 is an example of brainstorming for a unit on Farms.

The next step is to take this list of ideas and sort and classify them into related categories. New items may be added and original ideas deleted. Brainstorming and sorting is only the first stage in developing the topic web. Most of us will need to do further research in the library using textbooks, magazines, trade books, and/or the Internet to develop our knowledge of the topic. Depending on the subject matter, we may want to consult local experts or visit a local museum for more information. What is important at this stage is that we become knowledgeable about the topic so that, in

Planting—spring	Harvesting—fall
Vegetables—corn, tomatoes, beans, potatoes	Barns
Grains—wheat, alfalfa, millet, sorghum	Silo
Animals—cattle, sheep, pigs, chickens	Fields
Animal babies	Tractor
Thresher	Dairy
Milking	Stalls
Coop	Sty
Pastures	

· ► Figure 2.2

Brainstorming Information on Farms

turn, we can help the children find answers to their questions. Imagine a first-grader who is enamored with dinosaurs. He's thrilled when the class begins studying these prehistoric animals. During a class discussion about what happened to the dinosaurs, he volunteers that some dinosaurs "got stuck in the mud." Unfortunately, his teacher has predetermined answers in mind and is also unaware of the La Brea Tar Pits. She summarily dismisses the child's idea and moves on to another child. In this real-life scenario, a child's contribution was not valued because of his teacher's lack of knowledge and curiosity. Therefore, the whole class missed out on interesting factual information. Children's unexpected responses can and should be used as jumping-off points for further research. In this way, the classroom truly becomes a place where all are teachers and learners.

The final step is to create the actual web. Begin by placing the theme topic or core in the middle of a piece of paper. Then place each category of information around the core. These are called web strands. The bits of information for each category are called strand supports. Figure 2.3 is the completed topic web for the Farm unit.

DEVELOPING KEY CONCEPTS

Once we've determined the information the unit will cover, the next step is to formulate concepts. What do we expect children to learn from this unit? Each key concept is written in sentence format and explicates important facts or relationships between and among facts about the unit topic. These key concepts should be broadly focused as they form the basis for the development of the learning experiences. After writing the concepts, arrange them in order from the simplest to the most complex. This sequencing helps us plan activities each day based on one or two key concepts and moves the children from a basic understanding to a more complex understanding of the topic. Key concepts for the unit on Farms for kindergarten might include the following:

1. Animals such as cows, pigs, sheep, turkeys, and chickens are considered farm animals. There are different names for adult males, females,

and babies, and they make different sounds (e.g., cows moo, pigs oink, sheep baa, turkeys gobble, chickens cluck).

2. Farm animals live in different areas of the farm because of their diet and differences in their ability to escape: cows and sheep live in fenced pastures or barns and graze on grass and eat grains; pigs live in a fenced sty and eat mostly corn and soybeans; turkeys and chickens live in coops and eat grains.

3. Certain plants and animals are raised on farms because they provide us with food or other products (e.g., leather, wool) that we use in our daily lives.

4. Crops such as vegetables (e.g., corn, tomatoes, potatoes, beans) and grains (e.g., oats, wheat, rice, alfalfa) begin as seeds and need good soil, water, and sunlight to grow.

5. Farmers use large machines to help carry out different chores on the farm, such as a seeder for planting, combine for harvesting, and tractors for hauling. Hand tools such as rakes, shovels, hoes, and pitchforks also are used.

DESIGNING LEARNING ACTIVITIES

Once the key concepts have been formulated we're ready to develop learning activities. The framework includes all content areas: reading, language arts, math, science, social studies, and the arts. Using the long-range curriculum goals set forth by the school or district, we plan activities that meet those goals through the children's discovery of the thematic topic. For example, if kindergartners are working on counting skills in math, we would develop activities that encourage counting using farm-related objects. In addition, we select literature that will captivate children's interests as they explore the unit's content. Certainly, as teachers we need to have a good working knowledge of children's literature, but it is impossible to know all or even most of the books available on a given topic. We find that school librarians and children's librarians in public libraries are invaluable sources of information

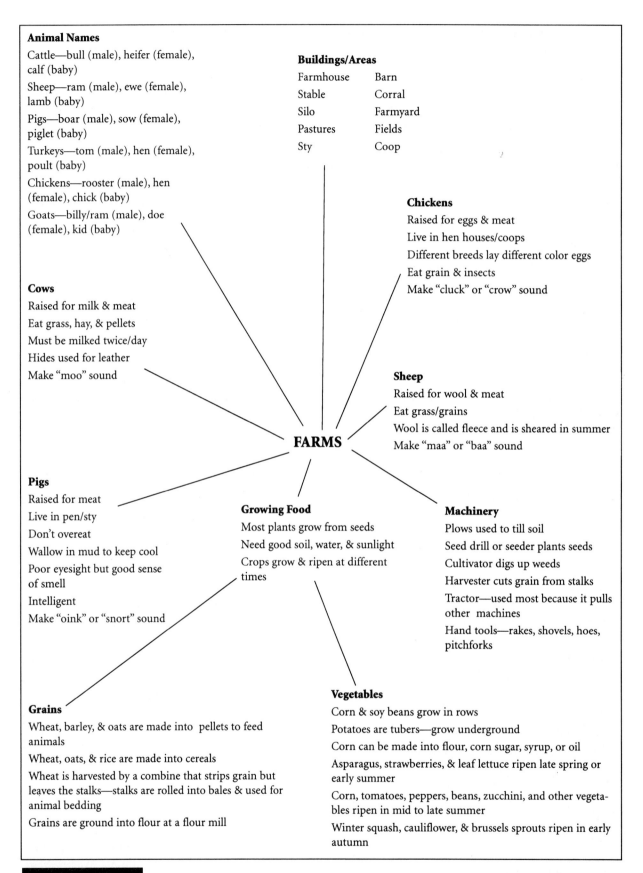

Animal Names

Cattle—bull (male), heifer (female), calf (baby)

Sheep—ram (male), ewe (female), lamb (baby)

Pigs—boar (male), sow (female), piglet (baby)

Turkeys—tom (male), hen (female), poult (baby)

Chickens—rooster (male), hen (female), chick (baby)

Goats—billy/ram (male), doe (female), kid (baby)

Cows

Raised for milk & meat

Eat grass, hay, & pellets

Must be milked twice/day

Hides used for leather

Make "moo" sound

Pigs

Raised for meat

Live in pen/sty

Don't overeat

Wallow in mud to keep cool

Poor eyesight but good sense of smell

Intelligent

Make "oink" or "snort" sound

Grains

Wheat, barley, & oats are made into pellets to feed animals

Wheat, oats, & rice are made into cereals

Wheat is harvested by a combine that strips grain but leaves the stalks—stalks are rolled into bales & used for animal bedding

Grains are ground into flour at a flour mill

Buildings/Areas

Farmhouse   Barn

Stable   Corral

Silo   Farmyard

Pastures   Fields

Sty   Coop

Chickens

Raised for eggs & meat

Live in hen houses/coops

Different breeds lay different color eggs

Eat grain & insects

Make "cluck" or "crow" sound

Sheep

Raised for wool & meat

Eat grass/grains

Wool is called fleece and is sheared in summer

Make "maa" or "baa" sound

FARMS

Growing Food

Most plants grow from seeds

Need good soil, water, & sunlight

Crops grow & ripen at different times

Machinery

Plows used to till soil

Seed drill or seeder plants seeds

Cultivator digs up weeds

Harvester cuts grain from stalks

Tractor—used most because it pulls other machines

Hand tools—rakes, shovels, hoes, pitchforks

Vegetables

Corn & soy beans grow in rows

Potatoes are tubers—grow underground

Corn can be made into flour, corn sugar, syrup, or oil

Asparagus, strawberries, & leaf lettuce ripen late spring or early summer

Corn, tomatoes, peppers, beans, zucchini, and other vegetables ripen in mid to late summer

Winter squash, cauliflower, & brussels sprouts ripen in early autumn

·⌣ Figure 2.3 ⌣·

Topic Web for Farm Unit

when selecting children's literature. There are also many fine periodicals that review children's books, provide annotated bibliographies, and suggest teaching ideas (see Figure 2.4).

For our unit on Farms, we have selected the children's books shown in Figure 2.5. Each book matches one or more of the key concepts and will be used as a focal point for cross-curricular activities. Most of the

books can be used for read-alouds; however, some were chosen for placement in the Literacy Center for individual reading or small-group shared reading.

Let's explore how to use some of these literature selections as springboards for activities within the Farm Unit. *Barnyard Banter, The Tortilla Factory, Tractor,* and *Growing Vegetable Soup* all lend themselves to large-group reading and discussion for con-

---

Book Links. American Library Association, 50 E. Huron Street, Chicago, IL 60611.

The Bulletin of the Center for Children's Books. University of Illinois Press, 54 E. Gregory Drive, Champaign, IL 61820.

Childhood Education. Association for Childhood Education International, 11501 Georgia Avenue, Suite 312, Wheaton, MD 20902.

The Horn Book Magazine. Horn Book, Inc., 11 Beacon Street, Boston, MA 02108.

Language Arts. National Council of Teachers of English, 1111 Kenyon Road, Urbana, IL 61801.

The New York Times Book Review. New York Times Co., 229 W. 43rd Street, New York, NY 10036.

The Reading Teacher. International Reading Association, 800 Barksdale Road, Newark, DE 19714-8139.

•⌐ Figure 2.4 ⌐•

Sources for Book Reviews

Concept 1: Animal names/sounds
Big Red Barn by M. W. Brown
Animal Lingo by P. Conrad
"Quack!" Said the Billy Goat by E. Carle, in *Animals Animals*
Barnyard Banter by D. Fleming
Old MacDonald Had a Farm illus. by G. Rounds
This Is the Farmer by N. Tafuri

Concept 3: Products
The Folks in the Valley by J. Aylesworth
Pancakes, Pancakes! by E. Carle
Bread Is for Eating by D. & P. Gershator
Kele's Secret by T. M. Mollel
The Tortilla Factory by G. Paulsen

Concept 5: Machines
Farming by G. Gibbons
Seasons on the Farm by J. Miller
Tractor by C. Llewellyn

Concept 2: Where animals live/eat
The Folks in the Valley by J. Aylesworth
Farming by G. Gibbons
Seasons on the Farm by J. Miller

Concept 4: Planting
Growing Vegetable Soup by L. Ehlert
Bread Is for Eating by D. & P. Gershator
The Tortilla Factory by G. Paulsen

Other Books
Gathering the Sun by A. F. Ada
The Chicken by E. Emberley
A Year in the Country by D. Florian
Rosie's Walk by P. Hutchins
Who Took the Farmer's Hat? by J. L. Nodset
There's a Hole in the Bucket by N. B. Westcott

•⌐ Figure 2.5 ⌐•

Children's Literature Selections for Farm Unit

Growing Vegetable Soup
Art—Vegetable prints or collage of paper vegetables
Math—Measuring ingredients for soup (measurement)
Math—Poll class for favorite soup and graph results (graphing)
Science—Plant vegetable seeds under different conditions (water and sunlight access). Over several weeks, compare the growth rate of the seedlings. (inquiry, life science)
Social Studies—Visit a nearby farm or farmers' market on a class trip (people, places, and environments)

Barnyard Banter
Art—Sponge-paint farm animals
Creative Dramatics—Children portray the different animals in the story
Language Arts—Match sound words to animals (vocabulary development)
Science—Incubate chicken eggs (inquiry; life science)
Math—Cornmeal in containers for measuring (measurement)

FARMS

The Tortilla Factory
Cooking—Making tostados
Art/Sensory—Playdough
Math—Measuring ingredients for tostados (measurement)
Science—Making secondary and tertiary colors from primary colors
Social Studies—Class discussion of production and distribution of farm products (production, distribution, and consumption)
Language Arts—Record children's reactions to making and eating tostados (language experience)

Tractor
Art—Paint with plastic tractors
Language Arts—Draw picture of farm machine and write a sentence about it (writing)
Social Studies—Discuss different kinds of farm machines of today vs. the past (time, continuity, and change)
Social Studies—Discuss ways new machines have changed farmers lives (science, technology, and society)

· Figure 2.6 ·

Sample Activities for Farm Unit Selections

cept development. Depending on student and teacher interest, cross-curricular activities can be developed for each. Figure 2.6 provides a sample of the different kinds of activities we generated for each book.

The Generative Curriculum

Those of us who have taught a particular grade over a period of time understand that there are some things that remain constant from year to year. We know, for example, if we teach first grade that early in the year many of the children will "fall" out of their chairs. Similarly, the excitement and trepidation that almost all our students experience as they get ready to move to middle school or junior high school is no surprise to a seasoned fourth- or fifth-grade teacher. In addition to our awareness of these developmental characteristics, we also gain understandings of the curricular experiences that work well for our students. In one of our favorite schools, the weekly cook-

ing class is greeted with enthusiasm by the primary students year after year. In the same school, fifth-graders consistently report that the best thing about the year is their participation in a community garden project. While these perennial favorites have an important place in our curriculum, we also know that each group of children we teach comes to us with unique interests, talents, and personalities.

In a generative curriculum, the interests, desires, and needs of the students and teachers are paramount. Rather than teachers predetermining the course of study, children and teachers work collaboratively to develop learning goals, to identify personal research goals, and to locate resources. In other words, the curriculum is generated and formed cooperatively by students and teachers. The learning is authentic, and the curriculum develops organically as expertise and interests evolve. The classroom becomes a learning community in which everyone is a researcher, learner, and teacher (Fisher & Cordiero, 1994).

For example, a group of upper-elementary students who are initially interested in learning about prehistoric life might decide, after reading about cave paintings, that they want to focus on pictographs and petroglyphs. As they learn more about these forms of expression, they begin to wonder about graffiti. Is graffiti the cave art of the twentieth century, they ask. Do people use graffiti today the way we think people in the past used petroglyphs and pictographs? Why do people make graffiti? Is graffiti vandalism or art? These new questions take the group's study off in a different direction. Their interest in and exploration of prehistory has evolved into a study of contemporary communication, art, and social issues.

Because sharing what we learn is an important part of the generative curriculum, opportunities for exchanging information is an integral part of each day. Individuals and groups are also expected to present their research projects to an audience of their peers, families, and/or the community at large. During their presentation, the group described in the previous example would talk about where their intellectual journey led them along with what they learned. These culminating activities may contain oral, written, physical, musical, and/or visual components. For example, the cave art group might design an exhibit entitled "From Ancient Petroglyphs to Modern Graffiti" and provide guided tours through the exhibit.

Clearly, the teacher is no longer at the center of instruction in this approach. She is more of a "guide on the side" learning along with the class and helping students to refine their questions and to locate and effectively learn from a variety of resources. In an article for the journal *Primary Voices*, Nikki Thomas (1994), an elementary school teacher, describes how her teaching changed when she shifted from thematic teaching to a generative approach. She says, "In the past, when I had done thematic units, my role was central. When my students asked questions, I gave them answers....I thought I knew what they wanted to know, and so I provided ways for them to learn that" (Thomas, 1994, p. 36). After embracing the generative approach, Thomas found that her class relished the idea of finding the answers to the questions they had developed. Students could be found at any time of the day reading books and magazines and sharing what they learned with each other and their teacher.

Obviously books and other materials are central to this approach. It is essential for teachers and children to have access to a large number of books, newspapers, and magazines that reflect the different interests, needs, and reading levels of the class. In addition teachers, with the help of librarians, must be able to identify appropriate Internet sites, films or videos, possible guest speakers, and opportunities for field trips. As students become immersed in finding answers to their questions, the teacher engages in purposeful strategy instruction and

---

1. Students and teachers choose a broad topic for study such as Egypt, Cycles, or Sports.
2. The teacher researches the topic in order to have a good working knowledge of the topic and location of resources for student use.
3. The teacher begins to gather resources: books, audiovisuals, magazines, people, Web sites, etc.
4. The teacher develops introductory lessons that provide opportunities for students to explore the possibilities the topic offers for further study.
5. Students and teachers develop a list of questions and research topics.
6. The teacher guides and supports students as they begin their investigations.
7. The teacher acts as a resource for students as they carry out their investigations and create their culminating projects.
8. The teacher arranges for a time and place for projects to be shared.
9. Students and teachers assess the learning that has occurred.

❧ Figure 2.7 ❧

Steps in Developing and Implementing a Generative Approach

facilitates student progress. Figure 2.7 outlines the steps we use in a generative approach.

CONCLUSION

Classrooms filled with stories, poems, and informational texts enhance the learning lives of children and teachers. In this chapter, we have explored three ways of using literature to teach across subject areas in meaningful ways. We see a natural progression from the "one book at a time" approach, to the thematic unit approach, to the generative curriculum. However, successful teachers come in many guises. Some adopt thematic units after becoming skillful with the one-book approach, while others embrace the generative curriculum at the beginning of their careers. No matter which approach we choose to use, the important thing to remember is that literature provides rich and meaningful learning experiences for the children.

Children's Literature Cited in the Chapter

Lionni, L. (1967). *Frederick.* New York: Pantheon.

Panzer, N. (Ed.). (1994). *Celebrate America in Poetry and Art.* New York: Hyperion.

Soto, G. (1995). *Chato's Kitchen.* Illustrated by S. Guevara. New York: Putnam.

Children's Literature Cited for the Farm Unit

Ada, A. F. (1997). *Gathering the Sun.* Illustrated by S. Silva. New York: Lothrop, Lee & Shepard.

Aylesworth, J. (1992). *The Folks in the Valley.* Illustrated by S. Vitale. New York: Harper.

Brown, M. W. (1989). *Big Red Barn.* Illustrated by F. Bond. New York: Scholastic Inc.

Carle, E. (1990). *Pancakes, Pancakes!* Saxonville, MA: Picture Book Studio.

Carle, E. (1989). *Animals, Animals.* New York: Philomel.

Conrad, P. (1995). *Animal Lingo.* Illustrated by B. B. Falk. New York: HarperCollins.

Ehlert, L. (1990). *Growing Vegetable Soup.* New York: Harcourt Brace.

Emberley, E. (1982). *The Chicken.* New York: Little Brown & Company.

Fleming, D. (1994). *Barnyard Banter.* New York: Henry Holt & Company.

Florian, D. (1989). *A Day in the Country.* New York: Greenwillow Books.

Gershator, D., & Gershator, P. (1995). *Bread Is for Eating.* Illustrated by E. Shaw-Smith. New York: Henry Holt & Company.

Gibbons, G. (1988). *Farming.* New York: Holiday House.

Hutchins, P. (1968). *Rosie's Walk.* New York: Macmillan Publishing.

Llewellyn, C. (1995). *Tractor.* New York: DK Publishing Inc.

Miller, J. (1986). *Seasons on the Farm.* Englewood Cliffs, NJ: Prentice Hall.

Mollel, T. M. (1997). *Kele's Secret.* Illustrated by C. Stock. New York: Lodestar Books.

Nodset, J. L. (1963). *Who Took the Farmer's Hat?* Illustrated by F. Siebel. New York: HarperCollins.

Paulsen, G. (1995). *The Tortilla Factory.* Illustrated by R. W. Paulsen. New York: Harcourt Brace.

Rounds, G. (Illus.). (1989). *Old MacDonald Had a Farm.* New York: Holiday House.

Tafuri, N. (1994). *This Is the Farmer.* New York: Greenwillow Books.

Westcott, N. B. (1990). *There's a Hole in the Bucket.* New York: HarperCollins.

References

Ellis, A. K., & Stuen, C. J. (1998). *The Interdisciplinary Curriculum*. Larchmont, NY: Eye on Education Inc.

Fisher, B., & Cordiero, P. (1994). Generating curriculum: Building a shared curriculum. *Primary Voices, 2*(3), 2–7.

Freeman, E. B., & Person, D. G. (1998). *Connecting Informational Children's Books with Content Area Learning*. Boston: Allyn & Bacon.

Morrow, L. M., Pressley, M., Smith, J. K., & Smith, M. (1997). The effect of a literature-based program integrated into literacy and science instruction with children from diverse backgrounds. *Reading Research Quarterly, 32,* 54–76.

Paley, V. (1997). *The Girl with the Brown Crayon.* Cambridge, MA: Harvard University Press.

Thomas, N. (1994). Working toward a generative curriculum. *Primary Voices, 2*(3), 34–40.

CHAPTER 3

Finding and Fostering the Reader in Every Child

We believe that within every student there is a life-long reader waiting to be discovered. The kind of reader we have in mind keeps a stash of books at the ready, haunts the local library in search of the latest book by her favorite author, reads to find out why her perfectly obedient PC has become positively persnickety, and shares what she's reading with the people around her. Sometimes it doesn't take much to uncover an avid reader. Some children seem to have been born to read. Take Andy, who from a very early age was fascinated by words. As a preschooler, he loved playing rhyming games in the car. Then in kindergarten, he spelled Dena's name and remarked that the end of her name was like the beginning of his, only reversed. By the end of second grade, Andy was hooked on the Hardy Boys, and soon after he became a devotee of the Harry Potter series. Andy took to words and stories like the proverbial duck to water.

Other children grow into reading more slowly; they need a good deal of support and often that support entails introducing them to just the right books. As teachers, it is our job to help these children discover the books that will delight and entice them into the world of words and story. Matt, for example, was less taken with words and books than any first-grader we've ever met. He told us repeatedly that there was no reason for him to read with us; frankly he was "too busy" to learn to read. Book after book was rejected. Then Matt met *How Many Bugs in a Box?* by David Carter. He adored the book's pop-ups. Moreover, the book's guessing game format encouraged Matt to take the risks he had so far been unwilling to take. He reread the book so many times that he soon had it memorized. He decided that he had to share this wonderful book, so he read it to anyone who would listen. With one beloved book under his belt, Matt was willing to keep trying this thing called reading. It took hard work on everyone's part, but little by little Matt began to grow into reading. All children, whether they are like Matt or Andy, need to be surrounded by books that delight, transport, tug at their hearts, and/or help them answer their questions about the world around them. An effective language arts program must not only help children to become competent readers, writers, speakers, and listeners, it must also help children care about what they read and wish for more (Sebesta, 1997; Sebesta, 2000).

We know we're on the right track when the before-school conversations center on something students are reading. We know we're on the right track when students enter our classrooms announcing that what they are reading is so interesting, heartbreaking, inspiring, or hilarious that they just have to talk about it right now. We know we're on the right track when students tell us that their conversations about the books they are reading extend beyond the classroom walls.

We know our students are wishing for more when they ask if there are any other books like *The Thief* by Megan Whalen Turner. We nod in agreement when students sigh and tell us that they didn't want Paul Fleischman's *Seedfolks* to end. We know when our first-graders shout "Read it again!" that they are deeply involved in the story and aren't quite ready to let go of the experience. These are magical moments for readers and their teachers. How can we ensure that all of our students not only become competent readers and writers but also have reading and writing lives filled with magical moments?

STANDARDS FOR THE LANGUAGE ARTS

In 1996, the National Council of Teachers of English (NCTE) and the International Reading Association (IRA) issued a joint report entitled *Standards for the English Language Arts* that attempts to answer the above question. The report, which relies upon research and best practices in the language arts, outlines through twelve standards those things all students "need to know about language and be able to do with language" (NCTE & IRA,1996, p. 1) if they are to successfully navigate an increasingly complex world and to construct productive and satisfying lives. The standards begin with a model of language and literacy instruction that places the learner at the center and that emphasizes the active nature of the learning process. Language learning according to this model is affected by content, purpose, and development. In terms of content, students must: 1) be exposed to a wide range of texts—everything from poetry to menus, 2) be able to use a variety of strategies to make meaning as they read and write, and 3) be able to use and adapt their knowledge of the conventions of print in a variety of settings.

While content outlines what is to be learned, purpose lays out the broad goals of the language arts curriculum. Students should take from their language learning an ability to "obtain and communicate information, respond to and create literary texts, learn from and reflect upon their reading and writing and the reading and writing of others, and solve problems" (NCTE & IRA, 1996, pp. 17–18). Finally, development requires that we keep in mind the ways in which students grow into reading, writing, speaking, listening, viewing, and visually representing. Teachers who are interested in supporting children in their journeys toward becoming lifelong readers know that they must 1) offer students a choice of what they will read, 2) build classroom and school communities that have reading and responding to books at their centers, 3) create many opportunities throughout the day for talking and writing about books in meaningful ways, and 4) be knowledgeable and enthusiastic readers themselves in order to help students navigate and appreciate a variety of texts.

READING ALOUD

In her book *The Art of Teaching Reading,* Lucy Calkins (2001) reminds us that one of the few things reading educators agree upon across the board is that children should have numerous opportunities throughout the school day to hear the very best fiction and nonfiction read aloud to them. She goes on to suggest that each day should begin with the teacher reading aloud. Furthermore, this type of experience should be an integral part of science and social studies as well as reading and writing instruction. In a similar vein, Cunningham & Allington (2000) believe that teachers should read different kinds of text to children every day. Their list includes informational material, poetry, tried and true favorites of the age group, and old favorites that are easy to read. We advocate using reading aloud to foster an appreciation of literature, to enrich content area instruction, and to provide transitions throughout the day. For instance, after a particularly boisterous activity, we read something that helps everyone catch their breath and calm down. Following a particularly intense experience, we read a piece that lets us blow off steam and have some fun. Whether you think of reading aloud the way we do or the way Calkins or Cunningham and Allington do, reading aloud should take place in your classroom every day and more than once a day.

Effective read-alouds take planning and preparation. First and foremost, the books we read should be books we love and are excited about sharing. They also should be developmentally appropriate. For example, because of their humorous and cartoonish illustrations, Paul Galdone's and James Marshall's versions of traditional fairy tales are perfect for kindergartners and first-graders. Other versions, because of their more sophisticated illustrations and text, are far too scary. One way to measure whether we have been successful in selecting books for reading aloud is to see how many children choose to revisit the books during free reading time.

We want the experience to be both enjoyable and meaningful. In order for this to happen, we need to consider how we will help the children to make personal connections with the characters, settings, problems, and solutions presented in the text. How familiar with each of these elements are students? Can the class dive into the book after a brief discussion of the title and/or cover, or will we need to provide an experience that builds prior knowledge before beginning? The children may surprise us by the connections they are able to make. We once developed an elaborate prereading experience for Lulu Delacre's *Vejigante Masquerader* because we thought many of our students would have difficulty relating to the setting, Carnival in Puerto Rico. Halfway through our introduction, one of the students exclaimed, "Oh, it's like the Mummers on New Year's!" "Yeah!" the class chorused, and they then began to relay their rich and varied experiences with the Mummers. Not being native Philadelphians, we hadn't made the connection to the Mummer's Parade, but the children certainly had. We scrapped our introduction and began reading the story.

We plan where to stop and to elicit comments or have the children make predictions. Our questions should be open-ended and thought-provoking. It is important to be flexible, knowing that as the children respond our plan may change. We make sure to spend time during and after finishing the text to solicit personal responses from the children. Students should feel free to ask questions, talk about their favorite part, and share how the book makes them feel. It is important that we share our thinking and feelings as well. This is also a time when we help students make connections to other texts. Reading researchers (Smith, 1988; Myers, 1992; Peterson & Eeds, 1990) believe that this kind of interaction helps students to both broaden and deepen their understanding of the written word. It also stimulates thinking and builds comprehension strategies as the teacher models how a skilled reader approaches and thinks about text.

We are careful not to "overtalk" the text. Too many questions turn the experience into a testing situation. Too much discussion causes the children to lose interest. A very conscientious praticum student of ours was mortified when one of her small charges announced, "I'm sick of this book! Get on with it!" His comment caused her to reevaluate her pacing and use of questioning. Table 3.1 provides suggestions for planning successful read-alouds.

READER RESPONSE

Louise Rosenblatt has much to tell us about what happens when readers enter the world of books. In her classic work, *Literature as Exploration*, Rosenblatt (1938/1995) explains that every reader creates her own meaning as she reads. Therefore, rather than simply absorbing the words and thoughts of the writer, the reader uses what she knows about the world both intellectually and emotionally as she makes sense of and responds to the writer's words. In this reciprocal process, which Rosenblatt describes as a "live circuit," reading is dynamic, not static.

A perfect example of the relationship between text as muse and reader as creator can be seen in a comment made by one of our students, Jennifer

---

1. Choose a text that both you and the children will love.

2. Plan and prepare the read-aloud:
   - Get to know the story or poem.
   - Decide how you will introduce the piece.
   - Choose stopping points for brief comments and discussion.
   - Practice reading the piece out loud so you are able to read it with feeling and expression.
   - Practice handling the book if illustrations are an important part of the story.

3. Pay attention to the children as you read the book. Let them be your guide in terms of pacing and discussion. Remember to solicit personal reactions, connections, and comments during and after the read-aloud.

4. Have a copy or copies of the book available in the classroom library so that children may read and revisit the book.

5. Enjoy!

· Table 3–1 ·

Guidelines for Read-Alouds

Neff, as she describes her interaction with the opening scenes in *The Hobbit* by J. R. R. Tolkien. "I wanted to really see the hobbit-hole, all the dwarves' hoods lining the hall, and of course Bilbo Baggins' comfortable kitchen filled with the dwarves and Gandalf. My picture of the opening scene is filled with color, and it has the warmth of a familiar place." Later, she goes on to tell us that "...my ideas of what dwarves and wizards look like were probably formed from other books. My understanding of Bilbo and his personality is largely personal/empathetic, for I see myself in Bilbo, in his appreciation of home, his pleasure in the quiet life, and his wanting to please and entertain his guests. I also wondered why the dwarves' hoods were different colors. Was it because of age, family relations, ranking, or special ability? I decided it most likely was because of age or special ability, though the hood color may have just been personal preference" (Student Response Paper, 03/15/00). We see in Jennifer's comments that she has put herself into the text. As she read, she made the story her own. She used the author's words along with her knowledge of life to recreate the story in her own image.

USING WHAT WE KNOW ABOUT THE WORLD TO CONNECT WITH TEXT

In the previous paragraph, Jennifer's comments tell us she has had personal and literary experiences that allow her to connect with the text. For example, although she has never been in a hobbit hole, the opening scene of *The Hobbit* evokes a familiar warmth. She wonders about the colors of the dwarves' hoods and makes predictions based upon both her knowledge of imaginary places and the creatures that inhabit them and the world in which she lives.

At first, she reads to make sense of this new place. How is it like her world and the other magical worlds about which she has read? As she creates her own images and understandings of the hobbits' world, she is also relating the characters

to herself and people she knows. Jennifer ends her response paper by saying that "He (Tolkien) lets and encourages the reader to find her own way through (the story), taking at the end what meant the most to her, rather than what she (the reader) was told to take" (Student Response Paper, 03/15/00). Readers using the author's signposts "find their own way through the text" and then take from the text what "means most to them." This statement beautifully sums up the very best of literary experiences.

There are many ways in which teachers can help students to learn how to use their real life and literary experiences so that they are able to 1) easily enter a text, 2) make their own way as they read, and 3) depart from the text with what has meant the most to them.

ENTERING A TEXT

Before students begin to listen to or read something, it is important that they have an opportunity to activate their prior knowledge, make predictions about whatever they are to listen to or read, and set purposes for listening/reading. Let's take a look at how these three things can be accomplished as part of a regular classroom routine.

Using the Cover and Title of a Book

Gayle Wood is about to read Mem Fox's *Night Noises* to her first-grade class. The story is about a 90-year-old woman, Lily Laceby, who lives in a cottage with her dog, Butch Aggie. One stormy night, with Butch Aggie at her feet, Lily Laceby falls asleep by the fire in her living room. As she dreams of the past, ominous sounds pierce the night. There's crunching on the walk, rattling at the windows, whispering in the bushes...who on earth could it be? To help her students relate to the book, Ms. Wood reads the title of the book to her students as she shows them the cover. She asks them to talk with a partner about the kinds of noises they hear at night when they go to bed and how those noises make them feel. After a minute or two, she calls on several children to share the noises they hear at night. She then directs the children's attention to the cover. As the children discuss the picture of the elderly woman and the dog, she asks the children to predict how the story will unfold. After affirming their predictions, she instructs the children to listen carefully in order to find out what night noises are in this book and what they have to do with the lady and the dog. As Ms. Wood reads the story, she stops periodically for the children to comment on the noises and to guess what those noises mean. She asks children to elaborate on their answers and also asks who agrees or who has a different idea. This interaction with the children is very important. Lucy Calkins (2001) suggests that when reading is a social activity children learn to value books and the role reading plays in their lives and the lives of their peers.

Relating a Book to Other Texts

Sometimes our experiences with other books help us in knowing what to expect and look for as we enter a text. For example, many children and adults like series books because they are comfortable: The characters seem like old friends, and readers generally know what to expect in terms of plot. A book that is enjoyed by a child may also lead her to and help her enter other books from the same genre or with similar subject matter or theme. A student we know who lived in Germany during second and third grade read Judith Kerr's *When Hitler Stole Pink Rabbit* in third grade. She became keenly interested in the Holocaust, and was thrilled when one of the choices in fourth grade was Lois Lowry's *Number the Stars.* Having read these two books, Melissa was able to make sense of and appreciate Jane Yolen's *The Devil's Arithmetic,* a time travel tale that blends fantasy, realistic fiction, and historical fact.

Teachers can easily help children relate a new book, story, or poem to already familiar works. For example, a second-grade teacher needs simply to ask as she shares the cover and title of Susan Lowell's *The Three Little Javelinas,* "Does this remind you of a story you already know?" Followed by, "I wonder how much it will be like the story of the three little pigs?" Similarly, a fourth-grade teacher may introduce Patricia Polacco's *The Butterfly,* a memoir about the French Resistance in picture book form, by asking students to think back to *Number the Stars.* Later he may ask the class to revisit *The Butterfly* and to look for similarities and differences between the two works.

Anticipation Guides

Anticipation guides (Herber, 1978; Readence, Bean, & Baldwin, 1981) are another way to encourage students to think about what they know and/or believe, share their ideas with others, and set purposes for reading or listening. This activity asks students to individually decide whether they agree or disagree with a series of three to six statements about the subject at hand. Often students are given individual copies of the statements, or the statements are projected for all to see through the use of an overhead or other technology projection system. After students have had an opportunity to respond individually to the statements, the class or group comes together to share and discuss each person's ideas. By keeping in mind both their answers and the class discussion, students now have several reasons for reading or listening to the text. It is important to revisit the statements following the reading for further discussion. Anticipation guides work equally well with pieces of fiction and nonfiction. The following are examples of anticipation guides for texts at different grade levels. Please keep in mind that the synopsis is not part of the anticipation guide. We have included it in case readers are unfamiliar with the book for which the guide was developed.

Example 1

Growing Frogs (2000) by Vivian French

Grade Level: K-2

Synopsis: With the help of her mother, a young girl begins to grow frogs at home. The reader learns vicariously through the girl's experiences as she witnesses the spawning of frog eggs into tadpoles and then into frogs. Step-by-step directions for raising frogs as well as a good deal of explanatory information is presented in a natural and engaging way.

Anticipation Guide: Please circle "agree" or "disagree" after you listen to each statement.

1. Frogs make good pets.

   AGREE   DISAGREE

2. Frogs lay eggs.

   AGREE   DISAGREE

3. Tadpoles turn into frogs.

   AGREE   DISAGREE

4. Tadpoles can breathe underwater.

   AGREE   DISAGREE

Example 2

One Good Apple: Growing Our Food for the Sake of the Earth (1999) by Catherine Paladino

Grade Level: 5-6

Synopsis: Well-researched text and beautiful photographs combine to make a case for a different approach to agriculture. The book explores the history of pesticides in the United States, their current use, and the benefits and dangers of pesticides. It then offers organic farming techniques as a viable alternative to current methods.

Anticipation Guide: Please circle "agree" or "disagree" after you read each statement.

1. The food we buy in the grocery store is safe to eat.

   AGREE   DISAGREE

2. Washing fruits and vegetables before we eat them removes any germs and/or harmful chemicals that may remain.

   AGREE   DISAGREE

3. The only good bug is a dead bug.

   AGREE   DISAGREE

4. Insects can outsmart humans.

   AGREE   DISAGREE

5. Small bruised apples are better to eat than big, bright, shiny, red apples.

   AGREE   DISAGREE

K-W-L

An extremely popular and effective way of helping students determine what they currently know about a topic and set their own purposes for listening to or reading an informational selection is the strategy known as K-W-L (Ogle, 1986). Three columns, one for each letter, are drawn on chart paper or an overhead. The "K" column is used to record what the children say they know (K) about the topic during a brainstorming session that takes place prior to reading or listening. After discussing what they know or think they know about the topic, the students then decide what they want (W) to learn about the topic. Their questions are recorded in the "W" column. It is easy to see how this strategy helps students enter the text in an informed and motivated way. After listening or reading, students share what they have learned (L), and this information is recorded in the "L" column. Most agree that the strategy is better suited for use with informational text rather than narrative text. For example, we might use a K-W-L chart with upper-elementary students before they begin reading a variety of books about a historical figure such as Sitting Bull or as they begin a science unit on the rain forest.

Story Cans, Book Boxes, and Container Clues

Book boxes (Yopp & Yopp, 2001), story cans, and container clues capitalize on students' interest in solving puzzles and mysteries. Objects relating to a book are placed in a decorated can, basket, box or any other type of appropriate container. The object or objects are removed from the container for all to see, and students are encouraged to use the clues to try to make predictions about the upcoming story. In some cases, the container itself may be a clue. Let's explore how this technique can be used with the book *Because of Winn-Dixie* by Kate DiCamillo.

In their discussion of book boxes, Yopp & Yopp (2001) point out that students should be given ample time to think and talk about the objects. It has been a common experience by those implementing this technique that students are very engaged in the text after participating in this activity.

Because of Winn-Dixie (2000) by Kate DiCamillo.

Grade Level: 4-6

Synopsis: A delightful modern day "girl and her dog" story that explores how loss and loneliness can be healed with time and the help of others. India Opal Buloni is new in town. Not knowing anyone gives Opal lots of time to think. What she thinks most about is why her mother left when she was three and how lonely she is in this new place. Enter Winn-Dixie, a dog as ugly as he is friendly. With Winn-Dixie as her guide, Opal becomes friends with a diverse cross-section of the town. It is these new friends who help her realize that life contains both the bitter and the sweet and that we must learn to savor the sweet.

Instead of a can or box, we might choose to use a paper bag from the grocery store because Opal finds the dog she names Winn-Dixie at a grocery store. A special cough drop, a pet store, a librarian, and a woman thought to be a witch by the neighborhood children figure prominently in the story, so we might place a dog collar, a cough drop, a container of bird food, a library card, and a witch hat or a picture of a witch in the bag.

· ꝏ Figure 3.1 ꝏ ·

Example of Container Clues for Because of Winn-Dixie by Kate DiCamillo

Freewriting

Freewriting or quickwrite (Moore, Readence, & Rickelman, 1989) asks upper-elementary students to write down everything they know or think about a topic in five minutes or less. Students are encouraged to concentrate on getting their thoughts down on paper. Ideas (rather than grammar, spelling, and punctuation) are the focus of this assignment. After completing the quickwrite, students share what they have written. For example, a group of students who have chosen to read *North by Night: A Story of the Underground Railroad* by Kathryn Ayres might be asked to do a quickwrite on what they know about the Underground Railroad. Their writing then becomes the basis for a discussion that helps their teacher assess their prior knowledge and aids the students in determining what the book might be about and what questions they have about the topic. We especially like this strategy because it gives less-vocal students an opportunity to generate and share their ideas in a comfortable way.

We've discussed six ways of guiding children as they first enter a text. Language arts, reading, and children's literature texts will also contain many other strategies for assisting students in activating prior knowledge and setting purposes for reading. It is important to remember that the strategy we choose should help children connect with the text in meaningful ways.

READING: FINDING OUR WAY THROUGH TEXTS

Today, many prominent researchers in the field of literacy (Anderson, Hiebert, Scott, & Wilkinson, 1985; Galda & Gucice, 1997; Marshall, 2000) agree with Rosenblatt (1938/1995) that reading is a dynamic and creative act. As we make our way through a piece of poetry or prose we are continuously predicting, making connections, forming pictures in our heads, reevaluating our ideas, and changing or confirming what we are thinking. It seems hard to believe that all of this is going on as we sit down with the morning paper, enjoy the latest best-seller, or read an e-mail message, but it is.

Let's revisit *One Good Apple*, the book about the use of pesticides in this country and organic farming. As we read the title, each of us pictures what for us is a "good apple." For some of us the apple is red, for others it is green. Many of us will think crunchy; others will think sweet or tangy. We may even have a certain type of apple in mind: Red Delicious, Granny Smith, or Gala. Our apples are certainly all apples, but they are each slightly different depending on our experience with apples. We can see from this example that as readers we've created a picture, connected the author's words "good apple" with what we know about the world, and even made a prediction about what the author means by a good apple.

However, after reading the opening paragraphs of the book, we find that we need to rethink our ideas about what makes for a good apple. The author suggests that a good apple is probably small, dull in color, and may have some spots or even a worm hole. "Wait a minute," we think, "Why is that kind of apple better than the kind I like?" We keep reading to try and make sense of the author's words and ideas. The cycle of predicting, connecting, questioning, affirming, and readjusting continues. The ability to predict, connect, picture, and question as we read is something all good readers must learn to do. When we are able to do this, we are reading strategically. Our students can become effective readers if we show them how to use these strategies and provide opportunities for them to practice. Let's see how this might be accomplished through the following scenario.

Strategic Reading Instruction

Paul Moran has noticed that his sixth-graders need to be prompted to picture and make connections as they read. He could make an announcement to that effect, but he believes it will be more compelling if his reminder shows rather than tells. In order to do this, he decides to share with the class the poem "The Vendors," from Paul Janeczko's *That Sweet Diamond*. He chose this particular poem because it creates a clear snapshot of the people who move about the stands selling refreshments at baseball games.

He begins by reading the title and asking students what they know about the word vendors. As students share their ideas and experiences, he joins the conversation and tells about the time he went to the Moscow Circus and bought peanuts and soft drinks from a vendor. He describes how once his daughter realized she didn't have to leave her seat for snacks, she began listening and keeping an eye out for the vendors. Then he explains that this poem really reminds him of that outing because the poet uses words that help him form pictures of vendors. These images in turn trigger memories of his trip to the circus.

Mr. Moran reads the poem once and solicits personal connections and responses. It is important that he does this so that his students have an opportunity to share their thoughts and feelings before beginning any strategy work. He then reads the poem again asking students to listen for words and phrases that help them create pictures. At the end of the poem, he encourages the class to share their visualizations along with the words and phrases that helped to evoke those images. As individuals share their words and pictures, Mr. Moran discusses how the ability to visualize helped him to make meaning. For example, at first he thought of the vendors at the circus, but the last lines of the poem caused him to see a ball park.

Later, when he works with a group of students who are about to read the short story "Baseball in April" by Gary Soto, Mr. Moran gives each student sticky notes and asks them to mark three places in the text where they are able to form pictures as they read. When the group meets to talk about the story, he solicits and explores personal responses before asking students to return to the text and share their visualizations and the words that triggered the images. It is only now, after he has taught and provided practice, that he verbally reminds students how important visualizing is when we read.

We said earlier that something we read often leads to another book, article, story, or poem. In this case, the student discussion led to an exploration of Latino baseball players. A perfect book to extend that exploration is *¡Beisbol! Latino Baseball Pioneers and Legends* by Jonah Winter. In the end, we base what we will take away from the book on what makes sense to us and what we need at this particular moment in our lives.

THE IMPORTANCE OF TALK

Talk is an important part of reading. We have a desire to talk about what we have learned and to share what we're thinking and feeling. We also want to know what others are thinking. Do they agree with us and/or the author? After reading *One Good Apple,* we may want to know how others feel about pesticides. What do they know about organic farming? As we read about the wax on fruit and vegetables in the grocery store, we are reminded of a recent conversation with a friend. We make a mental or written note to talk with Penny about this. We may decide to talk with someone who knows a good deal about organic farming. Perhaps he will be able to answer some of our questions. Through conversations, we sort out what we've learned, develop deeper understandings, and formulate new questions. A compelling book leads to a variety of conversations; it may lead us to other books as well. We need to provide time in our classrooms for these conversations to occur.

Of course, discussions before, during, and after reading or listening encourage children to share their thinking and feelings. Regular participation in literature circles, paired reading, and book groups also provide students with important opportunities for talk. These activities center around plenty of reading, personal response, and conversation. In an article entitled "Good Books, Good Talk, Good Readers," Holt and Bell (2000) explore the role literature circles play in the development of knowledge. They point out that when readers talk about what they are reading, they are exposed to different ways of organizing and thinking as they create a shared understanding of the text or topic. Moreover, when the teacher is an active participant in the discussion, he can model the thinking and intellectual risk-taking of a skilled reader and learner. As children follow his lead and practice taking intellectual risks and talking about text, the conversations become richer, the learning more meaningful.

EXTENDING THE CONVERSATION

At a book's end, we may be content to conclude our conversation with the text, or we may be inspired to extend the conversation and/or create something more permanent. This can be accomplished in a variety of ways. We may write a piece that mirrors or embellishes the text we've just left. We may dramatize, dance, or sing the text. We may decide

to conduct experiments or initiate some kind of social action based upon what we've learned or discovered. When teachers and students are inspired in these ways, the learning that takes place is rewarding.

We know a first-grade class, for example, that discovered *Hailstones and Halibut Bones*, Mary O'Neil's collection of color poems, during their investigation of the spectrum. The class was intrigued by how O'Neil was able to capture the spirit of each color as well as each color's reality. Because these poems rang so true, the class wondered if they, too, could write about colors the way O'Neil did. And so, after much polling and discussion, they chose to write about the color blue. Then they talked about what blue looked like and felt like to them. They brainstormed, sorted through their ideas, talked some more. They revised, and then when they had just the right images, they borrowed O'Neil's use of the phrase "Blue is ..." to structure their poem. We think you will agree that the end product is stunning. As you read the poem, notice how much the children learned about poetry, use of image, and the structure of language.

What Is Blue?

Blue is an ocean,
Blue is the sky,
Blue is a bluebird flying up high.
Blue is great and so am I.
Blue is a flower,
Blue is my tear,
Blue is the feeling that I fear.
Blue is the ceiling of my room,
and the color of a hot air balloon.
Some paper is blue and the cover of a book,
A fish, a lake, and the face of a piggy bank.
Blue is the bluest river where crocodiles dive.
Blue is a water ski and a shark,
Blue is the twilight before it's dark.
Blue is the bluest thing in my eye.
Blue is the bluest summer sky.
And the place where the sky meets the sea.
　　(Ms. Lee's Class, 1996)

Other primary students we know have created big-book versions of Pat Hutchins' *Rosie's Walk*, or have danced a poem. After reading *Juneteenth: Freedom Day* by Muriel Miller Branch, fifth-grade students were moved to write to the publisher of their social studies textbook asking for the inclusion of the event and Major General Gordon Granger in their textbook. *Salsa Stories* by Lulu Delacre inspired a group of students and their parents to recreate the dishes upon which the stories in the collection are based. Murals, videos, plays, songs, and Reader's Theater performances have all been used to continue classroom conversations with and about texts. Experiences like these actively engage children in the construction of their own knowledge. Furthermore, they create many opportunities throughout the day for talking and writing about books and build classroom and school communities that have reading and responding to books as their primary focus.

The remainder of this chapter provides examples of how books can be used in the language arts program to foster a love of literature, strategic reading, and literary understandings. We have included three "one-book-at-a-time" lessons as well as a framework for the generative approach. The first "one-book-at-a-time" sample lesson, "Pancakes and Jam," is appropriate for kindergarten or first grade. The second, "Social Action Soup," is suitable for second and third grade. "If This Hat Could Talk" is geared for fourth and fifth grades. It is important to keep in mind that these are only suggested levels. With the exception of "Pancakes and Jam," all the lessons can easily be adapted for a higher or lower level.

"Play Ball" is our example of a generative curriculum approach. It includes an explanation of how we would go about implementing the generative curriculum. This particular example was inspired by a sixth-grade class one of us once taught.

Sample Lessons for Younger Readers

One Book at a Time

Pancakes and Jam

Read aloud *Pancakes, Pancakes!* by Eric Carle.

Pancakes, Pancakes! is a cumulative tale that includes some repetitive sentences. In the story, Jack wakes up hungry for pancakes. His mother is more than willing to make them for breakfast, but she needs his help. The book follows Jack as he gathers the necessary ingredients: flour, eggs, milk, butter, and jam.

Preparation

1. Write the recipe on chart paper. Use rebus as much as possible.
2. Gather ingredients and equipment for making pancakes.
3. Obtain a copy of Christina Rossetti's poem "Mix a Pancake," and print it on chart paper. Words need to be large enough so all the children can see them. The poem may be found in *Dilly Dilly Piccalilli: Poems for the Very Young*, an anthology by Myra Cohn Livingston.
4. Practice reading *Pancakes, Pancakes!* out loud. Take note of the repetitive phrases. These are perfect places to invite the children to join in and read with you. You simply need to pause and signal through expression or gesture that the children should help you read. Phrases like "Here's the _____" use children's listening skills, whereas "Now we need _____" encourages children to make predictions based on picture clues.
5. Plan where else you will stop to solicit comments.

Introduction

Say something to the children like "I woke up hungry this morning for _____. It's my favorite thing to eat for breakfast. What do you like to eat for breakfast?" After you have solicited comments and/or children have shared their favorite food with a neighbor, read the poem by Rossetti to the children. The poem on chart paper allows you to point to the words as you read. Then reread the poem. This time invite the children to read with you (choral reading) or read a line and have them repeat it (echo reading). You may also want to develop gestures for mix, stir, and toss with the class.

Reading the Book

Tell the children that today's story is about a boy who wants something special for breakfast. Can they tell what it is? Read the title and author. Tell the children that Jack will have to help his mother if she is to make his favorite breakfast. They should listen for what Jack has to do as you read the story. Solicit personal reactions and comments from the children and discuss what Jack did.

Curriculum Connections

Interdisciplinary (Language Arts and Cooking)

Recipe: Use a recipe for pancakes that you like or the one that follows.

PANCAKES

1 1/2 C Flour	2 Eggs
1 t Salt	1 1/2 C Milk
2 T Sugar	2 T Melted Butter
2 t Baking Powder	

Extra butter for pancakes. Two or three kinds of jam.
Makes about 12–4" pancakes.

Directions:
1. Sift together dry ingredients.
2. Break eggs into medium bowl.
3. Add the milk and butter; whisk until well blended.
4. Pour the wet ingredients into the dry and whisk until you can't see the flour anymore.
5. Spray electric frying pan with cooking spray and heat to 325 degrees.
6. Measure 1/3 cup batter and pour into the pan.
7. When little bubbles appear all over the top, use a spatula to peek at the bottom. If it is golden brown, it's time to flip!
8. Wait a minute or two after flipping, then take a peek. If the bottom is golden brown, the pancake is ready.

After cooking and eating, record children's reactions to making and eating pancakes. Remember to provide an opportunity for children to read what they have written. (**Language Experience.**)

Brainstorm with the students' words to describe how the pancakes tasted. Arrange words in a web. (**Vocabulary.**)

Make a pancake book that describes either making pancakes or the students' reactions to making and eating pancakes. (**Writing.**)

Mathematics

After making and eating the pancakes, discuss the different items children put on their pancakes (butter and/or jam). Ask children to make a prediction about which combination of pancake and topping(s) was most popular with their classmates. Then survey the children as to how they like to eat pancakes. To represent their choices, children are given small quarter-size circles. Their choices are: plain (brown circle), with butter (yellow circle), with strawberry jam (red circle), with grape jam (violet circle), with butter and strawberry jam (orange circle), or with butter and grape jam (lavender circle). Children can then make a graph using the circles to depict their choices. Ask children questions using the completed graph as a point of reference. For example, "What was the most popular topping? What was the least popular topping? What topping was the second most popular?" (**Making Predictions**; **Counting**; **Graphing**.)

Science

As the children are making the pancakes, have them observe and discuss what happens to the liquid batter as it is introduced to heat. (**Observation and Communication**.)

Creative Dramatics

Have children act out the story *Pancakes, Pancakes!* Depending on the children's reading abilities, the first several times the teacher may have to narrate the story while the children carry out the actions. You may also use numbered rebus cards as cues for the children to act out the story independently. (**Oral Language**; **Sequencing**; **Listening Skills**.)

Connecting to Standards

Pancakes and Jam

Language Arts #3: Students use a variety of strategies to comprehend, interpret, and appreciate texts.

Language Arts #6: Students demonstrate their knowledge of language and its conventions to create and discuss print (NCTE & IRA, 1996).

Mathematics (Data Analysis & Probability): Students ask questions, and they collect and analyze data to find the answers to their questions.

Mathematics (Representation): Students use graphs to represent, record, and communicate results of research (NCTM, 2000).

Science (Physical Science): Students develop an understanding of properties of objects and materials. Students develop an understanding of light, heat, electricity, and magnetism (NRC, 1996).

Social Action Soup

Read aloud *Uncle Willie and the Soup Kitchen* by DyAnne DiSalvo-Ryan.

The narrator of *Uncle Willie and the Soup Kitchen* is a young boy who's not quite sure why his Uncle Willie chooses to work in a community soup kitchen. When he asks, his mother and uncle tell him that sometimes people need help and that the soup kitchen is a way to help. But the people the boy sees on his way to school that look like they might need help seem a little scary and a little sad. Is the soup kitchen a sad or scary place? He decides to find out for himself by spending a morning helping his uncle at the soup kitchen.

Preparation

1. Find out about the soup kitchens and food banks in your community. Arrange for someone from a soup kitchen or food bank to be interviewed by your class. Investigate the possibility of your class helping to prepare a meal at a local soup kitchen.
2. Construct a poster-size K-W-L chart.
3. Practice reading *Uncle Willie and the Soup Kitchen* aloud.

Introduction

Begin by showing your class the cover and reading the title of the book. Ask them what they know or think they know about soup kitchens. Some of your students may have volunteered or been a guest at a soup kitchen. Write the students' responses in the "K" column. Ask the students to listen for the things the boy in the story wants to know about the place his uncle works and what he learns.

Reading the Book

Read the book, stopping at places that confirm information in the "K" column or provide additional information. Since you don't want to disrupt the flow of the story, simply say, "Oh, that's something we knew, isn't it?" or "What has the boy found out about ____?" At the end of the book solicit personal responses. You might ask if your class thinks the boy will help at the soup kitchen again. Ask students to support their answers. Then ask what they and the boy learned. Record the children's responses under the "K." Move to the "W" column and share with the class a question you have after reading the book. For example, you might wonder how many people in the U.S. or the world go hungry every day, or you might wonder how much soup it takes to feed the 120 people who visited the soup kitchen in the book. Write your question in the "W" column and then solicit questions from the class. Once a series of questions has been developed under the "W," discuss how the class might find the answers. Divide the class into research partners or groups and formulate a research plan. As students find the answers to their questions, have them share the information with the class and record what they learned under the "L" column.

Curriculum Connections

Language Arts

Some of your class's questions may be best answered by a person involved with running a soup kitchen or food bank. If this is the case, arrange for an in-person visit, a telephone interview, or instant messaging over e-mail. Work with your students to develop questions that address the five "Ws" (who, what, when, where, and why). After brainstorming a number of questions, help students to refine their questions and arrange them in a logical order for the interview. Discuss the role of follow-up questions. During the interview, make sure that there is a mechanism for recording the interviewee's responses. Afterward go over the answers and add information to the "L" column. Remember to have the class write a thank-you letter to your guest. (**Interviewing**; **Writing**; **Speaking**; **Listening**.)

Art

Students may want to share what they've learned with others. One way to do this is to create posters. Work with your school's art teacher or a parent who has experience with graphic design to create lessons that will help children understand how to combine words and images to create an effective message. (**Visual Literacy**; **Graphic Design**.)

Social Studies

Try to arrange for the students to help prepare a meal at a soup kitchen. If this is not possible, your students may wish to raise money for an organization that helps feed the hungry. Selling homemade soup comes to mind, but a bake sale or any other "edible" sale works just as well. Through their investigation of hunger, students will learn about the causes of hunger as well as local and global solutions. They will also learn that communities large and small need individuals who are willing to work together to solve problems and make life better for everyone. Perhaps more importantly, students will learn that they can make a difference. (**Civil Ideals and Practices**; **Individuals, Groups and Institutions**; **Global Connections**.)

Mathematics

Depending on the cooking activity you choose to do, students will be reading recipes to calculate how much food to prepare, making shopping lists, calculating costs, deciding on a fair price if they are selling what they make, figuring out portion size, measuring, etc. (**Measurement**; **Problem Solving**.)

Connecting to Standards
Social Action Soup

Language Arts #4: Students adjust their use of spoken, written, and visual language to communicate effectively with a variety of audiences and for different purposes.

Language Arts #7: Students conduct research on issues and interests by generating ideas and questions, and by posing problems. They gather, evaluate, and synthesize data from a variety of sources to communicate their discoveries in ways that suit their purpose and audience.

Language Arts #8: Students use a variety of technological and informational resources to gather and

synthesize information and to create and communicate knowledge (NCTE & IRA, 1996).

Mathematics (Problem Solving): Students build new mathematical knowledge through problem solving, apply and adapt a variety of appropriate strategies to solve problems (NCTM, 2000).

Social Studies (Individuals, Groups, & Institutions): Students can engage in a social action project and experience how citizens can work together to create a better society.

Social Studies (Global Connections): Students explore and discuss important social issues (NCSS, 1994).

Creative Drama

Students may want to write individual pieces based upon what they have learned about hunger or their experiences volunteering in a soup kitchen or food bank. These pieces can then be used for a Reader's Theater presentation.

Sample Lesson for Intermediate Readers

One Book at a Time

If This Hat Could Talk

Read aloud *Aunt Flossie's Hats (and Crab Cakes Later)* by Elizabeth Fitzgerald Howard with paintings by James Ransome.

Aunt Flossie's Hats (and Crab Cakes Later) finds Sarah and Susan having a tea party at their Great-great-aunt Flossie's. The best part of the afternoon is when Aunt Flossie brings out her hat boxes. As the girls try on hats that strike their fancy, Aunt Flossie shares the story behind each hat. Some of the stories are from before the girls or their parents were born, but their favorite is about an adventure involving them and Aunt Flossie's "favorite best Sunday hat."

Preparation:

1. Create a story box. Find a hat box and choose a hat (baseball cap, baby bonnet, cowboy hat, "Sunday go to meeting" hat...) that has a story to tell about you or someone you know.
2. Practice reading *Aunt Flossie's Hats (and Crab Cakes Later)*. Plan where you will stop once or twice to elicit comments.

Introduction

Show the students your hat box and ask them to guess what might be inside. As students guess, ask them to explain their guesses. Open the hat box and reveal its contents. After talking a few minutes about the guesses and the importance of hats and hat boxes in the past, begin to tell the story of your hat. Then direct your students' attention to the cover of the book and the title. Solicit predictions and then ask students to listen carefully for the stories that Aunt Flossie's hats tell.

Reading the Book

Read the story, stopping periodically to address questions and comments. Solicit personal reactions to the story. When finished, ask what stories Aunt Flossie's hats told. See if anyone knows someone like

Aunt Flossie, who can tell stories about long ago, or who has a possession that tells a story. Have students share their stories.

Curriculum Connections

Language Arts

Revisit the text. Explain that the author does something very interesting with time in this book. Do students know what it is? Share the illustrations on pages 4 and 5, then share the text and illustrations on pages 10 and 11. Ask if the story is taking place in the present. How do we know? Is the story about to switch to the past? What clues does the author give us? Turn the page and direct the students' attention to the illustration. When does this part of the story take place? How do we know? You may want to discuss pages 14–17 and 22 and 23 in a similar manner. It may also be appropriate at this time to introduce the term "flashback." Solicit comments from the class on why writers might want to use flashbacks. Also talk about the fact that this book has illustrations that help us figure out when the story is going back in time, but many authors use just words. Depending on your curriculum, you may want to do a follow-up lesson using a piece of text that uses flashback(s). (**Literary Technique**; **Flashback**.)

Social Studies

Use your hat as an example of how everyday objects can tell us about the way people lived in the past. You may want to introduce the term "artifact." Ask students to bring an object to school that tells a story about their past. Help students develop a definition of past. You may want to call this activity an "Artifact Hunt." Since all will want to share their finds, have students present their artifacts in pairs or small groups. Bring students together to talk about what the objects tell us about the time in which we live and the individuals in our class. (**Culture**; **Oral History**.)

Visit a museum or a museum Web site that has a display of everyday objects. Have students guess the purposes of several unusual items. Then after learning about these objects and several that interest the students, compare the museum's artifacts with the class's artifacts. What can we tell about life during each of the time periods? How have our lives changed? Would you like to have lived in a time period other than our own? Why or why not? (**Social and Cultural History**.)

Connecting to Standards

If This Hat Could Talk

Language Arts #3: Students apply a wide range of strategies to comprehend, interpret, evaluate and appreciate texts. They draw on their prior experience, their interactions with other readers and writers, their knowledge of word meanings and other texts.

Language Arts #6: Students apply knowledge structure, language conventions, media techniques, figurative language, and genre to create, critique, and discuss print and nonprint texts (NCTE & IRA, 1996).

Social Studies (Time, Continuity & Change): Students will learn how to reconstruct the past and develop a historical perspective to interpret the present (NCSS, 1994).

The Arts (Music): Understanding music in relation to history and culture.

The Arts (Visual Arts): Understanding the visual arts in relation to history and cultures (CNAEA, 1994).

Music

Since the book mentions the Great War, play music from that time period. What do the lyrics tell us about life and what people thought at this time? Play a song you know is popular with your students. What might this song tell someone in the future about us? Have students work individually or in pairs to choose music that represents life today. Ask each student/pair to explain their choice on a 3 × 5 card so that their artifact can be displayed as if in a museum. (**Music**; **History/Culture**.)

Art

Have students design a cover for the song they have chosen to represent the present. As students present their covers to the class, remind them of how the words and artwork in *Aunt Flossie's Hats (and Crab Cakes Later)* worked together to help readers understand the story. (**Visual Arts and Culture**.)

Sample Generative Curriculum for Intermediate Grades

Play Ball!

The following plan was inspired by a class of sixth-graders who truly loved playing ball. They weren't just fans; they were fanatics! They played softball at recess, talked incessantly and ardently about how their favorite baseball and softball teams were faring, and were veritable fonts of information about baseball players and baseball lore. Their passion for the game has helped to guide us as we designed this unit. The focus of the unit is primarily baseball, but we have also included some selections that deal with softball.

To the uninitiated, baseball may seem a fairly simple game of bat meeting ball and ball meeting glove. But as anyone who loves the sport will tell you, baseball is a game that requires perfect timing and lightning reflexes. Balls thrown by major-league pitchers routinely travel at speeds above 80 miles per hour! In terms of rate, time, and distance, batters often have less than three-tenths of a second in which to make decisions about how they should react (Ritter, 1999). The question that immediately comes to mind is "How can they (batters) react so quickly?" This query can lead us to biology and the study of reaction times. In addition, physical science can be used to explain much of what goes on in terms of hitting and pitching. Any discussion of batting averages and other statistics requires an understanding of mathematical principles and operations.

Americans have been playing baseball for over 150 years. In a sense we have grown up with baseball and it with us. The game has much to tell us about who we are and perhaps who we hope to be. In baseball's history, we see America as it grapples with issues of race, ethnicity, and gender. Scandals in baseball may prompt an exploration of ethics and character. The salaries of major league players, ticket prices, stadium funding, and even the price of refreshments and souvenirs lead us to economics.

It's interesting that when we reflect upon what has been written about this sport, it is a poem that first comes to mind. "Casey at the Bat" by Ernest Lawrence Thayer was written over 100 years ago, and yet it is still being read and enjoyed today. Not only is the poem still in print, no small feat after 100 years, but new illustrated versions keep being created. One of our favorite versions, illustrated by

Christopher Bing, was named a Caldecott Honor Book in 2001. We feel certain that this particular version will be very appealing to upper-elementary students.

Like the poem "Casey at the Bat," baseball continues to be a topic about which people choose to read and write. Today, there are well over 500 titles in print about the sport for children. It makes sense that there would be a good deal of nonfiction written about the game itself, the players, and how to perfect one's game, but there are also many fine examples of poetry and fiction as well. May Swenson, Paul Janeczko, and J. Patrick Lewis are contemporary poets who have written about baseball. Fictional offerings for the intermediate grades include contemporary fiction such as *Joey Pigza Loses Control* by Jack Gantos and Chris Lynch's *Gold Dust. Choosing Up Sides* by John Ritter, *Bat 6* by Virginia Euwer Wolff, and Walter Dean Myers' *The Journal of Biddy Owens* are just a few examples of historical fiction that have been written about baseball and softball for this age group. Finally, titles such as *Moon Ball* by Jane Yolen, *Zachary's Ball* by Matt Tavares, and Dan Gutman's *Honus and Me: A Baseball Card Adventure* place baseball firmly in the realm of fantasy.

The possibilities for using the prose and poetry written about the game are seemingly endless. Figurative language, theme, point of view, character development, setting, as well as a study of genre(s) can all easily be taught. The topic also lends itself to exploring different forms of writing, including memoir, biography, sports writing, poetry, and the short story. Reading strategies such as predicting, visualizing, making connections, reading for a purpose, activating prior knowledge, and making meaning can all be taught and practiced in a unit on baseball. Obviously, this is a topic rich in curricular possibilities.

We explained in Chapter 2 that in a generative curriculum we work together with our students to decide what will be studied. Students then individually or in a group develop research questions and search for the answers to those questions. Initial questions or areas of interest often lead to new questions. As the teacher, it is up to us to help students refine their questions and develop the necessary literacy and research strategies. We also need to make sure that curricular goals are met. One such goal may be using primary documents to learn about the past. For example, students who are researching women in baseball can be directed to the primary documents about the All-American Girl's Professional Baseball League, which can be found on The National Baseball Hall of Fame's Web site. Once online, the students will likely find the league's rules and handbook—as well as some of the newspaper articles and editorials about women and baseball—fascinating, thereby experiencing firsthand the power of primary sources.

While our plan contains some whole-group activities, much of the work is accomplished through individual and small-group projects. Because we think it is important for our students to also share in some common experiences, literature circles and reading aloud activities are included in the plan.

Preparation

We begin by researching the topic. For us, this means reading adult books such as *Baseball for Dummies* by Joe Morgan and *Baseball: An Illustrated History* by Geoffrey C. Ward and Ken Burns. Lawrence S. Ritter's *The Story of Baseball* is an excellent nonfiction resource for both children and teachers alike. Once we feel we have sufficient background knowledge about how the game is played, the skills necessary to play the game, and the history of the game, we brainstorm ideas for a topic web (see Figure 3.2).

The topic web helps us visualize the curricular possibilities. We then begin (with the help of librarians, physical education teachers, colleagues, and friends) to gather resources. These resources include poems, fiction and nonfiction selections, newspaper and magazine articles, Web sites, people who might be available to visit our classroom, and field trip possibilities. Figure 3.3 is a suggested list of titles for a unit on baseball.

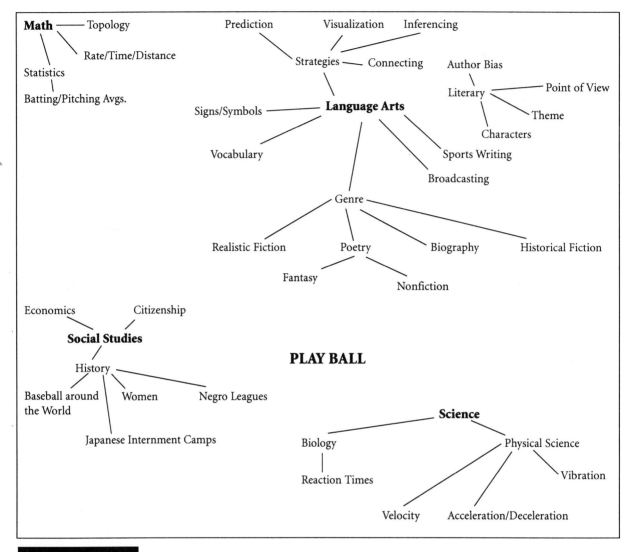

· ⌐ **Figure 3.2** ⌐ ·

Play Ball Topic Web

Beginning

Once we can see the possibilities, we are ready to begin creating the unit with our students. We do this by engaging in a week of exploration. We fill our classroom with books, magazines, newspapers, posters, photographs, the addresses of Web sites, and anything else we can think of that will spark everyone's curiosity. As we encourage students to be on the lookout for items to add to the classroom's resources, newspaper and magazine articles, books, and baseball paraphernalia begin to take over the classroom. Our school librarian is also on alert and is ready to help the class with its research questions for the next several weeks.

Each day we begin with a reading-aloud experience that gets us thinking and talking about the games of softball and baseball. On Monday, we ask students to do a quickwrite of what they know and/or feel about baseball/softball. Students share their writing with a partner, and then we ask several pairs to share their ideas to spark group discussion. At this point, we introduce the class to the poem "Analysis of Baseball" by May Swenson, which can be found in the anthology *Extra Innings: Baseball Poems* by Lee Bennett Hopkins. We explain that the poem contains Swenson's thoughts

Books for Read-Aloud Experiences

Satchel Paige by L. Cline-Ransome

The Bat Boy & His Violin by G. Curtis

Frank and Ernest Play Ball by A. Day

Dirt on Their Skirts by D. Rappaport & L. Callan

Zachary's Ball by M. Tavares

Baseball Saved Us by K. Mochizuki

Baseball in April by G. Soto

Moon Ball by J. Yolen

Books for Browsing

Baseball for Dummies by J. Morgan

Ballpark by E. Cooper

Belles of the Ballpark by D. S. Helmer

Bat, Ball, Glove by W. Jaspersohn

A Whole New Ball Game by S. Macy

The Story of Baseball by L. S. Ritter

Black Diamond: The Story of the Negro Baseball Leagues by P. & F. McKissack

Beisbol!: Latino Baseball Pioneers and Legends by J. Winter

Leagues Apart by L. S. Ritter

Shadow Ball: The History of the Negro Leagues by G. C. Ward

Fair Ball! by J. Winter

Game Day by R. Young

Baseball in the Barrios by H. Horenstein

Baseball: An Illustrated History by G. C. Ward

Fiction for Literature Circles

Choosing Up Sides by J. Ritter

Bat 6 by V. Wolff

The Journal of Biddy Owens by W. D. Myers

Yang the Youngest and His Terrible Ear by L. Namioka

Gold Dust by C. Lynch

The Trading Game by A. Slote

Thank You, Jackie Robinson by B. Cohen

Team Picture by D. Hughes

Joey Pigza Loses Control by J. Gantos

Poetry Selections

Casey at the Bat by E. L. Thayer

Extra Innings: Baseball Poems by L. B. Hopkins

Celebrate America in Poetry and Art by N. Panzer (Ed.)

That Sweet Diamond by P. B. Janeczko

· ⤳ **Figure 3.3** ⤳ ·

Children's Literature Selections for Baseball

about baseball. We wonder aloud about why the poet decided to call her thoughts about the game "Analysis of Baseball," and ask the class to share their ideas. Before reading the poem, we instruct students to listen for the ways in which their ideas about baseball are like Swenson's and how their ideas are different from those of the poet. After reading the poem, we talk about the similarities and differences between our quickwrites and Swenson's writing. As the children share their ideas, we revisit the poem and reread lines that they particularly like.

Next, we give each student a copy of the poem. We talk about how the words in this poem invite us to create pictures in our heads. Since the poem has four stanzas, we ask the students to take turns reading aloud alternating stanzas with their partners. The person who is not reading is instructed to see if he can create pictures in his head as he listens. Afterward, each pair revisits the poem and chooses several lines that evoked images. These lines are shared with the group and students are encouraged to talk about why the images are effective in describing the game. We encourage the students to try to create pictures in their heads as they read throughout the day.

It is at this point that we talk about the details of our investigation of baseball. We explain that by the end of the week all students must have choose a research idea and two books that they would like to read for literature circles. Our students know that part of the day for the next four days will be spent browsing through the classroom and school library resources, participating in reading-aloud experiences, and listening to us give book talks on the literature circle selections. Our hope is that the books we've chosen to read aloud will expand the class's awareness of the topic and peak their curiosity. Some of our students will know at the beginning of "exploration week" exactly what they want to research and learn. Others will change their topic over the course of the week as their knowledge grows. Either way is fine with us; our goal is to provide students with as many ideas and choices as possible.

Sample Lessons for Reading Aloud

Satchel Paige

Satchel Paige by Lesa Cline-Ransome with paintings by James E. Ransome is an engaging biography that introduces us to the complex nature of one of baseball's greatest players. The author does an excellent job of helping the reader understand both the man and the time in which he lived.

Preparation

1. Practice reading the book aloud.
2. Since one of the purposes for reading this book is to have students draw conclusions and offer support for their ideas, go through the text carefully and note information that offers support for conclusions. For instance, after reading the book readers may conclude that Paige liked doing things his own way. There are several examples of Paige's independence that can be used to support this conclusion.
3. Choose several stopping points in the book for discussion.
4. Obtain a copy of *That Sweet Diamond* by Paul Janeczko. Practice reading "the Pitcher." Or, obtain a copy of *Extra Innings: Baseball Poems* selected by Hopkins. Practice reading "To Satch" by Samuel Allen.

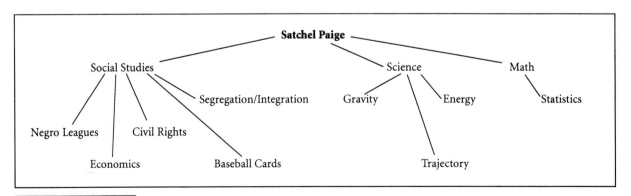

·⌣ Figure 3.4 ⌣·

Where Satchel Paige *Might Lead: Possible Research Topics*

Connecting to Standards
Satchel Paige

Language Arts #1: Students read a wide range of print and nonprint texts to build an understanding of texts, of themselves, and of the cultures of the United States and the world.

Language Arts #3: Students apply a wide range of strategies to comprehend, interpret, evaluate, and appreciate texts.

Language Arts #6: Students apply knowledge of language structure, language conventions, media techniques, figurative language, and genre to create, critique, and discuss print and nonprint texts.

Language Arts #11: Students participate as knowledgeable, reflective, creative, and critical members of a variety of literacy communities (NCTE & IRA, 1996).

Social Studies (Individual Development & Identity): Students explore how an individual's characteristics and abilities relate to development.

Social Studies (Power, Authority & Governance): Students define concepts such as role, status, justice, and power as they explore issues and social problems (NCSS, 1994).

Introduction

Begin by reading the poem "the Pitcher" or the poem "To Satch." Solicit student comments about the poet's description of the pitcher. Who do they consider to be great pitchers? Explain that the book is about one of the greatest pitchers of all time, Satchel Paige. Invite students to share what they know or think they know about this great pitcher.

Reading the Book

Ask students to listen for information that helps us understand the kind of person Paige was. Remind students to try to picture as they listen. Read the book, stopping when you or the students want to comment. For example, you may want to stop as early as page 1 to talk about what the description of the infant Paige might tell us and the images we have in our heads of Paige as a baby. At the close of the book, have students share their ideas. Ask students to support their ideas and revisit the text to confirm. (**Using Prior Knowledge; Visualizing; Drawing Conclusions; Providing Support; Critical Analysis of a Poet's Work.**)

The book *Satchell Paige* is likely to spark students' interest in a variety of related topics. Figure 3.4 outlines some of the possibilities that students may wish to pursue further.

Baseball Saved Us

Baseball Saved Us by Ken Mochizuki and illustrated by Dom Lee is a story about the coming of age of a young Japanese-American boy who is sent with his family to live in an internment camp during World War II.

Preparation

Prepare as suggested in 1 and 3 for the preceding book.

Introduction

Show students the front and back covers of the book as you read the title. Ask if they have an idea about where this story takes place. Explain briefly about the internment of Japanese Americans. Ask how the students would feel if this happened to them. Do they think what happened was fair or unfair? Why?

Reading the Book

Encourage students to think about how they connect with the boy and his story as they listen. Perhaps they have felt the same way he does or have been in similar situations. They may have read a book that reminds them of the boy or seen a television show or film that relates to the book. Read the book, stopping when you or students wish to comment. Solicit personal connections, responses, and questions at the end. Help students to see how their connections aid their understanding of the story. For example, if Sasha says that the part about the babies crying at night reminds her of when her aunt and new baby moved in with her family, you can point out that she has a very good feel for how stressful the living conditions were for the people in the story.

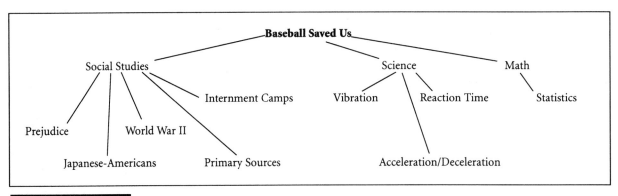

· ⌣ Figure 3.5 ⌣ ·

Where **Baseball Saved Us** *Might Lead: Possible Research Topics*

Connecting to Standards
Baseball Saved Us

Language Arts #1: Students read a wide range of print and nonprint texts to build an understanding of texts, of themselves, and of the cultures of the United States and the world.

Language Arts #3: Students apply a wide range of strategies to comprehend, interpret, evaluate, and appreciate texts.

Language Arts #6: Students apply knowledge of language structure, language conventions, media techniques, figurative language, and genre to create, critique, and discuss print and nonprint texts.

Language Arts #11: Students participate as knowledgeable, reflective, creative, and critical members of a variety of literacy communities (NCTE & IRA, 1996).

Social Studies (Individual Development & Identity): Students explore how an individual's characteristics and abilities relate to development.

Social Studies (Power, Authority & Governance): Students define concepts such as role, status, justice, and power as they explore issues and social problems (NCSS, 1994).

As a follow-up, you may want to share Dwight Okita's poem "In Response to Executive Order 9066: All Americans of Japanese Descent Must Report to Location Centers." We have often read this poem while playing Ray Charles' version of "America" softly in the background. The poem may be found in Norma Panzer's *Celebrate America in Poetry and Art.* Focus on how the narrator in the poem is feeling and the connections students can make to her situation. **(Making Personal Connections to Enhance Understanding; Appreciating Poetry**.)

As with the previous book, *Baseball Saved Us* is likely to inspire student research. See Figure 3.5 for possible ideas.

Dirt on Their Skirts

Dirt on Their Skirts by Doreen Rappaport and Lyndall Callan with pictures by E. B. Lewis is a fictional account of a baseball game played between the Rockford Peaches and the Racine Belles in 1946.

Preparation

1. Prepare as you have previously.
2. Log on to the Exploratorium Museum's Web site and/or the National Baseball Hall of Fame Web site to learn about women who played baseball and the All-American Girl's Professional Baseball League.
3. Obtain a copy of *That Sweet Diamond* by Paul Janeczko. Practice reading "NICKNAMES."

Introduction

Show students the front cover and read the title of the book. Solicit predictions about the book. Spend a few minutes talking about the history of women in baseball. Tell students that this story is about a championship game that was played in 1946 between the Rockford Peaches and the Racine Belles. Inform the class that at the end of the story, everyone should be able to talk about something they learned or something that was interesting to them. An alternative purpose could be to have students visualize as they listen.

Reading the Book

Read the book, stopping when you or the students want to comment or ask a question. Upon finishing the story, ask for personal reactions. Then have students share something they learned or found interesting with a neighbor. Pull the group together to discuss reactions and thoughts. You'll want to share something you learned or found interesting as well.

Since the book uses players' nicknames, you may want to read Janeczko's poem "NICK-NAMES" as a follow-up activity. Discuss why some people have nicknames; then read the poem. Students may notice that the poet is writing about the nicknames of male players. If so, this is a good opportunity to talk about how an author's experiences, purpose, and intended audience often influence his work.

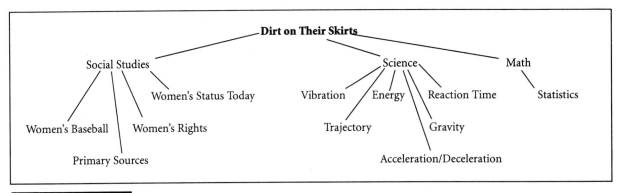

Where **Dirt on Their Skirts** *Might Lead: Possible Research Topics*

Connecting to Standards

Dirt on Their Skirts

Language Arts #1: Students read a wide range of print and non-print texts to build an understanding of texts, of themselves, and of the cultures of the United States and the world.

Language Arts #3: Students apply a wide range of strategies to comprehend, interpret, evaluate, and appreciate texts.

Language Arts #5: Students employ a wide range of strategies as they write and use different writing process elements appropriately to communicate with different audiences for a variety of purposes

Language Arts #6: Students apply knowledge of language structure, language conventions, media tech- niques, figurative language, and genre to create, cri- tique, and discuss print and nonprint texts

Language Arts #11: Students participate as knowl- edgeable, reflective, creative, and critical members of a variety of literacy communities (NCTE & IRA, 1996).

Social Studies (Individual Development & Identity): Students explore how an individual's characteristics and abilities relate to development.

Social Studies (Time, Continuity, & Change): Students develop an understanding of historical context as they study mores and actions of people in the past (NCSS, 1994).

Revisit *Dirt on Their Skirts* and make a list of the players' nicknames on the board or chart paper. Encourage students to add other nicknames to the list. Using Janeczko's poem as a model, create a class poem about female nicknames or male and female nicknames. Figure 3.6 depicts possible research topics for further investigation.

Literature Circles and Book Talks

In addition to pursuing individual interests, everyone will also participate in a literature circle. Literature circles provide a time for students to meet and talk about books they are reading indepen- dently. In this case, the students in each literature circle will be reading and discussing one of the fol- lowing six titles: *The Journal of Biddy* Owens by Walter Dean Myers, *Bat 6* by Virginia Euwer Wolff, *Yang the Youngest and His Terrible Ear* by Lensey Namioka, *Thank You, Jackie Robinson* by Barbara

Cohen, *Gold Dust* by Chris Lynch, and *The Trading Game* by Alfred Slote. The books vary in terms of reading level and sophistication, with *Gold Dust* and *Bat 6* as the most demanding of the six. Themes such as family relationships, friendship, and acceptance are common to all of the titles. Several of the books also deal with racism, segregation, stereotyping, and/or individual responsibility.

During the exploration period of this unit, multiple copies of each of the titles are available for student perusal. We encourage students to read a little bit of several books before they make their decisions about which book they will read. Because we want students to make informed decisions, we also give a book talk on each title. A good book talk is like a good movie trailer. It gets us interested in reading the book, but it doesn't give too much away. The following is a book talk we've given on *Bat 6*.

Book Talk Example: Bat 6

All of us girls had grown up hearing about Bat 6, the softball game that's pitted the sixth grade girls of Barlow against the girls of Bear Creek for as long as anyone can remember. Pitted is probably the wrong word to use because the game was originally played 50 years ago to bring our communities together. It worked way back then and has every year since. Until this year, that is. You have to remember that this was supposed to be our year just like the previous years had belonged to our sisters and mothers and even our grandmothers. Each one of us dreamed of helping our team win and of being named the most valuable player of the year. But it didn't turn out the way we thought it would. Something happened, and now we're all left wondering if maybe we aren't in some way to blame. If you'd like to find out more about us and what happened, read *Bat 6* by Virginia Euwer Wolff.

THE WORK OF THE UNIT

After spending the week exploring the topic, we ask students to talk with us about what they would like to research and choose a book for their literature circle time. We often ask students for first and second choices for the literature circle assignment, and we make sure that students who don't get their first choice this time do next time. Our students also know that they will present what they've learned at the end of the unit. Each presentation must have an oral, written, and visual component. Students, however, decide in consultation with us how they will meet each of the requirements. For example, one group may create and perform a piece for Reader's Theater on the Negro Leagues while another group may conduct and explain a scientific experiment using the sweet spots on baseball bats to explain vibration. The audience for the presentation may include class- and schoolmates, friends and family members, and/or the community at large.

CONCLUSION

Several years ago, we came across a T-shirt that perfectly expressed our sentiments about reading. The slogan on the shirt read, "So Many Books, So Little Time." We are constantly reminded of this slogan when we work with teachers and children because we believe that all children have the potential to become passionate about books and reading.

In this chapter, we have explored what happens when readers meet texts and engage in the dynamic and creative act of reading. In addition, we discussed the ways in which teachers can support students as they 1) use what they know about the world to enter texts, 2) find their way through texts, and 3) make use of what they have learned or experienced through their reading. We hope that readers will take away what meant most to them from this chapter and make use of our ideas and examples as they teach.

 *Visit ChildLit at* **www.mhhe.com/childlit** *for Web links related to this chapter.*

Children's Literature Cited in the Chapter

Ayres, K. (1998). *North by Night: A Story of the Underground Railroad.* New York: Delacorte Press.

Branch, M. M. (1998). *Juneteenth: Freedom Day.* Photographs by W. Branch. New York: Cobblehill/Dutton Books.

Carter, D. (1988). *How Many Bugs in a Box?* New York: Simon and Schuster Books for Young Readers.

Delacre, L. (2000). *Salsa Stories.* New York: Scholastic.

Delacre, L. (1993). *Vejigante Masquerader.* New York: Scholastic.

DiCamillo, K. (2000). *Because of Winn-Dixie.* Cambridge, MA: Candlewick Press.

Fleischman, P. (1997). *Seedfolks.* Illustrated by J. Pederson. New York: HarperCollins.

French, V. (2000). *Growing Frogs.* Illustrated by A. Bartlett. Cambridge, MA: Candlewick Press.

Fox, M. (1989). *Night Noises.* Illustrated by T. Denton. New York: Harcourt Brace.

Hutchins, P. (1968). *Rosie's Walk.* New York: MacMillan.

Janeczko, P. B. (1998). *That Sweet Diamond.* Illustrated by C. Katchen. New York: Atheneum Books for Young Readers.

Kerr, J. (1971). *When Hitler Stole Pink Rabbit.* London: Collins.

Lowell, S. (1994). *The Three Little Javelinas.* Illustrated by J. Harris. New York: Scholastic.

Lowry, L. (1989). *Number the Stars.* Boston: Houghton Mifflin.

O'Neil, M. (1989). *Hailstones and Halibut Bones.* Illustrated by J. Wallner. New York: Doubleday.

Paladino, C. (1999). *One Good Apple: Growing Our Food for the Sake of the Earth.* Boston: Houghton Mifflin.

Polacco, P. (2000). *The Butterfly.* New York: Philomel Books.

Soto, G. (1990). *Baseball in April.* New York: Harcourt Inc.

Tolkien, J. R. R. (1938). *The Hobbit.* Boston: Houghton Mifflin.

Turner, M. W. (1997). *The Thief.* New York: Greenwillow Books.

Winter, J. (2001). *¡Beisbol!: Latino Baseball Pioneers and Legends.* New York: Lee and Low Books Inc.

Yolen, J. (1988). *The Devil's Arithmetic.* New York: Viking Kestrel.

Children's Literature Cited in One Book at a Time Lessons

Carle, E. (1992). *Pancakes, Pancakes!* New York: Simon & Schuster.

DiSalvo-Ryan, D. (1997). *Uncle Willie and the Soup Kitchen.* Mulberry Books.

Howard, E. F. (1991). *Aunt Flossie's Hats (and Crab Cakes Later).* Paintings by J. Ransome. New York: Clarion Books.

Livingston, M. C. (1989). *Dilly Dilly Piccalilli: Poems for the Very Young.* Illustrated by E. Christelow. New York: Margaret McElderry Books.

Children's Literature Cited for Generative Curriculum Example

Cline-Ransome, L. (2000). *Satchel Paige*. Paintings by J. Ransome. New York: Simon & Schuster for Young Readers.

Cohen, B. (1974). *Thank You, Jackie Robinson*. Drawings by R. Cuffari. New York: William Morrow and Company.

Cooper, E. (1998). *Ballpark*. New York: Greenwillow Books.

Curtis, G. (1998). *The Bat Boy & His Violin*. Illustrated by E. B. Lewis. New York: Simon & Schuster for Young Readers.

Day, A. (1990). *Frank and Ernest Play Ball*. New York: Scholastic Inc.

Gantos, J. (2000). *Joey Pigza Loses Control*. New York: Farrar, Straus, and Giroux.

Gutman, D. (1997). *Honus and Me: A Baseball Card Adventure*. New York: Avon Books.

Helmer, D. S. (1993). *Belles of the Ballpark*. Brookfield, CT: The Millbrook Press.

Hopkins, L. B. (1993). *Extra Innings: Baseball Poems*. Illustrated by S. Medlock. New York: Harcourt Brace Jovanovich.

Horenstein, H. (1997). *Baseball in the Barrios*. San Diego, CA: Harcourt Brace.

Hughes, D. (1996). *Team Picture*. New York: Simon & Schuster for Young Readers.

Janeczko, P. B. (1998). *That Sweet Diamond*. Illustrated by C. Katchen. New York: Atheneum Books for Young Readers.

Jaspersohn, W. (1989). *Bat, Ball, Glove*. Boston: Little, Brown and Company.

Lynch, C. (2000). *Gold Dust*. New York: HarperCollins Publishers.

Macy, S. (1993). *A Whole New Ball Game*. New York: Henry Holt and Company.

McKissack, P. C. & McKissack, F. (1994). *Black Diamond: The Story of the Negro Baseball Leagues*. New York: Scholastic Inc.

Mochizuki, K. (1993). *Baseball Saved Us*. Illustrated by D. Lee. New York: Lee and Low Books Inc.

Myers, W. D. (2001). *The Journal of Biddy Owens*. New York: Scholastic Inc.

Namioka, L. (1992). *Yang the Youngest and His Terrible Ear*. New York: Little, Brown & Company.

Panzer, N. (Ed.). (1994). *Celebrate America in Poetry and Art*. New York: Hyperion.

Rappaport, D., & Callan, L. (2000). *Dirt on Their Skirts*. Illustrated by E. B. Lewis. New York: Dial Books for Young Readers.

Ritter, J. H. (1998). *Choosing Up Sides*. New York: Philomel.

Ritter, L. S. (1999). *The Story of Baseball*. New York: William Morrow & Company.

Ritter, L. S. (1995). *Leagues Apart*. Illustrated by R. Merkin. New York: Morrow Junior Books.

Slote, A. (1990). *The Trading Game*. New York: J. B. Lippincott.

Soto, G. (1990). *Baseball in April*. New York: Harcourt Inc.

Tavares, M. (2000). *Zachary's Ball*. Cambridge, MA: Candlewick Press.

Thayer, E. L. (2000). *Casey at the Bat*. Illustrated by C. H. Bing. Brooklyn, NY: Handprint Books.

Ward, G. C. (1994). *Shadow Ball: The History of the Negro Leagues*. New York: Alfred A. Knopf. Distributed by Random House.

Winter, J. (2001). *¡Beisbol!: Latino Baseball Pioneers and Legends*. New York: Lee and Low Books Inc.

Winter, J. (1999). *Fair Ball!*. New York: Scholastic Press.

Wolff, V. E. (1998). *Bat 6*. New York: Scholastic Press.

Yolen, J. (1999). *Moon Ball*. Illustrated by G. Couch. New York: Simon & Schuster Books for Young Readers.

Young, R. (1998). *Game Day*. Photographs by J. Watcher. Minneapolis, MN: Carolrhoda Books.

Adult Resources Cited for Generative Curriculum Example

Morgan, J., & Lally, R. (Contributor). (2000). *Baseball for Dummies* (2nd ed.). Foster City, CA: IDG Books Worldwide, Inc.

Ritter, L. S. (1999). *The Story of Baseball*. New York: William Morrow & Company.

Ward, G. C., & Burns, K. (Contributor). (1994). *Baseball: An Illustrated History*. New York: Alfred A. Knopf.

References

Anderson, R. C., Hiebert, E. H., Scott, J. A., & Wilkinson, I. A. G. (1985). *Becoming a Nation of Readers: The Report of the Commission on Reading*. Urbana, IL: Center for the Study of Reading, University of Illinois.

Calkins, L. (2001). *The Art of Teaching Reading*. New York: Addison, Wesley, Longman.

Cunningham, P. M., & Allington, R. L. (2000). *Classrooms That Work*. New York: Longman.

Galda, L. & Gucice, S. (1997). Response-based Reading Instruction in the Elementary Grades. In S. A. Stahl & D. A. Hayes (Eds.), *Instructional Models in Reading* (pp. 311–330). Mahwah, NJ: Erlbaum.

Herber, H. L. (1978). *Teaching Reading in the Content Areas* (2nd ed.). Englewood Cliffs, NJ: Prentice Hall.

Holt, J. & Bell, B. H. (2000). Good books, good talk, good readers. *Primary Voices K–6, 9*, 3–8.

Marshall, J. (2000). Response to Literature. In M. Kamil, P. Mosenthal, P. D. Pearson, & R. Barr (Eds.), *Handbook on Reading Research, Volume 3*. Mahwah, NJ: Erlbaum.

Moore, D. W., Readence, J. E., & Rickelman, R. J. (1989). *Prereading Activities for Content Area Reading and Learning* (2nd ed.). Newark, DE: International Reading Association.

Myers, J. (1992). The social contexts of school and personal literacy. *Reading Research Quarterly, 27*, 297–334.

National Council of Teachers of English & International Reading Association (1996). *Standards for the English Language Arts*. Urbana, IL: NCTE.

Ogle, D. (1986). K-W-L: A teaching model that develops active reading in expository text. *The Reading Teacher, 39*, 564–570.

Peterson, R., & Eeds, M. (1990). *Grand Conversations: Literature Groups in Action*. New York: Scholastic.

Readence, J. E., Bean, T. W., & Baldwin, R. S. (1981). *Content Area Reading: An Integrated Approach*. Dubuque, IA: Kendall/Hunt.

Rosenblatt, L. (1938/1995). *Literature as Exploration*. New York: Language Association of America.

Sebesta, S. L. (2000). The Haunted Library Strikes Back! In N. Padak et al. (Eds.), *Distinguished Educators on Reading: Contributions That Have Shaped Effective Literacy Instruction* (pp. 253–255). Newark, DE: International Reading Association.

Sebesta, S. L. (1997). Having my say. *The Reading Teacher, 50*(7), 542–551.

Smith, F. (1988). *Joining the Literacy Club*. Portsmouth, NH: Heinemann.

Yopp R. H., & Yopp, H. K. (2001). *Literature-based Reading Activities*. Boston: Allyn & Bacon.

CHAPTER 4

Books That Bring Out the Artists in Us

We can't imagine what life would be like if there were no painters, sculptors, dancers, writers, poets, or musicians. Art expresses who we are as individuals and offers avenues for making connections across countries, continents, hemispheres, and time. "The arts have been part of us from the very beginning. Since nomadic people first sang and danced for their ancestors, since hunters first painted their quarry on the wall of caves, since parents first acted out the stories of heroes for their children, the arts have described, defined, and deepened human experience... A society and a people without the arts are unimaginable, as breathing would be without air." (Consortium of National Arts Education Associations, 1994, p. 5).

To us, schools without the arts are unimaginable as well. Picture a long corridor painted an institutional gray, green, or beige leading from classrooms to the cafeteria. Children and adults walk through the corridor several times a day as they go to breakfast, lunch, and physical education. Now think of the corridor as an art gallery. This month's exhibition is entitled "Mona with a New Look." As part of an integrated unit focusing on the life and work of Leonardo DaVinci, students have created their own up-to-date versions of the Mona Lisa. The smiles on the portraits are timeless; the dresses are pure 21st century. A month or so later, the corridor is again transformed; this time into an undersea world. The first-grade classes have covered the walls with murals that depict the plant and animal life found in the ocean. Overhead, three-dimensional sea creatures are suspended from the ceiling. Watch a kindergarten class as they enter the transformed hallway. Some children are "swimming" down the corridor, others are holding their noses as if they are truly underwater, while still others excitedly comment on the fish, turtles, and plant life. The daily lives of all who walk down the corridor are enhanced. The first-graders who transformed the corridor into an ocean have the pleasure of not only making art but also having their art viewed and appreciated by an audience.

NATIONAL STANDARDS IN THE ARTS

Early in the 1800s, the United States began universal public education as the means to strengthen and preserve our democracy. Music education was part of the established curriculum for the "Common Schools." Soon after, art instruction was included. Drama and dance came much later (Gary, 1997). Today, 97 percent of public elementary schools provide instruction in music, while 85 percent offer instruction in the visual arts. Approximately 43 percent of public elementary schools offer dance instruction, with only 8 percent offering instruction in drama (Westat Inc., 1995).

In 1994, the Consortium of National Arts Education Associations (now known as the National Coalition for Education in the Arts) published the *National Standards for Arts Education*. The Consortium defines art as both the "...creative works and the process of producing them and the whole body of work in art forms that make up the entire human intellectual and cultural heritage" (Consortium of National Arts Education Associations (CNAEA), 1994, preface). Through the development of the national standards, the CNAEA has provided a set of competencies in dance, music, theater, and the visual arts that identify what children should know and be able to do by the end of twelfth grade. These standards reinforce the belief that instruction in the arts must be a part of every child's curriculum in order for children to be truly educated (CNAEA, 1994).

THE BENEFITS OF EDUCATION IN THE ARTS

We believe that children require opportunities to make music just as they require opportunities to add, subtract, multiply, and divide numbers. They need to express themselves through dance just as they need to express themselves verbally. And they need to paint, draw, or sculpt just as they need to write. While competence in reading, language arts, mathematics, and science are expected, children also need to develop competence in the arts. A society benefits when its citizens are able to think and solve problems creatively, use the arts to express their ideas, and experience the pleasure that comes with creating works of art.

Participation in the artistic process encourages us to think both critically and creatively. For example, when most of us think of baseball, we rarely think beyond the typical images of players, bats, balls, and gloves. What would happen if we looked beyond? How would the world be different? Moses Pendleton, the founder and choreographer of MOMIX, answers these questions in his work "Baseball." Through dance, he explores and plays with our preconceived notions of baseball. His vision of the game encourages us to think about not only baseball but also the world in new ways.

Like MOMIX, when children participate in the arts they too use their creative and analytical thinking. Let's return to our previous example of "Mona with a New Look." Before creating their versions of the Mona Lisa, the students learned about the ways in which Da Vinci used line, light, color, and space to create his masterpiece. For their assignment, the students were confronted with the problem of transforming Da Vinci's Mona Lisa into a woman of the 21st century. What elements would they need to consider as they began to plan their work? How would they use the visual arts to express their views of modern women? The answers to these questions and the students' solutions were revealed in their finished works. It was evident to us as we viewed the portraits that each student had solved the problem in his or her own way. From the arts, we learn there are many equally valid answers and approaches to questions and problems.

Artists, dancers, playwrights, and musicians often offer social commentary that has the power to reach people's hearts and minds. Pablo Picasso's painting *Guernica* is a searing indictment of war, while Betye Saar's work asks us to look critically at American society. Folk songs and spirituals, along with contempo-

rary music, frequently comment on social issues. Often it is artists who act to preserve political freedom through their works. In fact, in totalitarian regimes, artistic freedom and expression are considered to be so powerful and threatening that the kind of music, visual art, dance, and theater that can be made and performed is dictated by the government. Artists who express contrary ideas are frequently persecuted or condemned in such societies. As we can see, the arts serve society as a free expression of ideas.

In addition to serving as social commentary, the arts are also an expression of culture. Chicano Park in San Diego and the Mural Arts Program in Philadelphia serve as prime examples of art as an expression of culture and social commentary. In each of these cities, local artists and community members work together to paint murals that not only beautify these cities but communicate a message of cultural strength and pride. At the end of World War II, the neighborhood known today as Barrio Logan in San Diego was a vibrant residential community for many of the city's Chicano citizens. However, a change in zoning laws designating the area as industrial rather than residential brought unwelcome changes after the war. The neighborhood was soon filled with junkyards; highways crisscrossed overhead. In 1967, community activists decided to reclaim the land beneath the highways for a neighborhood park. After several years of fighting city hall, Chicano Park was born. The highway pylons that once symbolized the neighborhood's demise now form an outdoor art gallery. Murals celebrating Mexican and Chicano culture and history have transformed the highway overpasses and pylons into expressions of beauty and inspiration.

Similarly, the Mural Arts Program was founded in 1984 by Jane Golden under the auspices of the Philadelphia Anti-Graffiti Network. In the 1980s and 1990s, individuals who were found writing graffiti on city walls were provided an alternative to prosecution. They were invited to attend workshops where they could learn to become mural artists. Over the intervening years, the program has become focused more on afterschool programs than graffiti artists and is now housed within the Philadelphia Recreation Department. Neighborhood residents suggest ideas for murals and often help to create them. The murals celebrate famous people, ordinary citizens, and grand ideals. With over 2,000 murals completed and many more sites available for future works, Philadelphia has the largest collection of murals of any American city. Graffiti still exists in Philadelphia, but the program's goals remain: to educate children, produce fine art, and positively influence the sense of community within the city's neighborhoods.

In addition, the arts help us to understand and appreciate other cultures. Several summers ago, at the Smithsonian Folklife Festival, we happened upon a performance of Surialanga, a Zulu-Indian Fusion Dance Troupe from South Africa. We were fascinated by the way in which a classical dance form had been combined with tribal dance and the dances of miners. The performers were college students of South African Indian descent and Zulu descent. The troupe's director, Professor Suria Govender, explained that the troupe had been formed at the University of Durban–Westville in part in response to the ethnic barriers that had been created during apartheid. It was her hope that through dancing, students would gain an understanding and appreciation of each other's cultures. She believed that this was crucial to South Africa's success as a nation.

We were recently reminded of Professor Govender's comments as we watched a group of elementary students performing dances from Vietnam as part of a Lunar New Year presentation. The children were from an urban school with a diverse student body. The dancers mirrored that diversity. Dressed in traditional garb, children from a variety of ethnic backgrounds performed dances that celebrate various aspects of Vietnamese culture. Students who knew little about the culture came away from the experience with new knowledge and appreciation, while other children saw their home culture being affirmed in school.

The arts also help us to see the world in different ways. Arts education encourages us to explore and learn about different styles, forms, perspectives, and people. As we learn classical dance steps, folk dances, and modern dance, we can learn the history of these dances as well. Comparing atonal and tonal music provides us with opportunities to explore

why composers choose to incorporate different sounds in their works. As we listen to baroque, folk, jazz, blues, or rap music, we can learn about these different forms and about the musicians who created them. When we examine portraits by Alice Neel, Vincent Van Gogh, Pablo Picasso, Salvador Dali, Frida Kahlo, and Rembrandt, we see the varied perspectives and styles of different time periods. Additionally, we are often surprised by the films that are made from books that we have read. The actors' and directors' interpretations are often quite different from our own. We leave the film or the museum with interesting questions and fresh perspectives. These opportunities remind us that exposure to the arts allows us to experience the many different ways in which ideas can be viewed and expressed.

There is also great pleasure in creating art. Drawing, sculpting, playing an instrument, and dancing are intrinsically rewarding. Although we may not consider ourselves to be "talented" in a particular art form, we learn that we can still enjoy the creative process. We may never sing or act professionally, but we can still derive great pleasure from being part of a community chorus or theater group. As teachers, we can do much to encourage our students to develop their artistic talents.

Aimee Martin's middle-school language arts class serves as an excellent example of how arts education can help students develop an appreciation for their artistic endeavors and those of others. Ms. Martin's class is studying poetry by reading the works of Native American, African-American, and Latino poets. As part of the unit, they listen to a variety of music, including jazz, blues, world, contemporary, and Native American. They explore how the music and poetry make them feel, and they share their interpretations of the words and the music. After several weeks of study, Ms. Martin shares two poems she has set to music. The first piece she performs for the class is "Life Doesn't Frighten Me" by Maya Angelou, read to Dollar Brand's "African Marketplace." At the conclusion of the reading, Ms. Martin and her students discuss how the musical composition corresponds to the feelings and messages found in Angelou's poem. Students then begin reading poetry and listening to music on their own or with a partner. As a final project each student selects a poem to set to music. Students perform their pieces for classmates and a tape of their performances is made so that their artistic endeavors can be shared with family, friends, and future classes. In this way, the students develop not only their own talents but also an appreciation for the talents of others.

In this section, we have noted some of the ways that education in the arts benefits us all. Yet in many schools across the country art, music, and physical education classes are the first to be cut during budget battles. The reality of the situation makes it even more crucial that classroom teachers offer their students opportunities to explore and learn about the arts.

CLASSROOM TEACHERS AND ARTS INSTRUCTION

Planning and facilitating art activities may be more challenging for teachers because they feel less prepared in the arts than in academic subjects such as math, science, language arts, or social studies. However, as we have seen, the arts enrich and enhance instruction. Integrating the arts into the curriculum provides opportunities for children to use critical and creative thinking skills for different purposes. According to Albers (2001), the artistic process both mirrors and reinforces the recursive nature of reading and writing. For example, teachers can help children see that the writing process is similar to the artistic process of working and reworking a clay sculpture.

We believe that students should receive instruction in the arts from teachers who are specialists in these fields. But at the same time classroom teachers can and should provide students with opportunities to paint, draw, sing, act, and dance. Two excellent resources for teachers who are interested in developing basic understandings of art and music are *The Art Pack* (1992) by Christopher Frayling, Helen Frayling, and Ron Van Der Meer; and *The Music Pack* (1994) by Ron Van Der Meer and Michael Berkeley. In addition, many museums

and arts organizations have extremely fine Web sites that provide information, lesson plans, and activities. The Getty Museum and the Kennedy Center for the Performing Arts both have Internet sites that we feel are invaluable to classroom teachers who are interested in incorporating arts education into their curricula.

What's most important to remember about art activities is that the children should feel free to be creative. As teacher educators, we stress to our preservice and inservice teachers that art activities should not be teacher-directed. When all of the children's creations look or sound exactly the same, the purpose of the activity is not to create art but rather to practice motor skills or to practice following directions. As teachers we need to provide students with opportunities to use a variety of materials constructively and creatively but not uniformly. One simple way to motivate students in the visual arts is to discuss the art in picture books. The book cover or book jacket often contains information about the artist/illustrator and the types of media used to create the illustrations. Some of the activities we suggest use this information as a starting point for exploring artistic forms.

CHILDREN'S LITERATURE AND THE ARTS

Happily, today there are many fiction and nonfiction selections that focus on the arts or artists. Many of the books we already use are actually lyrics. *This Land Is Your Land* by Woody Guthrie, *What a Wonderful World* by George D. Weiss and Bob Thiele, and *Mary Wore Her Red Dress and Henry Wore His Green Sneakers* by Merle Peek can all be used to teach children these classic songs. Examples of other books that encourage us to explore the world of music include *The Farewell Symphony* by Anna Harwell Celenza; Katherine Patterson's *Come Sing, Jimmy Jo*; *Zin! Zin! Zin! A Violin* by Lloyd Moss; and *Duke Ellington: The Piano Prince and His Orchestra* by Andrea Davis Pinkney. *i see the rhythm* by Toyomi Igus presents a history of African-American music from drum beats in Africa to modern day rap and hip-hop. Moreover, Michele Wood received the Coretta Scott King Award in 1999 for her illustrations in *i see the rhythm*.

Books about artists abound. Laurence Anholt has written several children's books that feature artists such as Degas, Picasso, and Van Gogh. In her biographies *Leonardo Da Vinci* and *Michelangelo*, Diane Stanley combines her own images with those of the artists to give readers an intriguing glimpse into these artists' lives. Books that explore the artistic process are also wonderful additions to classroom collections. Some selections we like include Cynthia Rylant's *All I See*, Tomie DePaola's *The Art Lesson*, and *Children of the Clay* by Rina Swentzell.

Dance is explored in both poetry and prose. Two poetry collections suitable for elementary classrooms are *Dance with Me* by Barbara Juster Esbensen and *Song and Dance: Poems*, an anthology compiled by Lee Bennett Hopkins. Other books such as *Mirandy and Brother Wind* by Patricia McKissack, *Jingle Dancer* by Cynthia Leitich Smith, *Ten Go Tango* by Arthur Dorros, and *My Mama Had a Dancing Heart* by Libba Moore Gray invite us to join in the dance. We can also meet real-life dancers through books. Andrea Davis Pinkney's *Alvin Ailey*, Tobi Tobias's *Maria Tallchief*, and *Dancing Wheels* by Patricia McMahon introduce us to three remarkable dancers.

In this chapter and throughout this book, we suggest activities in the arts that classroom teachers can implement. If your school has music, art, drama, or dance teachers, consult with them in planning activities for your students. When teachers share their expertise, children benefit.

Sample Lessons for Younger Readers

One Book at a Time

Let's Dance

Read aloud *Let's Dance* by George Ancona. With its simple text and exuberant photographs, *Let's Dance* invites readers to join with people around the world as they dance.

Preparation

1. Practice reading the book. Plan where you will stop to solicit responses. For example, early in the book, Ancona lists various actions in dance (kicking, hopping, reaching, etc.); you might stop and ask students which of these movements they do when they dance. Later, the books points out that we can dance alone, with a partner, or in a group. Again, you may choose to ask students which kind of dancing they prefer or if they know particular dances done singly, in pairs, or in a group. Avoid using the word costume when discussing the clothing worn by the dancers. Costume implies clothing worn for make-believe or pretend, neither of which applies to the clothing worn by dancers in the book.

2. Locate recordings of different types of music. Choose pieces from a variety of musical styles and cultures. The music should provide clues to the children about how they might move. Include musical passages of different tempos and moods. Jazz, world music, marches, and waltzes are several types of music that lend themselves to dance.

3. Locate music and directions for some simple dances done in groups or with a partner. Two such dances from Latin America and the American Southwest can be found in *Diez Deditos: Ten Little Fingers and Other Play Rhymes and Action Songs from Latin America* by Luis Orozco.

4. Gather chart paper and markers.
5. Locate a copy of the poetry collection *Dance with Me* by Barbara Juster Esbensen.

Introduction

Rather than beginning with the cover and title, start by sharing the end pages. These pages contain a double-page spread photograph of the legs of three tap dancers. Ask students to predict what the people in the photograph are doing. How do they know? Then share the cover and title. Find out who likes to dance, if anyone knows a special dance, when/where students dance, or anything else you think will activate your students' background knowledge. Tell the children that as you read the book, they should listen for information about how and why people dance.

Reading the Book

Read the book, stopping at several points to solicit student responses. After finishing the book, ask the children which type of dancing they would like to see or try. Discuss how dancing makes us feel. Then return to the purpose that was set for listening. Record what was learned about dance on chart paper. Return to the text to assist students in clarifying or justifying their ideas. When the group is finished sharing what they have learned, quickly review and summarize the information. You might say something like, "Wow, look at all the things we learned about dancing!" Then quickly reiterate the important points.

Curriculum Connections

Dance

Play a piece of music. Ask the students a variety of simple questions about the music. For example, is it fast or slow? How does the music make you feel? Does the music make you want to march, jump, turn...? Then have the children dance to the music. This activity can extend over the course of a week, a month, or the year. Students should have many opportunities to dance to different types of music. (**Identifying and Demonstrating Movement Elements and Skills.**)

Teach the class simple pair or group dances. Directions for "La Tia Monica" and "La Raspa" can be found in *Diez Deditos*. (**Dance and Culture.**)

Children who are learning a particular type of dance such as ballet, clogging, tap, or African may wish to demonstrate what they have learned or, with adult help, can teach the class some simple steps. (**Dance and Culture; Choreographic Principles.**)

Arrange to attend a dance performance. This may be as simple as enjoying a dance presentation by another class or as elaborate as attending a performance by a professional dance company. Have the students discuss what they observed and felt as they watched the performance. (**Dance and Critical Thinking.**)

Art

Just as children can use large-motor skills in dance to demonstrate emotions, they also can explore the artistic concept of line. Provide children with paper and pencils. Explore with the children how emotions can be communicated through simple marks on paper. Have them make marks that express a variety of emotions. Talk with the children about how their marks for each of the emotions are similar. Then explore how different marks convey different feelings. You may also wish to discuss how tightly or loosely the students hold their pencils as they make their various marks. (**Structure and Functions of Art**.)

Language Arts

Brainstorm the ways in which dancing makes us feel. Use the generated ideas to create a poem about dancing, beginning with the phrase "Dancing is..." For younger children, you may want to do a Language Experience Chart that begins with each child's name and the word he says. For example, Jeremy said, "Dancing is awesome." Make sure the poem or chart is read upon completion and is available for students to read during free reading time. (**Creative Writing; Writing Process**.)

For vocabulary development, create a web of dance words. The focus may be on things we do when we dance or how dancing makes us feel. (**Vocabulary Development**.)

After students have danced with a partner, you may decide to teach the word "pair." At the Reading Center, the children can sort pictures into things that are pairs and things that are not. Remember to have a symbol on the back of each picture that will facilitate self-checking. (**Vocabulary Development**.)

Share a poem or poems from Esbensen's poetry collection *Dance with Me*. Talk with the students about how the poet discovers dance in things that we might not consider when we think of dancing (bubbles, rain, and dust). Discuss with the children how poets often see the world in new and interesting ways, and this is one of the reasons poetry has the power to delight. (**Appreciation of Figurative Language**.)

Science

Read the poem "Bubbles" by Esbensen. Then invite the students to become "bubbleologists," people who study bubbles. Bubbles can be used to study surface tension, geometric shapes, and the spectrum. Provide students with bubble solution and a variety of commercially made and student-made wands. Take them outside and let them make bubbles. Encourage them to describe their bubbles—color, shape, size, number, how long the bubbles last, etc. Have them determine which wands worked the best. (**Physical Science; Experimenting**.)

Connecting to Standards

Let's Dance

The Arts (Dance): Understanding choreographic principles, processes, and structures.

The Arts (Dance): Applying and demonstrating critical and creative thinking skills in dance.

The Arts (Dance): Demonstrating and understanding dance in various cultures and historical periods (CNAEA, 1994).

Language Arts #3: Students apply a wide range of strategies to comprehend, interpret, evaluate, and appreciate texts. They draw upon their prior experience, their interactions with other readers and writers, their knowledge of word meaning, and other texts.

Language Arts #6: Students demonstrate their knowledge of language and its conventions to create and discuss print (NCTE & IRA, 1996).

Science (Physical Science): Students develop an understanding of the properties of objects and materials (NRC, 1996).

Social Studies (Culture): Students investigate how different cultures, groups, and societies are similar and different across common situations (NCSS, 1994).

Social Studies

Dance is a cultural universal found in all parts of the world. Ancona's book has numerous examples of dancers from various cultures. After discussing the examples in *Let's Dance*, you and your class may want to learn more about a specific dance or dances. Informational books such as *Lion Dancer: Ernie Wan's Chinese New Year* by Kate Waters and Madeline Slovenz-Low and *Powwow* by George Ancona give cultural information about the dances. (**Culture.**)

Let There Be Music!

Read aloud *Musicians of the Sun* by Gerald McDermott. Using an Aztec myth as his framework, McDermott creates a tale that explores music's power to transform and enrich people's lives. The colors used in the illustrations set the mood as they move from dark to light, sadness to joy.

Preparation
1. Practice reading the story. Select stopping points for prediction and response. For example, when the Lord of the Night tells Wind that he will arm him, stop and ask the students what the Lord of the Night might give to Wind.
2. Locate world music from Central America that contains the instruments mentioned in the book (rattles, drums, and flutes).
3. Obtain the tape or CD *Under the Green Corn Moon: Native American Lullabies*.
4. Gather other books of lullabies such as *Hush: A Thai Lullaby* by Minfong Ho, *Northwoods Cradle Song: From A Menominee Lullaby* by Douglas Wood, *Abiyoyo* by Pete Seeger, *In the Hollow of Your Hand: Slave Lullabies* by Alice McGill, *Sleep Rhymes around the World* edited by Jane Yolen, and *Hush Little Baby: A Folk Song with Pictures* by Marla Frazee.
5. Have drawing paper and crayons assembled for the prereading activity.

Introduction

Ask the students when and where they sing, listen to, or make music. How do they feel when they are listening to or making music? Then tell students that you are going to play music from Central America. You may want to quickly point out Mexico and Central America on a map. Instruct students to draw how the music makes them feel as they listen. After students have shared their drawings with a neighbor, have several share their work with the entire group. Ask students what life would be like if there were no music. Share that the story they are about to hear is one that people told long ago to explain how music first came to be on earth and the difference music made in people's lives. Ask the students to listen for how music came to earth.

Reading the Book

Read the story, stopping to solicit predictions and comments. Upon finishing, take time for individual responses and reactions. Encourage students to share the part of the story or the illustration they liked best. You may want to revisit the text and point out to students how McDermott used different colors in the illustrations to create different feelings.

Curriculum Connections

Music

The yellow musician in the book plays a lullaby on his flute. Talk with the children about the definition of a lullaby. Do they know any lullabies? Have they ever heard a lullaby? Have the students discuss what they think the characteristics of a lullaby might be. Will the music be fast or slow? Soft or loud? If you have the CD *Under the Green Corn Moon*, play the "Aztec Lullaby." Have the students discuss whether the song matches their criteria for a lullaby. Play several other songs and have the children confer about which they think make good lullabies. (**Listening to and Analyzing Music**.)

Teach the children several different lullabies or arrange to have parents/caregivers and children teach a favorite lullaby to the class. (**Singing with Others**.)

Put tapes or compact discs of lullabies and music from Central America in the Listening Center. (**Music and Culture**.)

Art

Using three very different musical selections (for example, hard rock, an adagio, and Dixieland Jazz) have the students paint or draw what they are feeling while listening to the music. Talk with children about the mood of each piece of music and how their pictures reflect those moods. (**Connecting Visual Arts and Other Disciplines**.)

Language Arts

If the children are learning about story grammar, this tale lends itself nicely to story mapping. Students can identify the characters, setting, problem, and solution. (**Literary Elements**.)

Connecting to Standards
Let There Be Music!

The Arts (Music): Singing, alone and with others, a varied repertoire of music.

The Arts (Music): Listening to, analyzing, and describing music.

The Arts (Music): Understanding music in relation to history and culture.

The Arts (Visual Arts): Making connections between visual arts and other disciplines (CNAEA, 1994).

Language Arts #3: Students apply a wide range of strategies to comprehend, interpret, evaluate, and

appreciate texts. They draw upon their prior experience, their interactions with other readers and writers, their knowledge of word meaning, and other texts.

Science (Physical Science): Students develop abilities necessary to understand and do scientific inquiry (NRC, 1996).

Social Studies (Culture): Students investigate how different cultures, groups, and societies are similar and different across common situations (NCSS, 1994).

Students can choose sounds or rhythm instruments that might represent each of the characters or events in the story. As the story is reread, the children listen for their character/event and make the appropriate sound. (**Understanding Relationship between Music and Language Arts.**)

Science

Use the book as a jumping-off point to explore the spectrum. Take the children outside on a sunny day and demonstrate how a prism breaks or refracts light to form the spectrum. Talk about the order in which the colors appear (rainbow effect). Have the children work in small groups, giving each group a prism and large piece of white paper. Let each child have a chance to manipulate the prism to create the spectrum on the paper. Have the children focus again on identifying each color and the order of the colors. Then provide each child with white paper and markers to record their own spectrum. (**Physical Science; Experimenting.**)

Social Studies

Read several of the book-length lullabies suggested in the section on Preparation. Have the students compare the lullabies from different cultures. If you prefer shorter selections, use a variety of sleep rhymes from Jane Yolen's *Sleep Rhymes around the World*. Show children where each country is located on a map. (**Culture; Geography.**)

Sample Lessons for Intermediate Readers

One Book at a Time

Dancing Our Dreams

Read aloud *Dancing Wheels* by Patricia McMahon with photographs by John Godt. This book introduces us to Dancing Wheels, a dance company composed of "sit down" and "stand up" dancers. All the dancers in the troupe use their legs, arms, backs, necks, and faces as they dance; the "sit down" dancers also use their wheelchairs. The company is a dream come true for its founder Mary Verdi-Fletcher, a woman who was born with spina bifida. Meet Mary and the dancers and teachers in her company in this true story about people who are dancing their dreams.

Preparation

1. Practice reading *Dancing Wheels*. Because the book is 48 pages long, you may decide to read it in several sessions. Plan stopping points for questions and reactions.
2. Gather several examples of concrete poetry.
3. Prepare an Anticipation Guide. We have provided a sample below.

Anticipation Guide for *Dancing Wheels*

Dancers use their legs more than any other part of their bodies.

    AGREE   DISAGREE

Everyone can dance.

    AGREE   DISAGREE

No matter what, you should follow your dreams.

    AGREE   DISAGREE

Introduction

Begin by having the students respond individually to the Anticipation Guide. Then have individuals share and explain their answers. Tell students the title *Dancing Wheels* without showing them the cover. Solicit student ideas on how wheels might dance. Ask students to predict what the book might be about. Summarize the students' comments before showing them the cover. As students look at the cover, they will notice that some of the dancers are in wheelchairs while others are not. Remind them that they should be thinking about the statements in the Anticipation Guide as they listen.

Reading the Book

Read the book, stopping for students to comment, question, or relate what is being read to the Anticipation Guide. When you finish the book, solicit comments from the students. Revisit the Anticipation Guide. What do students think about Mary Verdi-Fletcher and Dancing Wheels?

Curriculum Connections

Dance

In the book, the choreographer for Dancing Wheels, Sabatino Verlezza, plays a dancing name game with the dancers. Follow his instructions and play the game with your students. This may be done before or after reading the book. (**Demonstrating Movement Elements**.)

Several other simple exercises that help students begin to think and act like dancers are explained in the book. You may want to collaborate with the physical education teacher in your school to implement these ideas. (**Demonstrating Movement Elements**.)

Art

The wheel revolutionized the making of pottery. If there is a potter's wheel available, have an art specialist demonstrate making a pot on the wheel. Have students make pots by another method (coil or slab) and compare their efforts to pots made on a wheel. If it's possible for students to use the wheel, they can compare the two experiences. (**Media, Techniques, and Processes**.)

Movement and rhythm can be found in the visual arts as well as in dance. Share reproductions of paintings that contain movement and/or rhythm. Some paintings that come to mind are Matisse's *The Dancers*, Van Gogh's *Crows over Wheatfields*, and *Under the Wave at Kanagawa* by Katsushika

Hokusa. Show the reproductions and talk with the students about how the artists conveyed movement and rhythm in their works. (**Structure and Function**.)

Language Arts

Share shape or concrete poetry with your students. "Egg" in *The Great Frog Race and Other Poems* by Kristine O'Connell George is a favorite of ours. *Splish Splash* and *Flicker Flash* by Joan Bransfield Graham and *Doodle Dandies* by J. Patrick Lewis are three very engaging collections of concrete poetry. Have the students brainstorm words and phrases that relate to wheels or objects that have wheels. Pairs or small groups can then arrange the words and phrases into an appropriate shape. Have students share their work and then display the poems. (**Literary Forms**; **Writing Process**.)

Science

Wheels are a very important technological innovation. Depending on your curriculum, you can use this book as a beginning point for exploring different types of wheels (cogwheel, flywheel, pulley) or scientific principles that pertain to rotating wheels such as precession, inertia, and centrifugal force. Another option is to study how wheels are used in machines. (**Physical Science**.)

Social Studies

Study the development of the wheel, and then explore the technological innovations that came as a result of the wheel (potter's wheel, machines that use pulleys, water wheels, wind mills, bicycles...). Over a 24-hour period, have the students record the ways in which they use wheels in daily life. How would our lives be different if we didn't have wheels? (**Science, Technology and Society**.)

Mary Verdi-Fletcher is living her dream of being a dancer. Research individuals who followed their dreams when others doubted them (e.g., inventors). Students can share their research by creating a living wax museum exhibit. Each student can pose with an appropriate prop and tell his/her person's story. (**Individual Development and Identity**.)

Connecting to Standards
Dancing Our Dreams

The Arts (Dance): Identifying and demonstrating movement elements and skills in performing dance.

The Arts (Visual Arts): Understanding and applying media, techniques, and processes. (CNAEA, 1994).

Language Arts #5: Students employ a wide range of strategies as they write and use different writing process elements appropriately to communicate with different audiences for a variety of purposes (NCTE & IRA, 1996).

Social Studies (Individual Development & Identity): Students explore how an individual's characteristics and abilities relate to development.

Social Studies (Science, Technology, & Society): Students investigate how science and technology have affected interactions with the social and natural world (NCSS, 1994).

Jubilee Singers

Read aloud *A Band of Angels* by Deborah Hopkinson with illustrations by Raul Colón. Just after the Civil War, a school for freed slaves that eventually became Fisk University was established in Nashville. In the early years, the school was so short of funds its very survival was threatened. *A Band of Angels* is the story of how the school's chorus, the Jubilee Singers, raised money to save the school and introduced the world to the power and beauty of Spirituals. This fictionalized account of the Jubilee Singers is told in the form of a family story or memorat. Colón's sepia-toned illustrations have the look of early photographs that help establish the setting.

Preparation

1. Practice reading the story, planning where you will stop for questions or comments.
2. Locate a recording of Spirituals that contains some of the songs sung by the Jubilee Singers. A list of the songs is provided at the back of the book. You will need to have "Swing Low, Sweet Chariot" to use during the introduction to this lesson.
3. Make an overhead transparency of the words to "Swing Low, Sweet Chariot," available on the CD *Golden Gospel Greats* by the Jordanaires.
4. Collect books containing Spirituals. We like Ashley Bryan's *All Night, All Day: A Child's First Book of African-American Spirituals,* as well as *How Sweet the Sound: African American Songs for Children* by Wade and Cheryl Hudson.
5. Locate a copy of the poem "Aunt Sue's Stories" by Langston Hughes. This poem may be found in *Words with Wings: A Treasury of African-American Poetry and Art* compiled by Belinda Rochelle.
6. Locate a copy or copies of *To Be a Slave* by Julius Lester.

Introduction

Play the song "Swing Low, Sweet Chariot" for the class. Ask how many of the students know or have heard the song. Where have they heard or sung the song? Project the transparency and read through it with the students. Show the cover of the book and read the title. Talk with the students about how the book might relate to the song. Ask them to think about why the author may have chosen the title *A Band of Angels* as they listen to the story.

Reading the Book

Read the story, stopping periodically to make and check predictions and to solicit comments and questions. When finished, solicit students' responses and thoughts. Revisit the title. As students offer their ideas, ask them to explain and support their answers. Play the song "Swing Low, Sweet Chariot" again. Explain that they will be listening to and learning about other songs known as Spirituals.

Curriculum Connections

Music

Two of the songs sung by the Jubilee Singers were "Go Down Moses" and "Steal Away," also available on the Jordanaires CD. Have the students listen to the songs. Analyze the lyrics of each. "Go Down

Moses" protests the enslavement of African-Americans, while "Steal Away" is thought to have been sung in conjunction with running away. After listening to these and other Spirituals, students also may enjoy learning and performing several songs. (**Music, History, and Culture**.)

Language Arts

Direct students' attention back to the text. Talk about the structure of the story and how the author has the character of Aunt Beth tell the story. Then tell the students that everyone is a storyteller. Do they or someone they know tell stories about what happened to them or other people in their families? Have they every heard someone say, "When I was a girl/boy" to begin a story? Do they know stories about when they themselves were babies or toddlers? Have the students either write a story about something that happened to them or about a family member or a person they know (neighbor, foster parent, friend...). Plan a time for students to share their stories. (**Writing Process**.)

You also may want to discuss how Colón's illustrations reflect the time period of the story. If they are illustrating their pieces, the students will want to consider how their illustrations reflect the settings in their stories. You might want to use the illustrations in books such as *Chato's Kitchen* by Gary Soto, *Uptown* by Bryan Collier, *McDuff Moves In* by Rosemary Wells, and *Henry Hikes to Fitchburg* by D. B. Johnson as you discuss the role illustrations play in helping readers understand when and where a story takes place. (**Literary Elements**.)

Social Studies

Share Langston Hughes' poem "Aunt Sue's Stories" with the class. In the poem, Hughes points out that some of the most compelling stories we read/hear are about real people. Do students agree or disagree with Hughes? Revisit the parts of *A Band of Angels* that describe the discrimination the Jubilee Singers faced. Have students discuss the incidents. Why did they happen? How would the students feel if these things had happened to them? Use several of the oral history pieces in *To Be a Slave* that deal with life after the Civil War. Explore the difficulties that the emancipated faced. Further investigation might

---

Connecting to Standards
Jubilee Singers

The Arts (Music): Understanding music in relation to history and culture.

Language Arts #3: Students apply a wide range of strategies to comprehend, interpret, evaluate, and appreciate texts. They draw upon their prior experience, their interactions with other readers and writers, their knowledge of word meaning, and other texts (NCTE & IRA, 1996).

Mathematics (Data Analysis & Probability): Students formulate questions that can be addressed with data and collect, organize, and display relevant data to answer them.

Mathematics (Representation): Students create and use representations to organize, record, and communicate mathematical ideas (NCTM, 2000).

Social Studies (Individuals, Groups, & Institutions): Students explore how people, events and elements of culture are impacted by groups and institutions.

Social Studies (Power, Authority & Governance): Students define concepts such as role, status, justice, and power as they explore issues and social problems (NCSS, 1994).

include learning about segregation and the Jim Crow Laws. (**Using Primary Sources; Power, Authority, and Governance.**)

Interdisciplinary (Mathematics and Social Studies)

When Ella arrived at the Fisk School, she had six dollars to her name. This was enough money to pay for three weeks of school. Use the cost of education today to have students apply their knowledge of mathematics. For example, have students find out how much it costs annually to educate a single student in their school. The class can explore issues related to cost. What expenses are included in the cost (materials, salaries, maintenance, utilities, etc.)? The data may be used to construct a pie graph. The chart can be used to generate a discussion on cost-saving ideas or to develop a list of questions about school costs. You may want to invite the person in charge of the school's finances to meet with your class as they explore this topic. (**Data Analysis and Probability; Representation; Individuals, Groups, and Institutions; Economics.**)

The Jubilee Singers raised money to keep their school open. Students may have a special project or charitable organization in mind for which they would like to raise money. After deciding on a project, students should investigate costs and formulate a fund raising plan that is feasible to implement. (**Individuals, Groups, and Institutions.**)

Vaudeville and Ragtime

Read aloud *The Piano Man* written by Debbi Chocolate and illustrated by Eric Velasquez. The author recounts her grandfather's career as a piano player for the silent movies, a vaudeville and musical comedy performer, and as a piano tuner when talking movies were created. She provides a glimpse into the musical styles and history of African-American music during the early part of the 20th century.

Preparation

1. Practice reading aloud *The Piano Man*, deciding where you will pause for questions or comments.
2. Locate a vintage silent movie preserved on videotape. Charlie Chaplin, the Keystone Kops, and old westerns are some to consider.
3. Have available recordings of Scott Joplin and Jelly Roll Morton for listening.

Introduction

Ask the students if they have ever seen an old silent movie. If anyone has, have them describe what they watched. How were the emotions of the actors conveyed? Show a short silent movie or movie clip. Explore with the students how music was used to convey actions, peril, sadness, and love. Have the students listen to find out what life was like for the man in the story.

Reading the Book

Read the book, stopping where you planned for questions and/or comments. Talk with the students about how technological advances can affect the work people do.

Curriculum Connections

Music

Play different types of instrumental music for the students (play the piano yourself if you know how, or use recorded music). Ask the children to think about what kinds of scenes might be happening in a movie for each type of music. What is it about the individual selections that brings to mind certain actions or scenes? **(Relationship between Music and Other Disciplines.)**

Introduce the students to recordings of Scott Joplin's and Jelly Roll Morton's ragtime music. They may be familiar with Joplin's "The Entertainer," but may not know that he composed the music. Invite your school's music teacher into the classroom to discuss syncopation, the rhythm used in ragtime music. If any of the students play the piano, they may want to practice and play a piece of ragtime music for the class. **(Listening to and Describing Music.)**

Interdisciplinary (Creative Drama, Music, Dance, Art, and Language Arts)

Invite students to work in groups to develop and produce Vaudeville-type acts. They can dance, sing, play instruments, create skits, etc. You may want to videotape the class's Vaudeville show and view it with the class. If the students are willing, they can perform the show for other classes. An excellent Web site to use to learn more about Vaudeville is provided by the Library of Congress.

Have the students write and produce a silent movie. They will need to write the script, select actors, make costumes and scenery, and decide on music. This activity will take several weeks, as students will need time to complete all the processes involved and practice their scenes. Videotape the movie and invite the students' families to view it. **(Relationship between Music and Other Disciplines.)**

Connecting to Standards
Vaudeville and Ragtime

The Arts (Music): Listening to, analyzing, and describing music.

The Arts (Music): Understanding relationship between music, the other arts, and disciplines outside of the arts

The Arts (Theater): Script writing by the creation of improvisations and scripted scenes based on personal experience, heritage, imagination, literature, and history. Acting by developing basic acting skills to portray characters who interact improvised and scripted scenes. Designing and developing environments for improvised and scripted scenes. Directing and organizing rehearsals for improvised and scripted scenes. Researching by using cultural and historical information to support improvised and

scripted scenes, Comparing and incorporating art forms by analyzing methods of presentation and audience response for theater, dramatic media, and other art forms (CNAEA, 1994).

Language Arts #4: Students adjust their use of spoken, written, and visual language to communicate effectively with a variety of audiences and for different purposes.

Language Arts #11: Students participate as knowledgeable, reflective, creative, and critical members of a variety of literacy communities (NCTE & IRA, 1996).

Social Studies (Power, Authority & Governance): Students define concepts such as role, status, justice, and power as they explore issues and social problems (NCSS, 1994).

Social Studies

Have students explore the historical period when Vaudeville was in its heyday (the 1890s to 1930s). These decades represent important periods in American history. Topics may include immigration, race relations, World War I, and the "Roaring 20s." The entertainment industry generally reflects the culture of the time. Vaudeville acts often included stereotypic views of immigrants, women, and African-Americans. Discuss how these performances operated to maintain the status quo of a segregated and racist America. (**Individuals, Groups, and Institutions**; **Power, Authority, and Governance**.)

Encourage the students to learn about the history of ragtime. They can research the music's roots, specific performers, and the music industry of the time. (**Culture**.)

Sample Unit for the Intermediate Grades

Rock Art

Many thematic units lend themselves to infusing arts activities into the curriculum. Conversely, some units that have a strong arts emphasis can also integrate other subjects into the study of the arts topic. We have provided such an example with our intermediate grades unit on Rock Art. We first developed this unit thinking only of the art aspects, but it soon became clear that the topic was much more than just a study of art—it was also a study of prehistoric peoples and our understanding of their daily lives. Art is an expression of one's culture. In this unit, we explore the culture and daily lives of prehistoric humans through a study of their art. We have chosen to study rock art from two areas: Europe and the southwestern United States. The concepts we developed may be used as they are written or may be changed to suit the need for a more focused study of rock art in a particular area.

Concepts for the Rock Art Unit

1. Around 100,000 years B.C., during the last Ice Age, our direct ancestors, *Homo Sapiens sapiens*, appeared in Africa. These modern humans migrated to Europe and Asia approximately 40,000 years ago. This is the period of time when the first known works of art were created.
   A. *Homo Sapiens sapiens,* also known as Cro-Magnons, created the cave paintings found in Europe in places such as Chauvet, Lascaux, and Altamira. The cave paintings at Chauvet are estimated to be 30,000 years old.
   B. Exactly how the first human inhabitants arrived in North America has recently come into question. The prevailing theory has been that they came across the Bering Strait during the last Ice Age. However, recent archaeological finds suggest that people may have come much earlier using ocean travel. Despite this controversy, the earliest known rock art in North America is estimated to be 16,000–18,000 years old.

2. Rock art includes drawings that are carved or engraved into stone (petroglyphs) as well as those that are painted on rock surfaces (pictographs). Line, shape, and color can be used to communicate ideas and feelings.

3. From a cross-cultural study of rock art, similarities in the images depicted by early humans can be found. The images these early humans left on rocks and in caves include animals, human figures, handprints, plants, and signs.

4. Archaeologists and others who study art have hypothesized about what the rock art might have meant to the prehistoric artists. They theorize that rock art may have been created for/as:

Concept 1: Prehistoric People
Early Humans by N. Merriman
The Stone Age by P. D. Netzley
The Ancient Cliff Dwellers of Mesa Verde by C. Arnold
A Personal Tour of Mesa Verde by R. Young
Anasazi by L. E. Fisher
Prehistoric Rock Art by M. Terzi
Stories in Stone: Rock Art Pictures by Early Americans by C. Arnold
Mystery of the Lascaux Cave by D. H. Patent

Concept 2: Petroglyphs/Pictographs
Native American Rock Art: Messages from the Past by Y. LaPierre
Mystery of the Lascaux Cave by D. H. Patent
Stories in Stone: Rock Art Pictures by Early Americans by C. Arnold
First Painter by K. Lasky
Stories on Stone, Rock Art: Images from the Ancient Ones by J. O. Dewey

Concept 3: Images Depicted
Native American Rock Art: Messages from the Past by Y. LaPierre
Painters of the Caves by P. Lauber
When Clay Sings by B. Baylor

Myths and Folktales
Crow and Hawk: A Traditional Pueblo Indian Story by M. Rosen
Coyote: A Trickster Tale from the American Southwest by G. McDermott
Coyote Walks on Two Legs by G. Hausman & F. Cooper
Arrow to the Sun: A Pueblo Indian Tale by G. McDermott
The People with Five Fingers by J. Bierhorst
How the Stars Fell in the Sky: A Navajo Legend by J. Oughton

Concept 4: Theories
Painters of the Caves by P. Lauber
Mystery of the Lascaux Cave by D. H. Patent
First Painter by K. Lasky
Native American Rock Art: Messages from the Past by Y. LaPierre
Quennu and the Cave Bear by M. Day
Stories on Stone, Rock Art: Images from the Ancient Ones by J. O. Dewey

Concept 5: Age of Rock Art
Painters of the Caves by P. Lauber
Stories in Stone: Rock Art Pictures by Early Americans by C. Arnold
Native American Rock Art: Messages from the Past by Y. LaPierre

Historical Fiction
Boy of the Painted Cave by J. Denzel
Return to the Painted Cave by J. Denzel
Noli's Story by P. Dickinson
Malu's Wolf by R. Craig
Anooka's Answer by M. Cowley
Dar and the Spear-Thrower by M. Cowley

·⌣ **Figure 4.1** ⌣·

Children's Literature Selections for Rock Art Unit

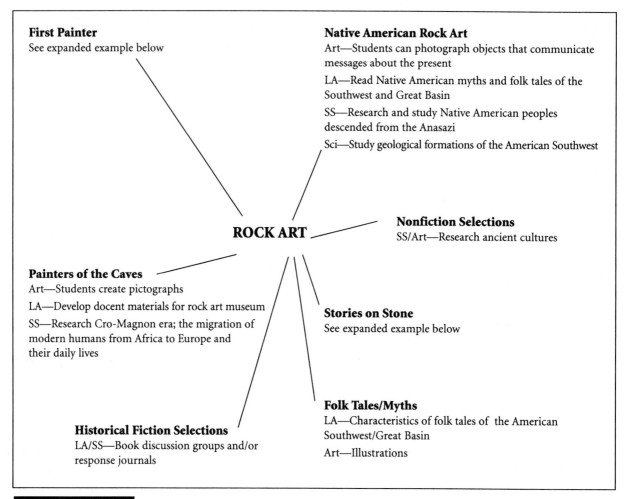

Web of Children's Literature for Rock Art Unit

A. Hunting magic—to help in the hunt for animals for food

B. Spiritual beliefs—to explain natural phenomena such as thunder and lightning or to ask spirits that had animal shapes for help

C. Ceremonial places—the caves are thought to be places where rites of passage took place

D. Recorded memory—before there were written words, the drawings served to tell stories or were prompts for stories elders would relay to younger members of the clan

5. The age of rock art is calculated through several methods. These include analyzing the subject of the art, the degree of erosion, the amount of lichen covering the drawing, and carbon-14 dating. By measuring the amount of carbon-14 in an object that was once living, scientists can closely estimate its age. Scientists measure the carbon-14 in the paints, tools, or human remains that are found at the sites.

Many of the books selected are appropriate for read-alouds. Others such as *The Stone Age* by Patricia Netzley and *The Ancient Cliff Dwellers of Mesa Verde* by Caroline Arnold are more suitable for independent reading and research. We have included several pieces of historical fiction that center around the lives of young people during the Ice Age. We also have listed several examples of Native American myths and folk tales to share some of the oral tradition of those societies. Although

Byrd Baylor's *When Clay Sings* deals with pottery, the designs depicted in the illustrations are those of ancient potters of the Anasazi, Hohokam, Mogollon, and Mimbres. We thought this book would be useful to show clearly the kinds of images that were created many centuries ago in the American Southwest.

Sample Lessons

Cave Painters

Read aloud *First Painter* by Kathryn Lasky with paintings by Rocco Baviera. *First Painter* is Kathryn Lasky's creative interpretation of the unknown history of Cro-Magnon era cave painting. In an afterword, she tells the readers that no one truly knows who the first cave painters were or why the paintings were done. She decided to let the First Painter be an adolescent girl, Mishoo, who paints the cave walls for spiritual reasons. Baviera's beautiful paintings are not actual copies of those found in Europe, but instead are original works made using natural materials similar to those of the prehistoric era.

Preparation

1. Practice reading aloud *First Painter*. Decide where you will pause for questions or comments.
2. Have chart paper on an easel or the chalkboard available to record students' responses.
3. Have available pictures of the real cave paintings from caves at Lascaux, Altamira, and Chauvet.

Introduction

Ask the children to close their eyes and to imagine that they live in prehistoric times. Give them a minute or two to think about what their lives would be like, what they would see and do. Have the children open their eyes and share with a partner what they imagined. Show the children the pictures of the cave paintings. Ask the students, "Why do you think cave paintings were created?" As the students offer their ideas, write them down on the board or chart paper. Tell the students the story is about a girl who is a cave painter and that they should listen to learn about her experiences.

Reading the Book

Read the book, stopping where you planned for questions or comments. Ask the students to imagine they are Mishoo. How would they feel as they went into the cave, as they were painting, or when the rain started?

Curriculum Connections

Art

If possible, use a large section of wall in the school to create a cave art mural. Invite the class to invent a prehistoric story and then illustrate it on the wall. Each student should have responsibilities for contributing to the story and painting the mural. Provide the students with an opportunity to look at the wall. Are there any bumps or gouges that can be used effectively in their design? How large a space do they have to fill? What other considerations do they need to address? The students should first draw their design to scale on regular-size drawing paper. As they talk about their ideas, they can revise their drawing until the class is satisfied with the design. They then will need to sketch the design onto the wall surface. Using the colors available during prehistoric times (yellow, red, ocher, and black), the students can add paints to create the finished mural. (**Choosing Subject Matter, Symbols, and Ideas**; **Arts and Culture**; **Connecting Visual Arts and Other Disciplines**.)

If it is not possible to use a school wall, provide each student with a large piece of butcher paper, approximately four to five feet in length. The students can create their own section of a prehistoric cave wall on their piece of butcher paper. They may crumble and then flatten the paper to get an interesting textured surface on which to draw and paint. The children may copy pictures from the book or those that you display of real cave paintings in Europe, or they can create their own original paintings to accompany a story they write. (**Arts and Culture**.)

The prehistoric cave paintings at Chauvet and other sites are considered to be the first-known attempts to create art. Graphic artists also believe that these images are the earliest examples of graphic design. These early artists used painting, drawing, engraving, and sculpture. Invite your art education teacher or a local art expert to the classroom to discuss these four art techniques. (**Understanding Artistic Techniques and Processes**.)

Language Arts

Read aloud pages 31–37, "What the Art May Tell," from Patricia Lauber's *Painters of the Caves*. After reading the chapter, discuss with students the theories scientists have devised to explain prehistoric paintings. Do the theories the students generated before listening to *First Painter* relate to those of the scientists? Then read aloud Lasky's Afterword, in which she explains her concept of the book. (**Comparing Texts**; **Evaluating Historical Fiction**.)

Just as Kathryn Lasky created a fictionalized version of the First Painter, students can write the story that is depicted in their "cave painting" from the art activity. Choosing one of the theories of why rock art was created, the students can write a story that corresponds with their painting. (**Creative Writing**.)

Social Studies

Share with the students the pictures you have gathered of real cave paintings. Discuss the figures that are depicted. In the cave paintings at Chauvet and elsewhere in Europe, only animals, humans, and signs were painted. No depictions of the environment or vegetation are present. Have students generate a list of questions about European cave art. Students then work in small groups to research the questions they have about the cave paintings at the sites of their choice. Students may use books or Internet resources to do their research. There are many Internet sites on rock art. Students then write a report and share what they learned with the class in an oral presentation. (**Research Skills**; **Geography**; **Communication**.)

Connecting to Standards
Cave Painters

The Arts (Visual Arts): Choosing and evaluating a range of subject matter, symbols, and ideas.

The Arts (Visual Arts): Understanding the visual arts in relation to history and cultures (CNAEA, 1994).

Language Arts #2: Students read a wide range of literature from many periods in many genres to build an understanding of the many dimensions of human experience (NCTE & IRA, 1996).

Social Studies (Culture): Students develop a knowledge of how culture influences behavior.

Social Studies (Time, Continuity, & Change): Students learn about ways scientists reconstruct and explain the past (NCSS, 1994).

Mathematics (Representation): Use representations to model and interpret physical, social, and mathematical phenomena (NCTM, 2000).

Discuss with students how we learn about early humans and what archaeologists do. If you live near a college or university that has an Archaeology or Anthropology department, invite an expert to visit with your class to discuss his or her profession. (**Culture; Time, Continuity, and Change.**)

Interdisciplinary (Art, Social Studies, and Language Arts)

In small groups, have the students discuss the following questions. "Why, when life was so difficult, would individuals take time to paint on rocks? What, if anything, was the benefit of their paintings to their society? Who painted and why?" Each group should have a recorder to write the group's responses. The groups then share their thinking with the whole class. This discussion may lead to an exploration of other communication systems (e.g., writing, drumming, sign language, mathematics, Morse code). (**Connecting Visual Arts and Other Disciplines.**)

Mathematics

Have students create a timeline depicting the earliest known art through today. On the timeline, the students can plot when specific artworks were done. (**Representation.**)

Science

Teach students about carbon-14 dating. (**Life Science.**)

Discuss with the students how the prehistoric painters mixed their own paints from the materials they had available. While these early humans used blood and animal fat as binders, the students can use gesso to mix with dry pigments to make their paints. (**Chemistry.**)

Native American Rock Art

Read aloud Jennifer Owen Dewey's *Stories on Stone, Rock Art: Images from the Ancient Ones*. In *Stories on Stone*, the author recounts family trips to visit rock art sites in the American

Southwest. She shares her enthusiasm for the mystery of American rock art and provides some possible answers to the questions of who created the rock art and why.

Preparation

1. Practice reading the book aloud, planning where you will stop for questions and comments.
2. Have available pictures of rock art from sites in the Southwest. Mimbres Valley, Nine Mile Canyon, Petroglyph National Monument, Chaco Canyon, and Mesa Verde are several options.
3. Have chart paper and an easel available for a "K-W-L."

Introduction

Show the students pictures of Native American rock art. Develop a "K-W-L." Ask the students what they know about rock art. Write what the students say on chart paper in the column labeled with a "K." Ask them what they would like to learn about Native American rock art. Write their responses in the column labeled with a "W." After everyone has had a chance to contribute, tell the students that they are going to begin their study of Native American rock art by listening to *Stories on Stone, Rock Art: Images from the Ancient Ones.*

Reading the Book

Read the book as you planned. If you come across information that the students specified on the "K-W-L" chart, stop and discuss it with them. "Is this enough information, or do we need to know more about this topic?" Following the read-aloud, provide an opportunity for students to add to the chart. As you and your students continue to study rock art and the ancient cultures of the American Southwest, add information to the "W" column for questions that still need to be investigated and to the "L" column for what you have learned.

Curriculum Connections

Art

Pair *Stories on Stone* with Byrd Baylor's *When Clay Sings.* As you read this poetic book, call students' attention to the illustrations. These illustrations reflect the images that Anasazi, Mogollon, Mimbres, and Hohokam potters used thousands of years ago. Allow the students opportunities to examine this book and the pictures of the Native American rock art that you gathered. Ask the art teacher to come into the classroom to discuss the elements of line, shape, and color found in the compositions. (**Reflecting upon Works of Others.**)

If you live near one of the rock art sites, plan a field trip to visit and learn. If that is not possible, use the Internet, to take a "virtual" rock art field trip. (**Arts and Culture.**)

Ask the students to recall the cave paintings of Europe and the Native American rock art. What similarities do they see in the art of these diverse cultures? Discuss the materials used and the designs created. (**Arts and Culture.**)

Revisit the hypothesized purposes of rock art. Discuss with the students contemporary artworks on walls. Share some photographs of murals. What are the purposes for these present-day works? Encourage the students to research information about murals and mural projects like those mentioned earlier in this chapter. The discussion may also lead to an investigation of graffiti and graffiti artists. (**Evaluating the Works of Others**.)

Music

Introduce students to Native American music. A recording that we mentioned earlier, *Under the Green Corn Moon: Native American Lullabies,* may be used in this lesson as well. There are many other recordings of Native American music. (**Listening to and Describing Music**.)

Social Studies

Using books such as Caroline Arnold's *The Ancient Cliff Dwellers of Mesa Verde* and Robert Young's *A Personal Tour of Mesa Verde,* along with the Internet and textbooks, have students study the culture of the Anasazi. What was daily life like for the Anasazi? How were their lives similar to ours today? How were they different? What were the roles of the men, women, and children? What was the political system? What may have happened to the Anasazi? (**Culture; Time, Continuity, and Change; Individuals, Groups, and Institutions; Power, Authority, and Governance; Production, Distribution, and Consumption**.)

Language Arts

No one knows for sure why the Anasazi abandoned their cliff dwellings. Using their Social Studies research, ask the students to speculate on what happened to the Anasazi. Have each student write a personal account from the viewpoint of a child his or her age that tells of the last day(s) at Mesa Verde. (**Writing Process; Creative Writing**.)

Share the poem "Magic Rocks" from Frank Asch & Ted Levin's *Cactus Poems.* Using "Magic Rocks" as a model, invite the students to write a class poem about one of the petroglyphs or pictographs that most inspires them or captures their imagination. (**Creative Writing; Writing Process**.)

Connecting to Standards
Native American Rock Art

The Arts (Visual Arts): Reflecting upon and assessing the characteristics and merits of their work and the work of others.

The Arts (Visual Arts): Understanding the visual arts in relation to history and culture.

The Arts (Music): Listening to, analyzing, and describing music (CNAEA, 1994).

Social Studies (Individuals, Groups, & Institutions): Students reflect on how groups and institutions impact people, events, and culture.

Social Studies (Production, Consumption, & Distribution): Students develop an understanding of historical developments in relation to economic concepts (NCSS, 1994).

Language Arts #5: Students employ a wide range of strategies as they write and use different writing process elements appropriately to communicate with different audiences for a variety of purposes (NCTE & IRA, 1996).

Early rock art communicated messages before people had written language. During the Great Depression, hoboes left signs along the way on their travels that communicated useful messages to those familiar with their meanings. Have the students research the signs and their meanings. You might have the students create new signs that would provide useful information for their classmates. (**Art and Culture**.)

CONCLUSION

Experiencing art is essential. As children grow and develop, opportunities to explore the arts allow them to see new perspectives, try fresh ideas, and practice different ways of sharing their thinking. Moreover, through art, children can express their feelings visually, kinesthetically, and musically as well as orally.

This chapter presented a rationale for and ways to integrate children's literature and instruction in the arts. It is our hope that the ideas we have suggested inspire you to look for the artist in yourself and in the children you teach.

 *Visit ChildLit at* **www.mhhe.com/childlit** *for Web links related to this chapter.*

Children's Literature Cited in the Chapter

Angelou, M. (1993). *Life Doesn't Frighten Me.* Illustrated by J. M. Basquiat. New York: Stewart, Tabori & Chang.

Celenza, A. H. (2000). *The Farewell Symphony.* Illustrated by E. Kitchel. Watertown, MA: Charlesbridge.

De Paola, T. (1989). *The Art Lesson.* New York: Putnam.

Dorros, A. (2000). *Ten Go Tango.* Illustrated by E. A. McCully. New York: HarperCollins Juvenile Books.

Esbensen, B. J. (1995). *Dance with Me.* New York: HarperCollins Publishers.

Gray, L. B. (1995). *My Mama Had a Dancing Heart.* Illustrated by R. Colón. New York: Orchard Books.

Guthrie, W. (1998). *This Land Is Your Land.* Paintings by K. Jakobsen. Boston: Little, Brown & Co.

Hopkins, L. B. (1997). *Song and Dance: Poems.* Illustrated by C. M. Taylor. New York: Simon & Schuster.

Igus, T. (1998). *i see the music.* Paintings by M. Wood. San Francisco, CA: Children's Book Press.

McKissack, P. (1988). *Mirandy and Brother Wind.* Illustrated by B. Pinkney. New York: Knopf.

McMahon, P. (2000). *Dancing Wheels.* Photographs by J. Godt. Boston: Houghton Mifflin Co.

Moss, L. (1995). *Zin! Zin! Zin! A Violin.* New York: Simon & Schuster Books for Young Readers.

Patterson, K. (1985). *Come Sing, Jimmy Jo.* New York: Dutton.

Peek, M. (1985). *Mary Wore Her Red Dress and Henry Wore His Green Sneakers.* Adapted and illustrated by M. Peek. New York: Clarion Books.

Pinkney, A. D. (1998). *Duke Ellington: The Piano Prince and His Orchestra.* Illustrated by B. Pinkney. New York: Hyperion Books for Children.

Pinkney, A. D. (1993). *Alvin Ailey.* Illustrated by B. Pinkney. New York: Hyperion Books for Children.

Rylant, C. (1988). *All I See.* Pictures by P. Catalanotto. New York: Orchard Books.

Smith, C. L. (2000). *Jingle Dancer.* Illustrated by C. Van Wright & Y. Hu. New York: Morrow Junior Books.

Stanley, D. (2001). *Michelangelo.* New York: HarperCollins Juvenile Books.

Stanley, D. (1996). *Leonardo Da Vinci.* New York: Morrow Junior Books.

Swentzell, R. (1992). *Children of the Clay: A Family of Pueblo Potters.* Photographs by B. Steen. Minneapolis, MN: Lerner Publications Co.

Tobias, T. (1970). *Maria Tallchief.* Illustrated by M. Hampshire. New York: Crowell.

Weiss, G. D., & Thiele, B. (1995). *What a Wonderful World.* Illustrated by A. Bryan. New York: Atheneum.

Children's Literature Cited in One Book at a Time Examples

Ancona, G. (1998). *Let's Dance.* New York: Morrow Junior Books.

Ancona, G. (1993). *Powwow.* New York: Harcourt Brace.

Bryan, A. (1991). *All Night, All Day: A Child's First Book of African-American Spirituals.* New York: Atheneum.

Chocolate, D. (1998). *The Piano Man.* Illustrated by E. Velasquez. New York: Walker and Company.

Collier, B. (2000). *Uptown.* New York: Henry Holt.

Esbensen, B. J. (1996). *Dance with Me.* Illustrated by M. Lloyd. New York: HarperCollins.

Frazee, M. (1999). *Hush Little Baby: A Folk Song with Pictures.* San Diego, CA: Browndeer Press.

George, K. O. (1997). *The Great Frog Race and Other Poems.* Illustrated by K. Kiesler. New York: Clarion Books.

Graham, J. B. (1999). *Flicker Flash.* Illustrated by N. Davis. Boston: Houghton Mifflin.

Graham, J. B. (1994). *Splish Splash.* Illustrated by S. Scott. New York: Ticknor & Fields.

Ho, M. (1996). *Hush: A Thai Lullaby.* Illustrated by H. Meade. New York: Orchard Books.

Hopkinson, D. (1999). *A Band of Angels.* Illustrated by R. Colón. New York: Atheneum Books for Children.

Hudson, W., & Hudson, C. (1995). *How Sweet the Sound: African American Songs for Children.* Illustrated by F. Cooper. New York: Scholastic Inc.

Johnson, D. B. (2000). *Henry Hikes to Fitchburg.* New York: Houghton Mifflin.

Lester, J. (1968). *To Be a Slave.* Illustrated by T. Feelings. New York: Dial Press.

Lewis, J. P. (1998). *Doodle Dandies.* Illustrated by L. Desimini. New York: Atheneum Books for Young Readers.

McDermott, G. (1997). *Musicians of the Sun.* New York: Simon & Schuster Books for Young Readers.

McGill, A. (2000). *In the Hollow of Your Hand: Slave Lullabies.* Paintings by M. Cummings. Boston: Houghton Mifflin.

McMahon, P. (2000). *Dancing Wheels.* Photographs by J. Godt. Boston: Houghton Mifflin.

Orozco, J. L. (1998). *Diez Deditos: Ten Little Fingers and Other Play Rhymes and Action Songs from Latin America.* Illustrated by E. Kleven. New York: Dutton Children's Books.

Rochelle, B. (Compiler). (2000). *Words with Wings: A Treasury of African-American Poetry and Art.* New York: HarperCollins Juvenile Books.

Seeger, P. (1986). *Abiyoyo.* Illustrated by M. Hays. New York: MacMillan.

Soto, G. (1995). *Chato's Kitchen.* Illustrated by S. Guevara. New York: Putnam.

Waters, K., & Slovenz-Low, M. (1990). *Lion Dancer: Ernie Wan's Chinese New Year.* Illustrated by M. Cooper. New York: Scholastic, Inc.

Wells, R. (1997). *McDuff Moves In.* Illustrated by S. Jeffers. New York: Hyperion Books.

Wood, D. (1996). *Northwoods Cradlesong: From a Menominee Lullaby.* Illustrated by L. Desimini. New York: Simon & Schuster Books for Young Readers.

Yolen, J. (Ed.). (1994). *Sleep Rhymes around the World.* Illustrated by 17 international artists. Honesdale, PA: Boyd's Mill Press.

Children's Literature Cited for Rock Art Unit

Arnold. C. (1996). *Stories in Stone: Rock Art Pictures by Early Americans.* Photographs by R. Hewett. New York: Clarion Books.

Arnold, C. (1992). *The Ancient Cliff Dwellers of Mesa Verde.* Photographs by R. Hewett. New York: Clarion Books.

Asch, F., & Levin, T. (1998). *Cactus Poems.* San Diego, CA: Harcourt Brace & Company.

Baylor, B. (1972). *When Clay Sings.* Illustrated by T. Bahti. New York: Charles Scribner's Sons.

Bierhorst, J. (2000). *The People with Five Fingers.* Pictures by R. A. Parker. New York: Marshall Cavendish.

Cowley, M. (1998). *Anooka's Answer.* New York: Clarion Books.

Cowley, M. (1994). *Dar and the Spear-Thrower.* New York: Clarion Books.

Craig, R. (1995). *Malu's Wolf.* New York: Orchard Books.

Day, M. (1999). *Quennu and the Cave Bear.* Toronto: Owl Books.

Denzel, J. (1997). *Return to Painted Cave.* New York: Philomel Books.

Denzel, J. (1988). *Boy of the Painted Cave.* New York: Philomel Books.

Dewey, J. O. (1996). *Stories on Stone, Rock Art: Images from the Ancient Ones.* Boston: Little, Brown & Co.

Dickinson, P. (1998). *Noli's Story.* New York: Grosset & Dunlap.

Fisher, L. E. (1997). *Anasazi.* New York: Atheneum Books for Young Readers.

Hausman, G., & Cooper, F. (1995). *Coyote Walks on Two Legs: A Book of Navajo Myths and Legends.* New York: Philomel Books.

LaPierre, Y. (1994). *Native American Rock Art: Messages from the Past.* Illustrated by L. Sloan. Charlottesville, VA: Thomasson-Grant & Lickle.

Lasky, K. (2000). *First Painter.* Paintings by R. Baviera. New York: Dorling Kindersley Publishing Inc.

Lauber, P. (1998). *Painters of the Caves.* Washington, DC: National Geographic Society.

McDermott, G. (1994). *Coyote: A Trickster Tale from the American Southwest.* San Diego, CA: Harcourt Brace & Co.

McDermott, G. (1974). *Arrow to the Sun: A Pueblo Indian Tale.* New York: Penguin Putnam Books for Young Readers.

Merriman, N. (1989). *Early Humans.* Photographs by D. King. New York: Alfred A. Knopf.

Netzley, P. D. (1998). *The Stone Age.* San Diego, CA: Lucent Books.

Oughton, J. (1992). *How the Stars Fell into the Sky: A Navajo Legend.* Illustrated by L. Desimini. Boston: Houghton Mifflin Co.

Patent, D. H. (1999). *Mystery of the Lascaux Cave.* New York: Benchmark Books.

Rosen, M. (1995). *Crow and Hawk: A Traditional Pueblo Indian Story.* Illustrated by J. Clementson. San Diego, CA: Harcourt Brace & Co.

Terzi, M. (1992). *Prehistoric Rock Art.* Chicago: Children's Press.

Young, R. (1999). *A Personal Tour of Mesa Verde.* Minneapolis, MN: Lerner Publications Co.

Recordings

Dollar Brand. (1994). *African Marketplace* [CD]. New York: WEA Distributing Corp.

Jordanaires (1995). *Golden Gospel Greats* [CD]. Richmond, VA: Time Life Music.

Various Artists. (1998). *Under the Green Corn Moon: Native American Lullabies* [CD]. Tom Wasinger (Producer). Boulder, CO: Silver Wave Records, Inc.

References

Albers, P. (2001). Literacy in the arts. *Primary Voices: K-6, 9*(4), 3–9.

Consortium of National Arts Education Associations. (1994). *National Standards for Arts Education: What Every Young American Should Know and Be Able to Do in the Arts.* Reston, VA: Music Educators National Conference.

Frayling, C., Frayling, H., & Van Der Meer, R. (1992). *The Art Pack.* New York: Alfred A. Knopf.

Gary, C. L. (1997). *Transforming Ideas for Teaching and Learning the Arts.* Washington, DC: U.S. Government Printing Office.

Van Der Meer, R., & Berkley, M. (1994). *The Music Pack.* New York: Alfred A. Knopf.

Westat Inc. under contract with the U.S. Department of Education, National Center for Education Statistics, and the National Endowment for the Arts. (1995). *Arts Education in Public Elementary and Secondary Schools, pp. iii–iv.* Washington, DC: U.S. Government Printing Office.

CHAPTER 5

Books That Bring Out the Mathematicians in Us

The five-year-olds were filled with delight as their teacher read and the class enacted *Caps for Sale* by Esphyr Slobodkina. As the peddler (teacher) fell asleep under the tree, the monkeys (children) crept quietly forward to take a cap off her head. And when the peddler awoke refreshed from her nap and noticed that all that remained on her head was her own checked cap, the monkeys giggled gleefully. The story continued to be read and enacted with the peddler finally regaining all of her caps before turning toward town to try to sell some of the caps.

Those of us familiar with the story *Caps for Sale* can readily see the math concepts presented in this wonderfully engaging book. In the large-group reading, the children listen and watch as the peddler sorts the caps by color (sorting and classifying) and positions each stack of caps upon his head (sequencing and ordinal numbers). They see one-to-one correspondence when each monkey takes one of the caps from the peddler and puts it on his head. All of these concepts—as well as others such as patterns, counting, addition, and subtraction—can be reinforced with follow-up small-group or individual activities. We, as many others, believe children's literature may be used to teach mathematics effectively.

NATIONAL STANDARDS FOR SCHOOL MATHEMATICS

In April 2000, the National Council of Teachers of Mathematics (NCTM) released *Principles and Standards for School Mathematics*. See the Appendix for a listing of the Standards. This document supports their continuing belief that standards can strongly influence the improvement of mathematics education. "Standards are descriptions of what mathematics instruction should enable students to know and do—statements of what is valued for school mathematics" (NCTM, 2000, p. 7). Of the ten Standards, five describe content goals for mathematics in number and operations, algebra, geometry, measurement, and data analysis and probability. The remaining five Standards deal with the processes of problem solving, reasoning and proof, connections, communication, and representation (NCTM, 2000).

In addition to the Standards, the NCTM (2000) proposed six principles that encompass characteristics of excellent mathematics education. The principles focus on equity, curriculum, learning, teaching, assessment, and technology. While all of these principles are important, we will address the Learning Principle here. The Learning Principle states that high-quality mathematics education requires that students understand the math theory they are learning by using their prior knowledge and through their active engagement with new knowledge (NCTM, 2000). Many of us may remember sitting in math classes and computing numbers correctly but never knowing why we were doing so or what the computations meant. We did it, the teachers corrected our work, and we moved onto the next topic, perhaps without any real understanding. We learned math by rote. Many students today also "do math" in class and have little understanding of how to use math applications in everyday life. Bransford, Brown, and Cocking (1999) found that being proficient in mathematics requires conceptual understanding as well as factual knowledge and procedural ability. "Students will be served well by school mathematics programs that enhance their natural desire to understand what they are asked to learn" (NCTM, 2000, p. 21).

MATHEMATICS AND STORIES

Societies have long used stories to educate in interesting and meaningful ways. Think about the folk tales, fables, and parables we have heard or read. These are examples of lessons presented in a story format. As readers and listeners, we identified with the heroes and heroines and understood the inherent messages of good triumphing over evil. Many years may have passed since we last encountered those stories, but we still remember them and their messages. When we transfer the idea of using stories to teach math, we can see the possibilities for interesting and meaningful instruction. In fact, the math concepts may be better understood and remembered because they are presented in a narrative format (Griffiths & Clyne, 1988; Hong, 1999; Welchman-Tischler, 1992).

Narrative Context

Children enjoy stories; they like to tell them and they like to listen to them. Most of us have first-hand experience listening to the stories of the children we teach. All we have to do is mention a familiar topic in a first-grade classroom and hands begin waving. Everyone wants to share a personal experience. These personal connections also create interest in listening to and learning from stories. *Six-Dinner Sid* by Inga Moore is a prime example of how a story on a familiar subject creates interest and can be used to initiate instruction. Sid is a cat who manages to "con" six families into adopting him as their pet. Life is grand for Sid as he moves from one home to another, living a most pampered existence. We listen and see as Sid first enjoys dinner at No. 1 Aristotle Street, then next at No. 2 Aristotle, and so on until he has had six different, delicious dinners. After listening to *Six-Dinner Sid*, the children are eager to share their cat stories. Sarah tells us about Emma, her wide-bodied cat, who loves to eat. When Brad relays the time his cat, Hissy Face, got stuck in a tree, telling the story in very meticulous detail, we now have an opportunity to use his story in combination with the book to reinforce the concept of ordinal numbers. We ask Brad to repeat his story. "Brad, what was the first thing that happened in your story?" As he relates the information, we write it on chart paper, and then ask him what happened next and so on. After Brad's story is complete, we review it with the children, emphasizing the ordinal sequence of events. An activity in the Math Center is planned to continue the emphasis on ordinal numbers. The children are provided with cutouts of Sid and two sets of doors numbered one through six for Aristotle Street and for Pythagoras Place. They can practice retelling the story of *Six-Dinner Sid* using the manipulatives and integrating math terminology. Some additional examples of children's books that contain math content within an engaging story include Sharon Bell Mathis's *The Hundred Penny Box* (money and time), Patricia McKissack's *A Million Fish...More or Less* (large numbers), *Grandfather Tang's Story* (tangrams) by Ann Tompert, and Kathryn Lasky's *The Librarian Who Measured the Earth* (geometry and spatial sense).

Motivation for Learning

We all recognize that learning new information is easier for us if we want to or need to learn it. It helps, too, if the new material is related to our previous experiences and if we have some background knowledge on which to build (Hong, 1999; Kouba & Franklin, 1995). In teaching mathematics, we know that children learn content better when they have opportunities to work with concrete materials and to share their thinking with peers and adults. These kinds of learning experiences allow children to grasp the abstract mathematical concepts and to learn the formal procedures for computation. One way we can begin to help children make connections between mathematical concepts and what they already know is through children's literature. A classic example is Pat Hutchins' *The Doorbell Rang*. All children have had the experience of sharing treats with siblings and/or friends. This story leads them gently into the mathematical concept of division. In *The Doorbell Rang*, the mother has just baked chocolate chip cookies and has given a plate of 12 cookies to her two children to share. But before they can eat the cookies, the doorbell rings and two friends join them at the table making it necessary to divide the 12 cookies by 4 instead of 2. The story continues with more friends arriving until 12 children are sharing the 12 cookies, but then the doorbell rings again. Following the reading and discussion of *The Doorbell Rang*, children can use manipulatives (brown circles for cookies) and practice dividing the cookies by different numbers. In this story 12 cookies are used, but teachers can increase or decrease the number to match the abilities of the children in their classroom.

Through conversations with children, Whitin and Wilde (1995) found that pairing mathematics and literature helps students to see the relevancy of mathematics in their own lives. Moreover, this pairing helps children to develop a broader view of the discipline; mathematics becomes a tool for solving problems rather than just number facts and meaningless computations.

Children's literature also has the power to engage those children who view math as difficult. Whitin and Wilde (1995) believe that children's literature helps to change many students' negative attitudes about math. When we use stories with students who are anxious about math, they often become so involved in the story that their anxiety dissipates. These students now feel "empowered" as learners of mathematics (Whitin & Wilde, 1995).

With this new confidence, these students are willing to explore mathematical concepts. For example, after listening to Steve Jenkins' *Biggest, Strongest, Fastest,* a book that presents interesting factual information about animals, students are excited about exploring the ideas in the book. Some will want to use classroom objects to weigh, measure, calculate, estimate, or compare with the records given in the book. Others may choose to research other animal records to make a book of their own. They might research to find the animals living in the coldest regions of the world or those that have the longest life spans. Mathematics becomes exciting and relevant. Books that are sure to delight and inspire children to explore the world of math include *Count!* by Denise Fleming, *Eating Fractions* by Bruce McMillan, *Sam Johnson and the Blue Ribbon Quilt* by Lisa Campbell Ernst, *Measuring Penny* by Loreen Leedy, *Splash* by Ann Jonas, *Anno's Mysterious Multiplying Jar* by Masaichiro and Mitsumasa Anno, and Greg Tang's *The Grapes of Math.*

It is important to note that while we strongly believe that pairing children's literature with mathematics instruction can facilitate children's learning of concepts and content, this is not the only method that should be used in the classroom. Some students may benefit from a more didactic teaching approach. Lubienski's (2000) qualitative research suggests that social-economic status (SES) and gender may influence the type of math instruction students prefer. She found that lower SES students, particularly females, tended to prefer more traditional mathematics instruction and curriculum. This finding reminds us that teachers need to use a variety of instructional strategies in order to meet the different learning styles of their students. Using children's literature to teach mathematics is one method teachers should incorporate into their repertoire of instructional strategies.

CHILDREN'S LITERATURE RESOURCES

As we have seen, many children's books are available to use in a variety of ways for mathematics instruction. Some of the books we have cited are recognized as quality children's literature and should be enjoyed first and foremost for their literary merits. Others have been written to teach specific mathematical concepts. While these books might not be considered quality literature, they do present math concepts in engaging ways. An excellent resource for teachers looking for children's literature related to mathematics is *The Wonderful World of Mathematics: A Critically Annotated List of Children's Books in Mathematics* (Thiessen, Matthias & Smith, 1998). In this second edition, the authors review over 550 children's books that deal with mathematical concepts. Additionally, they include sections on "Series and Other Resources" and "Incidental Geometry—Quilting" as well as listing some suitable out-of-print books that may still be available in public or school libraries.

Two more resources are *Read Any Good Math Lately? Children's Books for Mathematical Learning* (Whitin & Wilde, 1992) and *It's the Story That Counts: More Children's Books for Mathematical Learning, K–6* (Whitin & Wilde, 1995). In addition to listing children's literature selections, each of these resources suggests ways to use the books in the classroom.

The remainder of this chapter includes examples of curriculum planning based on children's literature selections for younger and intermediate readers. We demonstrate both the "one book at a time" approach as well as outlining a primary-grade unit covering the topic of measurement. Each example includes a read-aloud and follow-up activities. While the main focus of this chapter is pairing children's literature with mathematics instruction, we also include cross-curricular activities for each book.

Sample Lessons for Younger Readers

One Book at a Time

Stuck Ducks

Read aloud *One Duck Stuck* written by Phyllis Root and illustrated by Jane Chapman.

This engaging, rhyming counting book begins when one duck gets stuck in the muck and calls for help. A succession of animals (two fish, three moose, and so on) come to aid the duck but to no avail. Finally, all the animals work together, and the duck flies free.

Preparation

1. Practice reading aloud *One Duck Stuck*, planning where you will stop to ask questions or solicit comments.
2. Have the number words one—ten, the numerals 1–10, and corresponding animal cutouts available for use on a flannel board.

Introduction

Show the children the cover of the book and ask them to predict what it might be about. Suggest that they look carefully at the cover illustration to see that the duck has a problem. Lead them to say it is stuck. Then you can point to the words and tell them the title is *One Duck ___*, pause and allow them to fill in the word stuck. Repeat the title, "Yes, that's right. *One Duck Stuck.* Let's listen to find out how the duck solves his problem."

Reading the Book

Read the book, stopping where you planned. You can encourage the children to read the repetitive phrases in the book along with you. As the children join in, you can stop reading those words and let the children read them.

Curriculum Connections

Mathematics

In the Math Center, place the number words, numerals, and animal cutouts in three separate containers. The children will match the number word, numeral, and correct number of animal cutouts and place them on the flannel board. An extension of this activity is to have the children count the total number of animals in the story. (**Counting; Representing Numbers**.)

Depending on your students' understanding of counting and number operations, you can create simple single-digit addition problems for them to solve. They can use the animal cutouts to help them figure out the answers. For example, 1 duck + 2 fish = ___animals. (**Counting; Addition; Representing Numbers**.)

Science

In the Science Center, you can provide the opportunity for the children to play in mud. (Don't worry, it washes out!) Using the empty sand/water table, fill it half full with potting soil or dirt. Set out 2 or 3 small watering cans partially filled with water. Have the children don smocks and make mud. Be sure to limit the number of children in the area and set your rules before beginning. If you have plastic animals that coincide with the book, add them to the mud table to further reinforce the math concept. The children may retell the story using the props. (**Experimenting; Communication**.)

Language Arts

Be sure to have some informational books on marshes on your book shelf. Children can read and learn about marshes and the animals that live in or near them during independent reading time. (**Nonfiction Texts; Informational Resources**.)

In the Language Arts Center, put out a set of rimes that are from the animal names found in the book (e.g., uck, og, ish) and a set of onsets. (An onset is the initial consonant or consonants in a word; a rime includes the vowel and all the letters that follow.) Encourage the children to match the onsets to the rimes to form different words. As a special note, if you provide the children with the onsets and rimes, you can control the words they form. (**Vocabulary; Word Identification**.)

The children can create their own simplified versions of *One Duck Stuck*. Begin this activity by having the children brainstorm animals for each number 2 through 10 and what those animals do. For example, someone might suggest foxes for the number four. Ask the children to think of an action that foxes can do. They can run, jump, leap, etc. Next ask the children to think of words that rhyme with foxes—boxes works well. Each page will have the format:

1. Number word and brainstormed animals   Four foxes
2. -ing word and phrase that rhymes with animals   hopping over boxes
3. brainstormed action and the words "to the duck."   leap to the duck.

Working with each group, print the words on paper. Every page will start and end with the repetitive phrases in the book. (**Writing Process; Vocabulary**.)

Art

Children may create the illustrations for their books. They may draw the animals and accompanying background items directly onto the pages or they may draw and cut them out separately, then glue them to each correct page. (**Media, Techniques, and Processes**.)

Connecting to Standards:

Stuck Ducks

Mathematics (Number & Operations): Students understand numbers, ways of representing numbers, and number systems.

Mathematics (Number & Operations): Students understand the meaning of operations and how they relate to one another (NCTM, 2000).

Science (Earth Science): Students develop abilities necessary to understand and do scientific inquiry (NAP, 1996).

Language Arts #1: Students read a wide range of print and nonprint texts to build an understanding of texts, of themselves, and of the cultures of the United States and the world; to acquire new information; to respond to the needs and demands of society and the workplace; and for personal fulfillment.

Language Arts #3: Students apply a wide range of strategies to comprehend, interpret, evaluate, and appreciate texts.

Language Arts #4: Students adjust their use of spoken, written, and visual language to communicate effectively with a variety of audiences and for different purposes (NCTE & IRA, 1996).

Social Studies (Individual Development & Identity): Students can meet objectives through independent and cooperative means.

Social Studies (Civic Ideals & Practices): Students explore what it means to be a good citizen (NCSS, 1994).

The Arts (Theater): Acting by assuming roles and interacting in improvisations (CNAEA, 1994).

Social Studies

Often the focus of the kindergarten–first-grade social studies curriculum is self and group relations—learning how to get along with others in different social settings. The book *One Duck Stuck* can foster a discussion of helping one another. Talk with the children about how the different animals came to help the duck and how it took all of them working together to free him from the muck. You can have the children role-play the book. You can also have them think about ways they can help each other in the classroom. (**Individual Development and Identity; Civic Ideals and Practices**.)

Creative Drama

Using the story's characters or the children's own improvisations, invite the students to act out *One Stuck Duck*. (**Acting**.)

Estimating

Read aloud *Betcha!* written by Stuart J. Murphy and illustrated by S. D. Schindler.

This book is part of the MathStart series. In *Betcha!* two friends read about a contest at Planet Toys that involves guessing how many jelly beans are in the jar displayed in the store's window. As the boys ride the bus to the store, they challenge each other to guess how many people are on the bus, how many cars are in the traffic jam, and so on. Each estimate is graphically depicted in the illustrations so that readers see how to use estimation strategies. Notes for adults and children are included at the back of the book for estimation activities.

Preparation

1. Practice reading *Betcha!*, planning where you will stop to engage children in the estimation strategies.
2. Plan several scenarios where children can practice using estimation strategies, for example, books on a book shelf, mittens or gloves in the lost and found box, or children in the school.
3. Have a jar filled with a snack food such as pretzel nuggets or animal crackers for display.

Introduction

Begin by showing the students the cover of the book and soliciting predictions about the book. Ask the children if they have ever used the expression "betcha." Have them relate personal examples. From their responses, develop a definition of the word. Once it is established that the two boys in the story are challenging each other to estimate the number of jelly beans in the jar, ask the children what the boys would have to do to make an accurate estimate. Allow time for children to respond. Talk with the children about how estimating and guessing are different. A guess can be any answer. Estimates are reasonable answers derived from using available information and thinking carefully.

Reading the Book

Read the book, stopping where you planned. Page nine, where the boys make their first bet, is a good place to stop and ask the students how they would estimate how many people were on the bus. Give children an opportunity to express their strategies, then continue reading to see how the boy in the story estimated the number of bus riders. You can ask for your students' input at each challenge, or just continue reading if you feel stopping frequently is tedious.

Curriculum Connections

Mathematics

After reading the book *Betcha!*, discuss with the children what it means to estimate and how it is different than actual counting. We estimate when having an accurate number isn't necessary. Select one of your planned scenarios (see Preparation section) and ask the children to make an estimate. For example, you might ask the children to estimate the number of children in the school. Refer to the book and talk again about how the boy derived his estimates. Have each child write down an estimation and the reasoning he or she used to come up with his/her number. Then the whole class can share their estimates and strategies. Discuss with the children which estimates seem most reasonable and why. Talk about what they did to make a good estimate in order to make the reasoning as explicit as possible. Depending on your time constraints, you can do another estimation scenario that you planned or one that the students suggest. It is important to have the children make their estimations and write out their estimation strategies or reasonings. NCTM (2000) believes that conceptual understanding and procedural fluency are enhanced when students are given opportunities to problem-solve, reason, and discuss. (**Estimation**; **Reasoning**; **Communication**.)

Discuss with students how we use estimation in daily life. Some examples include estimating how many hot dogs to cook for a backyard barbeque, how long it will take us to travel to the dentist's office, and the temperature (in order to decide how to dress). Encourage the children to think about ways people use estimation in their daily lives. (**Estimation**; **Communication**.)

Have the students work in pairs to decide on a scenario to challenge their classmates' abilities in estimating. Each pair writes an idea on a 4" x 6" note card. The cards are placed in a large box. Then the teacher pulls one or two of the challenges out of the box each day during math time to present to the children. The pair who wrote the challenge read it to the class and organize the estimation activity with the teacher's help. (**Estimation**; **Reasoning**; **Communication**.)

In the Math Center, set out different-size jars containing different items such as counting chips, pencil erasers, marbles, crayons, 1-inch cubes, and the like. Children estimate and then count the items in each jar. You can rearrange the contents of the jars periodically—the same items are put in different-size jars—in order to provide the children with new estimation challenges. (**Estimation, Counting**; **Reasoning**; **Communication**.)

Refer back to the story *Betcha!* and the contest the boys entered. Show the children the jar filled with the snack food (See Preparation section). Have each child submit in writing an estimate of the number of items in the jar and his or her estimation strategy. The "winner" is the child who comes closest to guessing the correct number of items in the jar. He or she gets to share the contents with the class. In essence, all are "winners." Be sure that none of your students are allergic to the food item in the jar. (**Estimation**; **Counting**; **Reasoning**; **Communication**.)

Language Arts

As part of the mathematics activities, the students write their estimation strategies and challenge scenarios. (**Writing**.)

All of us use informal speech patterns such as "betcha." Discuss with the students the words that are combined to make betcha, bet and you. Have students brainstorm other words like betcha (e.g.,

---

Connecting to Standards:
Estimating

Mathematics (Number & Operations): Students understand numbers, relationships among numbers, and number systems. Students compute fluently and make reasonable estimates.

Mathematics (Reasoning & Proof): Students recognize reasoning and proof as fundamental aspects of mathematics. Students make and investigate mathematical conjectures. Students develop and evaluate mathematical arguments and proofs. Students select and use various types of reasoning and methods of proof.

Mathematics (Communication): Students organize and consolidate their mathematical thinking through communication. Students communicate their mathematical thinking coherently and clearly to peers, teachers, and others. Students analyze and evaluate the mathematical thinking and strategies of others. Students use the language of mathematics to express mathematical ideas precisely (NCTM, 2000).

Language Arts #5: Students employ a wide range of strategies as they write and use different writing process elements appropriately to communicate with different audiences for a variety of purposes (NCTE & IRA, 1996).

Social Studies (People, Places & Environments): Students can use available resources and tools to provide information (NCSS, 1994).

dontcha, gotta, gimme, gonna). Talk with students about the differences between formal and informal language. Most writing is formal, and so these words are spelled differently than they sound when we say them. (**Oral and Written Language**.)

Social Studies

In many second-grade classrooms, the focus of the social studies curriculum is the neighborhood. As a way to introduce or explore the components of a neighborhood, you can have the children practice their estimation skills using neighborhood scenarios. For example, the students can estimate the number of houses, restaurants, or pets in the neighborhood. Then, through follow-up research of their neighborhood, they can find out the actual numbers of each. A discussion of what constitutes a "house" is important. Do apartments count as houses if the neighborhood contains apartment buildings? These kinds of discussions can enrich children's understanding of housing. Discuss with children when it is important to have exact numbers of people, businesses, recreational facilities, etc., and when using estimates is satisfactory. (**People, Places, and Environments**.)

Sample Lessons for Intermediate Readers

One Book at a Time

Circles, Triangles, and Squares

Read aloud *A Cloak for the Dreamer* written by Aileen Friedman and illustrated by Kim Howard.

A tailor has three sons, two of whom enjoy sewing and wish to follow in their father's footsteps. The third son is more interested in traveling the world. The tailor receives a commission from the Archduke for three cloaks and other clothing. He asks each of his sons to make one of the cloaks. The oldest uses rectangular pieces of fabric to make a beautiful cloak. The middle son makes two cloaks, one using squares and the other, triangles. The youngest son relies on his fascination with the globe to fashion a cloak made of circular pieces of fabric. As can be expected, his cloak is full of open spaces and cannot be used. The tailor understands and accepts his youngest son's dreams of traveling the world, and devises a way to refashion his cloak made of circles into a warm garment he can use in his travels. Notes at the back of the book explain the geometric concepts.

Preparation

1. Practice reading aloud *A Cloak for the Dreamer,* planning where you will stop to ask questions or solicit comments.
2. Plan a mini-lesson on geometric shapes and angles. Have available examples of the different shapes: rectangles, squares, triangles (equilateral, isosceles, and scalene), parallelograms, rhombuses, and hexagons to show the students as you discuss the geometric concepts.

Introduction

Ask the students to brainstorm all the synonyms they know for coat. As the children name them, write them down on the board or easel paper. If the children do not mention "cloak," ask them if they know what a cloak is. Ask the children if there is a difference between a coat and a cloak. Have them explain their answers. Read the title, and then ask the children what they think a cloak for a dreamer would be like. Solicit responses. "Let's find out as we listen to the story."

Reading the Book

Read the story, stopping occasionally to ask questions or solicit comments. After reading the book, encourage the students to give their personal responses to the story. They may focus on the math concepts, or they may wish to discuss the father's ability to accept his youngest son's different dreams. You might also ask the students to think of their dreams for the future—what they want to be or do.

Curriculum Connections

Mathematics

Follow the read-aloud with your mini-lesson on shapes and angles. After you present the information on angles, provide the students with different shapes and encourage them to put the shapes together to make a 360-degree rotation around a point with no spaces. Students can work alone, in pairs, or in small groups depending on your class size and the availability of materials. After the lesson, place these shapes in the Math Center to allow the children further opportunities for exploration. (**Geometry; Problem Solving.**)

In the Math Center, provide the students with graph paper, protractors, and 3" x 5" cards that give the directions for making different shapes. For example, you might write: "Draw a shape with four sides of equal length, and four right angles. What is it?" Or, "Draw a triangle with one right angle and two sides of equal length. What kind of triangle did you draw?" Or, "Draw a triangle with three equal sides. Measure the angles using the protractor and write your answer on your drawing. What kind of triangle is this?" (**Geometry; Problem Solving; Communication.**)

Art

Using shapes cut out of construction paper, students can create a pattern collage. (**Art-Math Connections.**)

An alternative art activity is to use tile pieces or colored posterboard cut into small squares, triangles, and hexagons for students to create a mosaic design. Show the children some examples of mosaics. You will need strong cardboard squares, one for each student. The students draw a design or picture on the cardboard, then fill in the design by gluing the shapes onto the cardboard. (**Art-Math Connections.**)

Interdisciplinary (Social Studies and Language Arts)

Misha, the youngest son in the story, dreams of traveling the world. Lead a discussion on why someone might want to travel the world. Where have the children traveled? What did they see and do on the

---

Connecting to Standards:

Circles, Triangles, and Squares

Mathematics (Geometry): Students apply transformations and use symmetry to analyze mathematical situations.

Mathematics (Problem Solving): Students build new mathematical knowledge through problem solving. Students solve problems that arise in mathematics and in other contexts. Students apply and adapt a variety of appropriate strategies to solve problems.

Mathematics (Communication): Students organize and consolidate their mathematical thinking through communication. Students communicate their mathematical thinking coherently and clearly to peers, teachers, and others. Student analyze and evaluate the mathematical thinking and strategies of others. Students use the language of mathematics to express mathematical ideas precisely.

Mathematics (Connections): Students recognize and use connections among mathematical ideas.

Students recognize and apply mathematics in contexts outside of mathematics (NCTM, 2000).

Language Arts #7: Students conduct research on issues and interests by generating ideas and questions and by posing problems. They gather, evaluate, and synthesize data from a variety of sources to communicate their discoveries in ways that suit their purpose and audience.

Language Arts #12: Students use spoken, written, and visual language to accomplish their own purposes (NCTE & IRA, 1996).

Social Studies (People, Places, & Environments): Students understand and use maps and globes. Students can describe how people create the environments in which they live (NCSS, 1994).

The Arts (Visual Arts): Making connections between visual arts and other disciplines (CNAEA, 1994).

---

trips? Ask the students to study the globe or world map and to choose places they would like to visit. Encourage them to think globally. Each student will research the place she has selected either through books in the library or computer/Internet resources. Each then writes why she chose this place and what she would see and do there. Provide an opportunity for students to share their dream place. (**People, Places, and Environments; Thinking Skills; Writing Process.**)

As a follow-up activity, have the students design posters that represent their favorite places. These posters should be visually attractive, demonstrate knowledge of the places selected (e.g., geographic location, climate, customs, etc.), and serve to entice others in class to visit. (**People, Places, and Environments; Visual Communication.**)

This book can also lead to a discussion of the importance of creative thinking in the arts, technology, industry, and science.

Doubling Rice

Read aloud *One Grain of Rice: A Mathematical Folktale* by Demi.

A raja makes the farmers of the province give him almost all of the rice that they produce. He promises that if there should ever be a famine he will share the stored rice so no one goes hungry. As can be expected, when a famine does occur, he refuses to share the rice. A young girl, Rani, tricks the raja into rewarding her for a good deed that she has done. He agrees to give her one grain of rice that is to be doubled each day for 30 days. By the end of the 30 days, Rani has accumulated over a billion grains of rice, and the raja is left with none. She shares the rice with all the people and offers a basketful to the raja if he promises to collect only as much as he needs in the future.

Preparation

1. Practice reading the book aloud, and plan where you will stop to ask questions or solicit comments. The foldout page with the camels is an interesting 3-D visual effect that you might want to discuss with the students.
2. A note at the front of the book states that Demi's illustrations were inspired by 16th and 17th century Indian miniatures. Collect some photographs of these miniatures to share with the students as well as background information on this art form.

Introduction

Introduce this book with an Anticipation Guide. Possible Anticipation Guide statements include: 1) Greedy people get what they deserve; 2) Children can sometimes outsmart adults; and 3) I would rather get $5,000 today than a penny a day doubled for 30 days (e.g., 1 cent today, 2 cents tomorrow, 4 cents the third day, and so on). Students mark agree or disagree for each question. After students individually respond to the statements, have them discuss their answers with the class. Ask the students to keep their responses in mind as they listen to the book.

Reading the Book

Read the book, stopping where you planned. Solicit personal responses to the book. Revisit the responses to the statements in the Anticipation Guide. Check to see if anyone has changed his responses. Explore the changes. Talk with the children about large numbers. You might ask, "How much is a million? A billion?" Encourage students to think of how much those numbers are in different ways.

Curriculum Connections

Mathematics

Give each child (or pair of children) a 30-day calendar grid. Ask the students to estimate how many grains of rice Rani received in all. How did they come up with their estimates? Ask for written or verbal estimation strategies. Have the students calculate the number of grains of rice Rani received each day and place that number on the calendar in the appropriate square. Then, have the students add all 30 days to get the total number of grains of rice. This information is printed at the back of the book. Have children check their estimate against the actual total. Were their estimations close or not? Students can use calculators for some of the calculations if you would like them to work on calculator skills. **(Numbers and Operations; Problem Solving; Communication.)**

In the Math Center, provide the children with a container of rice, a measuring cup, and a scale. Ask them to count the number of grains of rice it takes to fill a measuring cup and then to weigh the cup full of rice. The children will have to subtract the weight of the empty cup to get the weight of the rice. Then ask the students to calculate the weight of the rice Rani received on any three consecutive days between day 15 and day 30. (**Number and Operations**; **Measurement**; **Problem Solving**; **Communication**; **Connections**.)

Art

If you are not adverse to using food items for activities, students may glue dyed rice to paper to make designs. They may either draw a design first, then glue the rice to the design (similar to the mosaic activity) or they may create a freeform design with the rice. This can be a painstaking activity since grains of rice are so small. Students will want to make small designs. The rice can be dyed by mixing rubbing alcohol and food coloring together, then adding the rice to the mixture. Stir to color the rice, then drain off the liquid and spread the rice on trays covered with waxed paper to dry. (**Creating with Novel Media**.)

Demi created the illustrations with paints and ink. You can provide the students with these materials and encourage them to create a picture of their choosing. You might want to focus on the Indian miniatures that inspired Demi's illustrations. If so, share pictures of these miniatures with the students. (**Visual Arts and Culture**.)

Language Arts

Introduce students to folktale variants. Share with them three variants of Demi's *One Grain of Rice: A Mathematical Folktale*. These include *The King's Chessboard* by David Birch, *A Grain of Rice* by Helena Clare Pittman, and *The Rajah's Rice: A Mathematical Folktale* by David Barry. Discuss the elements of a folktale and have the students analyze and compare all four variants for plot structure, characterization, style, theme, and/or motif. (**Exploring Genre**; **Interpreting, Evaluating, and Appreciating Texts**.)

Social Studies

This book works well as part of an interdisciplinary unit on India. Depending on the students' interests, the geography, history, culture, and socio-political foundations of India may be explored. This is an opportunity to implement the generative approach. (**Culture**; **People, Places, and Environments**; **Global Connections**.)

Students may also research the production of rice. For example, they may research where most of the world's rice is grown, the varieties of rice, which cultures have rice as a staple part of their diet and why, and the like. (**Production, Distribution, and Consumption**; **Global Connections**; **Culture**.)

Cooking

Cook and eat rice. Share the book *Everybody Cooks Rice* by Norah Dooley. You may want to use one of the recipes in the book, or you may simply cook a variety of rice grains such as white, brown, basmati, and wild rice. Have the students measure the amount of rice before and after cooking. Why did

Connecting to Standards:
Doubling Rice

Mathematics (Number & Operations): Students understand numbers, ways of representing numbers, relationships among numbers, and number systems. Students understand meanings of operations and how they relate to one another. Students compute fluently and make reasonable estimates.

Mathematics (Problem Solving): Students build new mathematical knowledge through problem solving. Students solve problems that arise in mathematics and other contexts. Students apply and adapt a variety of appropriate strategies to solve problems. Students monitor and reflect on the process of mathematical problem solving.

Mathematics (Measurement): Students understand measurable attributes of objects and the units, systems, and processes of measurement. Students apply appropriate techniques, tools, and formulas to determine measurements.

Mathematics (Data Analysis & Probability): Students formulate questions that can be addressed with data and collect, organize, and display relevant data to answer them.

Mathematics (Connections): Students recognize and use connections among mathematical ideas.

Students recognize and apply mathematics in contexts outside of mathematics (NCTM, 2000).

Language Arts #2: Students read a wide range of literature from many periods in many genres to build an understanding of the many dimensions of human experience.

Language Arts #3: Students apply a wide range of strategies to comprehend, interpret, evaluate, and appreciate texts.

Language Arts #5: Students employ a wide range of strategies as they write and use different writing process elements appropriately to communicate with different audiences and for a variety of purposes (NCTE & IRA, 1996).

Social Studies (Production, Distribution, & Consumption): Students can describe the processes involved in a competitive market system.

Social Studies (Global Connections): Students explore how exposure to the similarities found in cultural universals may lead to global understanding (NCSS, 1994).

The Arts (Visual Arts): Understanding the visual arts in relation to history and culture (CNAEA, 1994).

the amount of rice change? As the children cook and taste each variety, they can select which they like best and graph the results. (**Measurement**; **Graphing**; **Connections**.)

Sample Unit for Primary Grades

Measurement

From an early age, children make comparisons based on size and quantities. "I'm bigger than you," "Hey, he's got more blocks than me," and from the top of the jungle gym, "Look, I'm taller than the teacher," are the kinds of expressions we hear every day in kindergarten and primary classrooms. Comparisons occur naturally as children pay attention to the attributes of objects and each other. These spontaneous comparisons lead appropriately to a mathematics unit on measurement.

The NCTM states that measurement is one of the most frequently used mathematics applications. Through measurement activities, children develop an understanding of attributes, learn to use

correct methods and tools for measuring, and strengthen their understanding of other math concepts such as number, estimation, and geometry (NCTM, 2000). Children should have many opportunities to make comparisons, to measure objects using nonstandard and standard measuring tools, and to discuss what and how they are measuring in order to consolidate their understanding of measurement. Based on the NCTM (2000) expectations for children in grades pre-K–2, we have developed the following concepts.

Concept 1: Length, Volume, Weight, Area

Mr. Archimedes' Bath by P. Allen
Who Sank the Boat by P. Allen
Inch by Inch by L. Lionni
How Big Is a Foot? by R. Myller
Measuring Penny by L. Leedy
Just a Little Bit by A. Tompert
The Gigantic Turnip by A. Tolstoy
Measuring (Mini Math) by D. Kirkby
Capacity by H. Pluckrose
Weight by H. Pluckrose

Concept 2: Time

Clocks and More Clocks by P. Hutchins
Pigs on a Blanket by A. Axelrod
Anno's Sundial by M. Anno
The Grouchy Ladybug by E. Carle
Telling Time with Big Mama Cat by D. Harper
Bats around the Clock by K. Appelt
Time to... by B. McMillan
Telling Time: How to Tell Time on Digital and Analog Clocks by J. Older
Morning, Noon, and Night by J. C. George
Morning, Noon, and Night: Poems to Fill Your Day by S. Taberski
When This Box is Full by P. Lillie
Chicken Soup with Rice: A Book of Months by M. Sendak
A Child's Calendar by J. Updike
It's Justin Time, Amber Brown by P. Danziger
Jump Back, Honey: Poems by Paul Laurence Dunbar by P. L. Dunbar

Concept 3: Units of Measurement

How Tall, How Short, How Faraway by D. A. Adler
How Big Is a Foot? by R. Myller
Twelve Snails to One Lizard: A Tale of Mischief and Measurement by S. Hightower
Measuring (mini math) by D. Kirkby
Capacity by H. Pluckrose
Weight by H. Pluckrose
Telling Time: How to Tell Time on Digital and Analog Clocks by J. Older

Concept 4: Comparisons

A Pig Is Big by D. Florian
Is It Larger? Is It Smaller? by T. Hoban
Super Sandcastle Saturday (MathStart) by S. Murphy
How Big Is a Foot? by R. Myller
Twelve Snails to One Lizard: A Tale of Mischief and Measurement by S. Hightower
Measuring Penny by L. Leedy

ᴗ Figure 5.1 ᴗ

Children's Literature Selections for a Measurement Unit

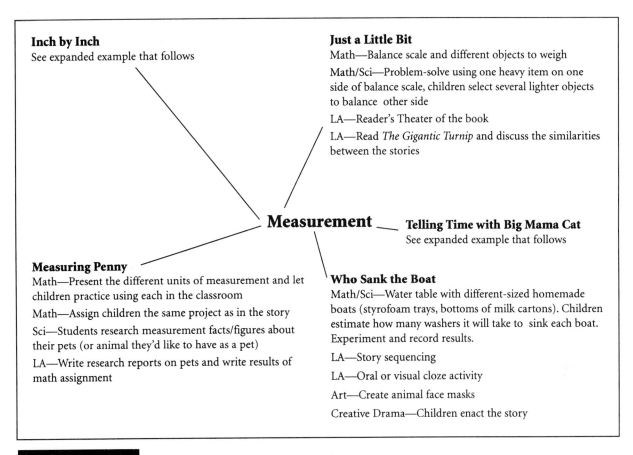

Inch by Inch
See expanded example that follows

Just a Little Bit
Math—Balance scale and different objects to weigh
Math/Sci—Problem-solve using one heavy item on one side of balance scale, children select several lighter objects to balance other side
LA—Reader's Theater of the book
LA—Read *The Gigantic Turnip* and discuss the similarities between the stories

Measurement

Telling Time with Big Mama Cat
See expanded example that follows

Measuring Penny
Math—Present the different units of measurement and let children practice using each in the classroom
Math—Assign children the same project as in the story
Sci—Students research measurement facts/figures about their pets (or animal they'd like to have as a pet)
LA—Write research reports on pets and write results of math assignment

Who Sank the Boat
Math/Sci—Water table with different-sized homemade boats (styrofoam trays, bottoms of milk cartons). Children estimate how many washers it will take to sink each boat. Experiment and record results.
LA—Story sequencing
LA—Oral or visual cloze activity
Art—Create animal face masks
Creative Drama—Children enact the story

·⤳ Figure 5.2 ⤳·

Sample Web of Children's Literature for Measurement Unit

Concepts for the Measurement Unit

1. Objects can be measured to determine their length, width, weight, volume, or area.

2. Time is measured by keeping track of seconds, minutes, hours, days, weeks, months, and years on clocks, watches, and calendars.

3. Two or more objects or times can be compared through measurement.

4. People can measure using nonstandard units (e. g., paper clips) or standard units (e. g., inches). Measurements must have a number and a unit (e .g., Martha is 50 paperclips tall).

The books we have selected for this topic cover measurement of length, weight, volume, and time. You may choose to focus more specifically on one type of measurement for a shorter period of time or cover all the types of measurement over a longer period. The choice is yours, depending upon your children's understanding of measurement and their level of interest, as well as other curricular considerations you may need to address. As you plan your own unit, read the suggested books and choose which ones work for you and your children. These books span children's development of the concept of measurement. We have included Tana Hoban's *Is It Larger? Is It Smaller?* and Douglas Florian's *A Pig Is Big* for introducing children to basic size comparisons. Books such as *Telling Time: How to Tell Time on Digital and Analog Clocks* by Jules Older and *Measuring Penny* by Loreen Leedy require greater understanding and more experience with measuring.

Sample Lessons

Inching Along

Read aloud *Inch by Inch* by Leo Lionni.

In order to save himself from being eaten by several hungry birds, a clever inchworm offers to measure different parts of the birds. All goes well until a nightingale asks the inchworm to measure his song. After some fast thinking, the inchworm tells the nightingale to begin singing as he inches away until he is out of sight.

Preparation

1.   Practice reading aloud *Inch by Inch*.
2.   Gather realistic pictures of each of the birds mentioned in the story to share with the children.

Introduction

Show the cover of the book and read the title to the children. Ask them to predict what the story might be about. After the children have made their predictions, tell them to listen as you read to see if their predictions were correct.

Reading the Book

As you read the book, stop where children have comments. Pause on the page where the nightingale asks the inchworm to measure his song. Ask the children what they think the inchworm might do. After children have responded, continue reading to the end. Discuss the children's earlier predictions and the inchworm's solution to measuring the nightingale's song, and solicit their thoughts about the story.

Curriculum Connections

Mathematics

At the Math Center, provide children with a container of inchworms constructed from green posterboard and many different objects to measure. The children use the inchworms to measure the objects in whatever way they wish. (**Using Nonstandard Measures**.)

Design a game on posterboard that features the inchworm at the bottom left corner and the birds mentioned in the book at several places around the board. Draw inch squares in a path from the bottom left corner to the top right corner. At the top right corner add a thicket of grass. The idea is for the children to move their inchworm (game piece) from the start to the finish to "save the inchworm." Two ways to design the game are as follows. One way is to simply have the children roll a die and move their inchworm the correct number of spaces. On each space there are directions to measure something (e.g., pencil, crayon, toothpick, paintbrush, a finger, etc.) using the posterboard inchworms. The children continue playing until they reach the thicket at the top. A second way to design the game is to draw three sets of the birds mentioned in the story on 5" x 8" cards.

Connecting to Standards

Inching Along

Mathematics (Measurement): Students understand measurable attributes of objects and the units, systems, and processes of measurement.

Mathematics (Measurement): Students apply appropriate techniques, tools, and formulas to determine measurements (NCTM, 2000).

Science (Life Science): Students have knowledge of the characteristics of organisms, life cycles, and environments (NRC, 1996).

Language Arts #3: Students use a variety of strategies to comprehend, interpret, and appreciate texts (NCTE & IRA, 1996).

The Arts (Visual Arts): Understanding and applying media, techniques, and processes (CNAEA, 1994).

The children shuffle the cards and place them in a stack face down. They then take turns turning over the top card and measuring the bird on the card with inchworms. What part of the bird they choose to measure is up to them. The child who measured the bird moves his/her inchworm game piece that many spaces. (**Using Nonstandard Measures**; **Counting**.)

Interdisciplinary (Science, Language Arts, and Art)

Place realistic pictures of the birds in the Science Center. The children choose one of the birds to research. For each, they must find an interesting measurement fact to include in a class book. Each of the facts will become a page in "Fantastic Facts about Our Feathered Friends."

Leo Lionni's illustrations are collages. Show the children the illustrations and talk with them about how they were created. Then provide the children with paper, crayons, paint, scissors, and glue. Children may paint or draw on the paper, then cut out shapes to make their own collages of their birds for the class book. (**Research**; **Communication**; **Media, Techniques, and Processes**.)

Language Arts

Make flannel board pieces for each of the characters in the story and encourage the children to retell the story using the flannel board. (**Comprehension**.)

What Time Is It?

Read aloud *Telling Time with Big Mama Cat* written by Dan Harper and illustrated by Barry and Cara Moser.

Big Mama Cat takes us through a day in her "busy" life. On each page she tells us what she does at certain times of the day. Each illustration includes an analog clock with the time depicted on the clock face. The front cover folds out to provide a clock with moveable hands for children to manipulate as the story is read. This feature can be used for individual or small-group reading times.

Preparation

1. Practice reading aloud *Telling Time with Big Mama Cat.*
2. Have available a cardboard analog clock for each child. These may be commercially produced or homemade, depending on your school's resources.

Introduction

Before you show the book to the children, move the clock hands on the cover to show an appropriate hour (morning or afternoon) depending on when you are reading the story. Then show the cover to the children and ask them if anyone knows what time the clock is showing. After children respond, tell them you will be reading a book entitled *Telling Time with Big Mama Cat.* Encourage the children to listen for things the cat does at different times of the day.

Reading the Book

As you read the book, talk with the children about what the cat is doing at different times of the day. At the end of the book, solicit personal reactions. Then ask the children to relay the things the cat did during the day. As the children relate each of the cat's daily activities, revisit the text to find the time of day the activity occurred. Using an analog clock, move the hands to the correct positions.

Curriculum Connections

Mathematics

Give each child a cardboard analog clock. As you reread the story, have the children move the clock hands to the correct time. Have partners compare their clocks to see if they agree. Then place several of the clocks and a copy of the book in the Math Center for children to use independently. **(Understanding Time Units.)**

Interdisciplinary (Mathematics and Language Arts)

Have the children write their schedules for a day, noting important times and what they do at those times. Each entry should include an analog clock face drawn by the child depicting the

Connecting to Standards
What Time Is It?

Mathematics (Measurement): Students understand measurable attributes of objects and the units, systems, and processes of measurement.

Mathematics (Measurement): Students apply appropriate techniques, tools, and formulas to determine measurements (NCTM, 2000).

Language Arts #12: Students use spoken, written, and visual language to accomplish their own purposes (e.g., for learning, enjoyment, persuasion, and the exchange of information).

The Arts (Visual Arts): Reflecting upon and assessing the characteristics and merits of their work and the work of others (CNAEA, 1994).

time and a sentence or two stating the time and what he does at that time. (**Understanding Time Units**; **Writing**.)

Language Arts

Share several poems about times of the day with children. Some possible selections include "Cat Kisses" by Bobbi Katz from *Morning, Noon and Night: Poems to Fill Your Day* and "Dawn," "Morning," "Good-Night," and "The Sand-Man" by Paul Laurence Dunbar from *Jump Back, Honey: Poems by Paul Laurence Dunbar*. (**Appreciating Poetry**.)

Art

Talk with children about how cats look and move. Have them practice moving like cats. Revisit the text and show the children the illustrations. Call their attention to how the illustrators' pictures realistically depict cats. Using an easel or book stand, prop open the book on the first two-page spread where Big Mama Cat talks about the busy day she has planned. Talk with the children about the illustration of Big Mama Cat. Invite them to use a pencil and draw her as they see her. After they have finished drawing her, they may paint her using watercolors if they wish. (**Understanding and Appreciating Illustrations**; **Drawing Realistic Pictures**.)

CONCLUSION

In this chapter, we have demonstrated how children's literature can be used to teach mathematics. Many children's books are explicitly about math, for example *Anno's Counting House* by Mitsumasa Anno or *Eating Fractions* by Bruce McMillan. Other stories lend themselves to teaching mathematics only through the teacher's creative planning. For instance, stories such as *The Three Billy Goats Gruff* by Glen Rounds may be used to teach ordinal numbers and size comparisons after the children have listened to and/or read the story several times for the sole purpose of literary enjoyment. The books we have suggested in this chapter are only some of the many selections available to use in your mathematics curriculum. We know that children's books are magical. As you discover new children's books, ask yourself, "Is this book also mathematical?"

 *Visit ChildLit at* **www.mhhe.com/childlit** *for Web links related to this chapter.*

Children's Literature Cited in the Chapter

Anno, M. (1982). *Anno's Counting House*. New York: Philomel Books.

Anno, M., & Anno, M. (1983). *Anno's Mysterious Multiplying Jar*. New York: Philomel Books.

Ernst, L. C. (1983). *Sam Johnson and the Blue Ribbon Quilt*. New York: Lothrop, Lee & Shepard Books.

Fleming, D. (1992). *Count!* New York: Henry Holt & Co.

Hutchins, P. (1986). *The Doorbell Rang*. New York: Greenwillow Books.

Jenkins, S. (1995). *Biggest, Strongest, Fastest*. New York: Scholastic.

Jonas, A. (1995). *Splash*. New York: Greenwillow.

Lasky, K. (1994). *The Librarian Who Measured the Earth*. Illustrated by K. Hawkes. Boston: Little, Brown & Company.

Leedy, L. (1997). *Measuring Penny*. New York: Henry Holt & Co.

Mathis, S. B. (1975). *The Hundred Penny Box*. Illustrated by L. & D. Dillon. New York: Viking.

McKissack, P. (1992). *A Million Fish...More or Less*. Illustrated by D. Schutzer. New York: Alfred A. Knopf.

McMillan, B. (1991). *Eating Fractions*. New York: Scholastic.

Moore, I. (1991). *Six-Dinner Sid*. New York: Simon & Schuster Books for Young Readers.

Rounds, G. (1993). *The Three Billy Goats Gruff*. New York: Holiday House.

Slobodkina, E. (1947). *Caps for Sale*. New York: Harper & Row.

Tang, G. (2001). *The Grapes of Math*. Illustrated by H. Briggs. New York: Scholastic.

Tompert, A. (1990). *Grandfather Tang's Story*. Illustrated by R. A. Parker. New York: Crown Publishers.

Children's Literature Cited for One Book at a Time Examples

Barry, D. (1994). *The Rajah's Rice: A Mathematical Folktale*. New York: Scientific American Books for Young Readers.

Birch, D. (1988). *The King's Chessboard*. New York: Dial Books for Young Readers.

Demi. (1997). *One Grain of Rice: A Mathematical Folktale*. New York: Scholastic.

Dooley, N. (1991). *Everybody Cooks Rice*. Illustrated by P. J. Thornton. Minneapolis, MN: Carolrhoda.

Friedman, A. (1994). *A Cloak for the Dreamer*. Illustrated by Kim Howard. A Marilyn Burns Brainy Day Book. New York: Scholastic.

Murphy, S. J. (1997). *Betcha!* Illustrated by S. D. Schindler. New York: HarperCollins Publishers.

Pittman, H. C. (1986). *A Grain of Rice*. New York: Hastings House.

Root, P. (1998). *One Duck Stuck*. Illustrated by J. Chapman. Cambridge, MA: Candlewick Press.

Children's Literature Cited for Measurement Unit

Adler, D. A. (1999). *How Tall, How Short, How Faraway*. Illustrated by N. Tobin. New York: Holiday House.

Allen, P. (1983). *Who Sank the Boat*. New York: Penguin Putnam Children.

Allen, P. (1980). *Mr. Archimedes' Bath*. New York: Lothrop, Lee & Shepard Books.

Anno, M. (1987). *Anno's Sundial*. New York: Philomel.

Appelt, K. (2000). *Bats around the Clock*. Illustrated by M. Sweet. New York: HarperCollins Juvenile Books.

Axelrod, A. (1996). *Pigs on a Blanket*. Illustrated by S. McGinley-Nally. New York: Simon & Schuster Books for Young Readers.

Carle, E. (1977). *The Grouchy Ladybug*. New York: Crowell.

Danziger, P. (2001). *It's Justin Time, Amber Brown*. Illustrated by T. Ross. New York: G. P. Putnam's Sons.

Dunbar, P. L. (1999). *Jump Back, Honey: Poems by Paul Laurence Dunbar.* Selected by Ashley Bryan and Andrea Davis Pinkney. Illustrated by A. Bryan, C. Byard, J. S. Gilchrist, B. Pinkney, J. Pinkney, and F. Ringgold. New York: Hyperion Books for Children.

Florian, D. (2000). *A Pig Is Big.* New York: Greenwillow Books.

George, J. C. (1999). *Morning, Noon, and Night.* Illustrated by W. Minor. New York: HarperCollins Juvenile Books.

Harper, D. (1998). *Telling Time with Big Mama Cat.* Illustrated by B. Moser & C. Moser. New York: Harcourt Brace.

Hightower, S. (1997). *Twelve Snails to One Lizard: A Tale of Mischief and Measurement.* New York: Simon & Schuster Books for Young Readers.

Hoban, T. (1985). *Is It Larger? Is It Smaller?* New York: Greenwillow Books.

Hutchins, P. (1994). *Clocks and More Clocks.* New York: Aladdin Books.

Kirkby, D. (1996). *Measuring (Mini Math).* Crystal Lake, IL: Rigby Interactive Library.

Leedy, L. (1997). *Measuring Penny.* New York: Henry Holt & Co.

Lillie, P. (1993). *When This Box Is Full.* Illustrated by D. Crews. New York: Greenwillow Books.

Lionni, L. (1960). *Inch by Inch.* New York: Astor-Honor, Inc.

McMillan, B. (1989). *Time to...* New York: Lothrop, Lee & Shepard Books.

Murphy, S. J. (1999). *Super Sandcastle Saturday (MathStart).* Illustrated by J. Gorton. New York: HarperCollins Publishers.

Myller, R. (1962). *How Big Is a Foot?* New York: Atheneum.

Older, J. (2000). *Telling Time: How to Tell Time on Digital and Analog Clocks.* Illustrated by M. Halsey. Watertown, MA: Charlesbridge Publishing.

Pluckrose, H. (1995). *Capacity.* Illustrated by C. Fairclough. Chicago: Children's Press.

Pluckrose, H. (1995). *Weight.* Illustrated by C. Fairclough. Chicago: Children's Press.

Sendak, M. (1962). *Chicken Soup with Rice: A Book of Months.* New York: HarperCollins Children's Books.

Taberski, S. (Ed.). (1996). *Morning, Noon and Night: Poems to Fill Your Day.* Illustrated by N. Doniger. Greenvale, NY: Mondo Publishing.

Tolstoy, A. (1999). *The Gigantic Turnip.* Illustrated by N. Sharkey. New York: Barefoot Books.

Tompert, A. (1993). *Just a Little Bit.* Illustrated by L. Munsinger. Boston: Houghton Mifflin Company.

Updike, J. (1999). *A Child's Calendar.* Illustrated by T. S. Hyman. New York: Holiday House.

References

Bransford, J. D., Brown, A. L., & Cocking, R. R. (Eds.) (1999). *How People Learn: Brain, Mind, Experience, and School.* Washington, DC: National Academy Press.

Griffiths, R., & Clyne, M. (1988). *Books You Can Count On: Linking Mathematics and Literature.* South Melbourne, Victoria, Australia: Thomas Nelson Australia.

Hong, H. (1999). Using Storybooks to Help Young Children Make Sense of Mathematics. In J. V. Copley (Ed.), *Mathematics in the Early Years* (pp. 162–168). Reston, VA: National Council of Teachers of Mathematics Inc.

Kouba, V. L., & Franklin, K. (1995). Multiplication and division: Sense making and meaning. *Teaching Children Mathematics, 1*(9), 574–577.

Lubienski, S. T. (2000). Examining problem-solving through a class lens. *Journal for Research in Mathematics Education, 31*(4), 454–482.

National Council of Teachers of Mathematics. (2000). *Principles and Standards for School Mathematics.* Reston, VA: NCTM.

Thiessen, D., Matthias, M., & Smith, J. (1998). *The Wonderful World of Mathematics: A Critically Annotated List of Children's Books in Mathematics* (2nd ed.). Reston, VA: National Council of Teachers of Mathematics Inc.

Welchman-Tischler, R. W. (1992). *How to Use Children's Literature to Teach Mathematics.* Reston, VA: National Council of Teachers of Mathematics Inc.

Whitin, D., & Wilde, S. (1992). *Read Any Good Math Lately? Children's Books for Mathematical Learning.* Portsmouth, NH: Heinemann.

Whitin, D., & Wilde, S. (1995). *It's the Story That Counts: More Children's Books for Mathematical Learning, K–6.* Portsmouth, NH: Heinemann.

CHAPTER 6

Books That Bring Out
the Scientists in Us

Almost from the time of their birth, children engage in scientific activities. As infants they continuously observe the world around them through all of their senses. They watch, listen, smell, touch, and always taste new objects. It's their way of finding out about the properties of objects and how they work. As toddlers and preschoolers they classify, infer, predict, and experiment. They use these processes as they develop their schema. For example, if Billy shares his home with the family's pet cat, he learns that cats are furry and have four legs and a tail. Billy has created a schema for cats. The first time he encounters a neighbor's beagle, he infers that it is a cat. It fits his schema: It has four legs, fur, and a tail. But then mom tells him, "No, that's a dog. Listen, he barks; cats meow." So Billy interprets this new information (barking versus meowing) and alters his schema accordingly. As children develop schema they are continuously classifying, inferring, and reinterpreting data.

Cognitive developmentalists define learning as an interactive process that occurs within and is influenced by the individual (Yager, 2000). The learner constructs schema as she organizes new information through "hands-on-mind-on" experiences. It is in the act of doing that one creates his or her own understanding of concepts. Preschoolers are active experimenters. As they build with blocks, they discover the challenges of gravity and spatial awareness. Through trial and error, they find ways to connect buildings by bridging and learn to build from a wide base for a sturdier construction. At the water table, they learn that some objects float, some sink, and some do both, depending on the amount of water they have absorbed. At the art table, they experiment with paints and discover that when they mix red and blue, they make purple. Each of their discoveries is fascinating and new. Children are actively engaged in finding out how the world works.

Once children reach elementary school, their experiences with science should continue to foster the experimenter in every child. For many children, the natural curiosity and desire to find answers through experimentation continue throughout the school years. Their teachers enjoy teaching science and convey that enjoyment to the students. Unfortunately, for some children science classes become ones in which they must listen to boring recitations and attempt to learn intimidating amounts of information. These are the students who tell us that they hate science or that science isn't important to them. However, we know that science literacy is important, perhaps more so today than at any time previously. Our society is becoming more technologically sophisticated. The citizens of today and tomorrow need to understand how science and technology impact daily life and how decisions made today influence the future.

NATIONAL SCIENCE EDUCATION STANDARDS

In 1996, the National Research Council (NRC) published the National Science Education Standards (NSES). The NRC proposed four main goals for science education for grades K–12. The goals state that students should:

1. Experience the richness and excitement of knowing about and understanding the natural world.

2. Use appropriate scientific processes and principles in making personal decisions.

3. Engage intelligently in public discourse and debate about matters of scientific and technological concern.

4. Increase their economic productivity through the use of the knowledge, understanding, and skills of the scientifically literate person in their careers (NRC, 1996).

These standards bring into focus the kinds of instructional practices, assessments, and curricular content that should be provided to students. Research on how students interpret, understand, and use scientific concepts suggests that even academically talented students often have many misconceptions about scientific phenomena (Miller, 1996). Listening to a teacher's explanation or reading about scientific concepts is not sufficient for real understanding to occur. Yager (2000) states that instructional practices that involve students in authentic experiences of the application of scientific knowledge and skills embodies the kind of teaching proposed in the NSES.

EFFECTIVE TEACHING AND LEARNING OF SCIENCE

Science is inquiry. Scientists use the processes of observation, prediction, measurement, analysis, and interpretation to attempt to answer questions (Austin & Buxton, 2000). Teaching science is teaching students to ask meaningful questions about the natural world, use resources and hands-on activities to generate answers, verify those answers, and communicate findings to an audience in an appropriate format. What is most essential is engaging children in the learning process. If students are given the opportunity to pursue topics or issues that are relevant to them, if they are challenged by developmentally appropriate expectations, if they are encouraged to seek answers to their questions, and if they have teachers who model an interest and excitement about science then they will be engaged in learning (Yager, 2000).

Gallagher (2000) and his colleagues have developed a model for teaching for understanding and application of science knowledge. Their tripartite model, the Mercedes Model for Teaching and Learning, involves building a knowledge base, generating understanding, and finding applications of science information in daily life. The first aspect, building a knowledge base, involves transmitting factual information to students. Lectures, reading in texts, and hands-on activities have traditionally been the way we teach factual information to students. While this is what occurs in most science

education programs, Gallagher (2000) suggests that teaching factual information is not enough. We need to add to our repertoire instructional practices that encourage the understanding and application of science concepts. Understanding and application can be encouraged by having students develop concept maps, write to learn, represent concepts with pictures and models, work in groups to develop explanations and describe applications, write about applications, and use newspapers to find science applications in everyday life (Gallagher, 2000). If we look carefully at these instructional practices, we see that many involve reading and language arts. Armbruster (1993) states that good readers and good scientists use the same skills. They use prior knowledge, make predictions, develop plans, assess understanding, describe patterns, compare and contrast, evaluate sources, etc. We, like many others, believe that making connections between children's literature and science enhances children's learning.

SCIENCE AND CHILDREN'S LITERATURE

Which is more likely to engage the interests of elementary students, reading a science textbook chapter on dinosaurs, or reading *Dinosaur Ghosts: The Mystery of Coelophysis* by J. Lynett Gillette and *Digging Up Tyrannosaurus Rex* by Jack Horner and Don Lessem? We think students are likely to choose the latter. Authors who present science in dynamic and accessible language and use fascinating photographs or illustrations get children excited about the topic and eager to learn more. Access to a wide variety of fiction and nonfiction science-themed trade books and poetry is a vital part of an elementary science curriculum. Cerullo (1997) and Savage (2000) state that science and literature make natural partners. These authors suggest that through the integration of science and literature children are able to explain events they observe, question, problem-solve, learn to write and write to learn, correct their science misconceptions, learn what scientists do, and learn how science affects us all.

In this era of accountability with standardized test scores in reading and math used as indices for determining the quality of the education provided by schools, some districts are increasing the amount of instructional time for reading and mathematics. This results in a reciprocal reduction in time spent on science, social studies, and the arts. One way some school districts are solving this time dilemma is by combining science and social studies with reading instruction. Integrating science and literature provides teachers with the opportunity to spend more time on both and to engage children in a variety of learning experiences (Cerullo, 1997).

Selecting Science-Themed Trade Books

As any other good children's literature, science-themed books need to be interesting and well written. The books we select should cultivate children's natural curiosity. If the trade books read like dry textbook chapters, then children are no more likely to read and learn from them than from the textbook. We need to also consider the illustrations or photographs that accompany the text. Do they contribute to children's understanding of the content?

In addition to these general guidelines, Cerullo (1997) suggests other criteria for science-themed literature selections. She states that teachers should look for accuracy and currency of the information, clear explanations, nonstereotypic representations, and organizational clarity. Anthropomorphism (attributing human characteristics to nonhumans) may be used in fiction, but should not be used in nonfiction books (Cerullo, 1997). One way that teachers can use science trade books that reflect inaccuracies in text or illustrations is to engage students as "science sleuths." In this way, students are able to work as detectives to discover what is incorrect in the book or books and furnish corrections. This is an authentic way to assess that children have learned the content.

When choosing children's literature for science themes, we should keep in mind that we will need texts for a variety of purposes and activities. Our classroom collections should include books that can be used for read-alouds, materials for independent reading, informational texts for individual or small-group research projects, and, when possible, poetry

selections. For example, when planning a thematic unit on the solar system for the intermediate grades, we can select any or all of Seymour Simon's books on the subject. *Comets, Meteors, and Asteroids* and *Stars* are examples of books that cover content related to objects in the solar system. The author's individual books on the planets—for example, *Destination Jupiter* and *Destination Mars*—provide details about the characteristics of these planets. Simon's books are excellent choices for reading aloud, for independent reading, and for student research. Other texts might include *First on the Moon: What It Was Like When Man Landed on the Moon* by Barbara Hehner, *To Space and Back* by Sally Ride and Susan Okie, *You're Aboard Spaceship Earth* by Patricia Lauber, *Maria's Comet* by Deborah Hopkinson, *The Mystery of Mars* by Sally Ride and Tam O'Shaughnessy, and *The Magic School Bus Lost in the Solar System* by Joanna Cole. It is interesting to note that all of the books mentioned as other possible selections for the solar system theme were written by women authors. While more females are choosing science as a career, women are still in the minority in most, if not all, scientific fields. By selecting good-quality science trade books written by and about women, teachers can encourage the girls in their classrooms to think of themselves as current and future scientists.

A typical science theme in the primary grades is insects. There is an abundance of excellent children's books to choose from for this unit. This topic may take on a more narrow focus, studying a single type of insect, for example butterflies, or it may be broadly focused on insects native to where we live. Books to consider for the butterfly unit include *An Extraordinary Life: The Story of a Monarch Butterfly* by Laurence Pringle, *The Butterfly Alphabet* by Kjell Sandved, *Are You a Butterfly?* by Judy Allen and Tudor Humphries, *Gotta Go! Gotta Go!* by Sam Swope, *Waiting for Wings* by Lois Ehlert, and *A Monarch Butterfly's Life* by John Himmelman. These are just some of the children's books available about butterflies.

Notable books about other insects include *Are You a Ladybug?* by Judy Allen and Tudor Humphries, *Insectlopedia: Poems and Paintings* by Douglas Florian, *I Didn't Know That Some Bugs Glow in the Dark* by Claire Llewellyn, *The Very Quiet Cricket* by

Eric Carle, *Fireflies in the Night* by Judy Hawes, *What Is an Insect?* by Robert Snedden, and *Flit, Flutter, Fly! Poems about Bugs and Other Crawly Creatures* by Lee Bennett Hopkins. Again, there are many, many more books to choose from for a thematic unit on insects. We might start this unit with a K-W-L and then make children's literature selections that meet the interests and needs of the children and are focused on what they want to learn about insects.

The remainder of this chapter is devoted to three examples of science-themed units for the elementary curriculum. For each unit, we identify key concepts, suggest appropriate trade books, and offer activity ideas based on several of the children's literature selections. The first unit is on ponds and is designed for first grade. The other two units are for the intermediate grades and cover the topics of rain forests and weather.

Sample Unit for Primary Grades

The Pond

Most young children love to explore the world outside, and they revel in muck and mud. Many of us have fond memories of tromping through the woods, building dams in creeks, or climbing trees to see the world from a different perspective. A thematic unit on ponds provides children with the opportunity to learn about the natural world. For children who live in suburban or rural areas near ponds, the unit offers a chance to learn more about ponds and to correct misconceptions they may have developed through their own explorations. For children who do not have access to ponds, the unit offers an opportunity to bring the natural world and all its excitement into the classroom.

Concept 1: Pond Formation

A Freshwater Pond by A. Hibbert

Life in a Pond by A. Fowler

Concept 2: Pond Plants

Life in a Pond by A. Fowler

Pond Year by K. Lasky

Concept 3: Pond Insects

All Eyes on the Pond by M. Rosen

Turtle in July by M. Singer

Joyful Noise: Poems for Two Voices by P. Fleischman

Concept 4: Small Animals

Box Turtle at Long Pond by W. George & L. B. George

What Newt Could Do for Turtle by J. London

At the Pond (Look Once, Look Again) by D. M. Schwartz

In the Small, Small Pond by D. Fleming

All Eyes on the Pond by M. Rosen

Concept 5: Frog Lifecycle

Growing Frogs by V. French

Frogs, Toads, and Tadpoles, Too by A. Fowler

Concept 6: Larger Animals

A Freshwater Pond by A. Hibbert

Beaver at Long Pond by W. George & L. B. George

·— **Figure 6.1** ⌣·

Children's Literature Selections for the Pond Unit

The following is a list of suggested concepts that are appropriate for a unit on ponds. Teachers may choose to use these concepts or refine them to meet the needs and interests of the children in their classrooms.

Concepts for the Pond Unit

1. Ponds are small, shallow bodies of water. Most are made when rainwater fills natural hollows in the land, but others are constructed by humans. All of the pond's inhabitants contribute to the pond's ecosystem.

2. North American ponds contain many different kinds of plants—for example, algae, duckweed, bladderwort, pond lilies, reeds, and rushes.

3. North American ponds are natural homes for many varieties of insects and arachnids, including water fleas, mosquitos, diving beetles, water striders, swamp spiders, and dragonflies.

4. Very small fish like minnows and sticklebacks live in ponds. Other animals like frogs, toads, and turtles live near ponds for feeding and mating purposes.

5. Frogs are amphibians, spending part of their life in the pond and part out on land. Frogs begin as spawn (frog eggs), then develop into tadpoles, and finally into adult frogs.

6. Larger animals such as raccoons, herons, deer, and ducks visit ponds for water and food. They eat the plants and smaller animals that live in or near the pond.

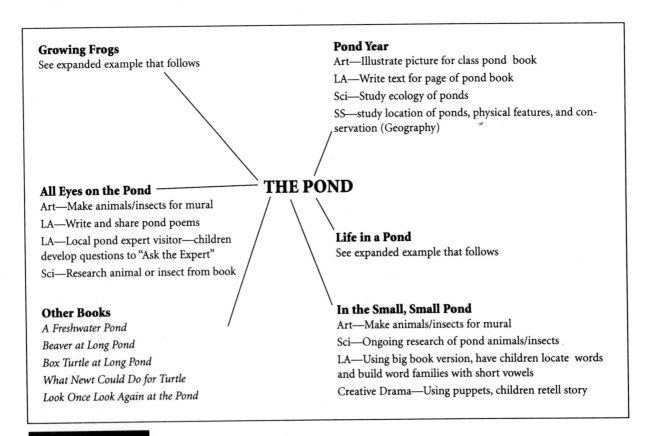

Growing Frogs
See expanded example that follows

Pond Year
Art—Illustrate picture for class pond book
LA—Write text for page of pond book
Sci—Study ecology of ponds
SS—study location of ponds, physical features, and conservation (Geography)

All Eyes on the Pond ——— **THE POND**
Art—Make animals/insects for mural
LA—Write and share pond poems
LA—Local pond expert visitor—children develop questions to "Ask the Expert"
Sci—Research animal or insect from book

Life in a Pond
See expanded example that follows

Other Books
A Freshwater Pond
Beaver at Long Pond
Box Turtle at Long Pond
What Newt Could Do for Turtle
Look Once Look Again at the Pond

In the Small, Small Pond
Art—Make animals/insects for mural
Sci—Ongoing research of pond animals/insects
LA—Using big book version, have children locate words and build word families with short vowels
Creative Drama—Using puppets, children retell story

·⌣ **Figure 6.2** ⌣·

Web of Children's Literature for the Pond Unit

Sample Lessons

Pond Life

Read aloud *Life in a Pond* written by Allan Fowler. This is a nonfiction "Rookie Read-About Science" book. In this book, the author introduces children to the plant and animal life that lives in or near ponds. Through the text and photographs, he explains the difference between ponds and lakes and helps children understand the ecology of ponds.

Preparation

1. Practice reading Life in a Pond, planning where you might stop to solicit comments or questions. This is a wonderful book to introduce the pond unit.
2. Have available an easel with paper and markers for children to begin listing pond vocabulary.

Introduction

Begin by showing the children the cover of the book and soliciting predictions about the text. Ask the children to define the word pond. After several children have given their definitions, ask them what makes a pond different from a lake. Again, pause to allow several children to give their answers. Tell the children you will read the book *Life in a Pond*, emphasizing that they should listen to find out what a pond is like and what lives in a pond.

Reading the Book

Read the book, stopping where you planned to ask questions or solicit comments from the children. When finished, ask the two introductory questions again. What is a pond? What lives in a pond? As the children answer, quickly revisit the text to check understanding.

Curriculum Connections

Science

Have the children work in small groups to sort and classify the pond's inhabitants into the following groups: plants, mammals, amphibians, reptiles, and insects. Children will need to research what makes an animal a mammal, reptile, amphibian, or insect in order to classify each of the pond's inhabitants correctly. (**Sorting and Classifying.**)

Children choose a favorite pond inhabitant (plant or animal) and write a research report about it. Encourage children to use the books in the classroom as well as other library or Internet resources to gather their information. Children write a first draft of their report and discuss it with the teacher. They then revise it as needed for the final draft. You may choose to have the children present their reports orally to the class. (**Library Research**; **Communication.**)

Art

Provide children with an abundance of different materials to create a Pond Mural for the classroom. Use butcher paper to create a large canvas (5' x 8') and draw an outline of a pond. Throughout the week as children learn about the different plants and animals that inhabit a pond, they may add new creations to the mural. If your school is located near a pond, the children might scavenge for twigs or dead grasses to add to the mural. Suggest to children that they leave growing plants at the pond to preserve the pond's ecology. (**Media, Techniques, and Processes**; **Using Art to Communicate Knowledge**.)

Children can make pond lilies from green construction paper and pink and yellow tissue paper. Show the children the picture of the pond lilies in the book *Life in a Pond*. Encourage them to make pond lilies to add to the mural and to take home. (**Media, Techniques, and Processes**.)

Language Arts

Title easel paper "Our Pond Vocabulary." Have the children add new words to the list as they learn them. Some examples from the book *Life in a Pond* include plankton, algae, dragonfly, shallow, and lodges. As the children add new words and fill the easel paper, hang each page on the wall and add a new sheet for the children to use for more words. (**Vocabulary**.)

Share poems with the children about insects that live around ponds. Some possible choices include "Dragonfly" by Marion Singer from *Turtle in July* and "Water Striders," "Water Boatmen," and "Whirligig Beetles" by Paul Fleischman from *Joyful Noise: Poems for Two Voices*. (**Figurative Language**; **Genre**.)

Print the concrete poem "Pond" written by Joan Bransfield Graham on chart paper. The poem may be found in Graham's *Splish Splash*. Read the poem to the children. Discuss how the words and shape of the poem help us visualize a pond. Help the children to write a class pond poem. In the middle of a piece of chart paper write the word pond and circle it. Ask the children to think back to the book *Life in a Pond* and/or the field trip, and to brainstorm words that describe a pond. As the children offer suggestions, draw lines from the circled word and write them down to form a web diagram. Then using those words, create a poem using the word pond (or ponds) to begin each sentence. Arrange the lines in the shape of a pond. (**Figurative Language**; **Writing Process**.)

Social Studies

Using the information from the book *Life in a Pond*, discuss with children where ponds are located, distinctive features of ponds, and conservation efforts to preserve ponds and their inhabitants. As children gain more knowledge throughout the week, this topic can be reintroduced for further discussion and clarification. (**Geography**.)

Connecting to Standards
Pond Life

Science (Life Science): Students have knowledge of characteristics of organisms, life cycles, and environments (NRC, 1996).

Language Arts #3: Students use a variety of strategies to comprehend, interpret, and appreciate texts (NCTE & IRA, 1996).

Social Studies (People, Places, & Environments): Students can find and compare and contrast various geographic formations. Students can explain the interplay of people and their physical environment (NCSS, 1994).

The Arts (Visual Arts): Understanding and applying media, techniques, and processes (CNAEA, 1994).

Rrr-bit!

Read aloud *Growing Frogs* written by Vivian French and illustrated by Alison Bartlett. After reading stories about frogs, a mother asks her daughter if she would like to watch real frogs grow. The pair venture out to a neighboring manmade pond and gather some frog spawn, pond water, and weeds in a bucket to take home. When they arrive home, they put everything into a fish tank in order to watch the frogs develop. Throughout the text, the author provides helpful hints on how to properly care for the developing frogs. At the end of the book, the mother and little girl return the baby frogs to the pond.

Preparation

1. Practice reading *Growing Frogs*, planning where you will stop to ask questions or solicit children's comments.
2. Draw pictures of the girl, her mother, and the things they did to collect the frog spawn. Include the different stages of the life cycle of a frog and the release of the frogs. Back each picture with flannel or velcro.
3. Have the "Our Pond Vocabulary" easel paper nearby for children to add new words they learn from the story.

Introduction

Begin by showing the children the cover of the book and soliciting predictions about the story. Use an Anticipation Guide to begin discussion of the life cycle of frogs (refer to Chapter 3 for our Anticipation Guide on *Growing Frogs*). Using information from the Anticipation Guide, explain the term "life cycle." Offer a few examples of life cycles. Tell the children that you are going to read a story about a little girl and her mother who grow frogs in order to learn about their life cycle. Remind the children to listen carefully for how a frog develops.

Reading the Book

Read the story, pausing where you planned to ask questions or solicit comments. Revisit and discuss the Anticipation Guide statements and student responses. When finished, ask children to recall the different stages of the frog's life cycle. Draw the life cycle to visually represent it for the children. Revisit the text in order to discuss some important rules to keep in mind when collecting frog spawn. As you discuss the rules and their importance, write them on easel paper.

Curriculum Connections

Science

If you have a manmade pond near your school and can arrange a field trip for the class, plan to take a trip to the pond to collect frog spawn and study the pond ecosystem. Follow the directions listed in the book *Growing Frogs* for collecting frog spawn. (If your school is not located near a pond, visit a pet store for some frog spawn.) Over the course of a few weeks, children will observe and record the development of the frogs. Each child is responsible for keeping a journal detailing what they observed about the frogs each school day. (**Observation; Communication**.)

Mathematics

On the day that you get the frog spawn, ask the children to estimate how many frogs will develop from the eggs. Each child is to record their estimate in their journal. When all of the frogs have developed, the class will count the frogs to see whose estimate was closest to the actual number of frogs. Discuss the difference between estimating and counting. (**Estimation**; **Counting**.)

Language Arts

Children will write a report on the frog's life cycle using the information they gather in their science journals. (**Writing**.)

Using a flannel board and the pictures you have drawn from the story, have the children retell the story. (**Comprehension**; **Sequencing**.)

Art

Make papier-mâché frogs. Inflate small balloons, one for each child. Using newspaper strips and wheat paste, the children cover the balloon with several layers. Show children pictures of the shape of frog bodies, but don't expect that their papier-mâché frogs will be perfect. Let them dry overnight. Children then cut thin cardboard and shape it into short tubes for the back and front legs. They tape these onto their frog with masking tape. Children then add several layers of newspaper strips with the wheat paste to cover the legs and tape. (They may need help with this part.) The final two layers are white newsprint. Let them dry completely. When dry, the children can paint their frogs with tempera paint and glue on webbed feet and googly eyes. (**Media, Techniques, and Processes**.)

Social Studies

If you gathered your frog spawn from a local pond, schedule another field trip to return the frogs to their natural habitat. A teacher we know calls this the "Born Free" day. As the children release the frogs into their natural habitat, she and the children break into song singing the theme from the movie *Born Free*. If you bought the frog spawn at a pet store, you might return the frogs to the store. (Check with the store manager beforehand!) You also may need to drive out to a rural area by yourself and

Connecting to Standards
Rrr-bit!

Science (Life Science): Students have knowledge of characteristics of organisms, life cycles, and environments (NRC, 1996).

Mathematics (Number & Operations): Students compute fluently and make reasonable estimates (NCTM, 2000).

Language Arts #7: Students conduct research on issues and interests by generating ideas and questions, and by posing problems. They gather, evaluate, and synthesize data from a variety of sources to communicate their discoveries in ways that suit their purpose and audience (NCTE & IRA, 1996).

Social Studies (People, Places, & Environments): Students can explain the interplay of people and their physical environments (NCSS, 1994).

return the frogs to nature. If you do this, videotape the release and share it with your students. Discuss why it's important to return the frogs to a natural habitat. (**People, Places, and Environments.**)

Sample Unit for Intermediate Grades (Fourth Grade)

Rain Forest

Children in the intermediate grades are interested in the wider world. Some of the more intriguing places on Earth are the rain forests. The mystery, beauty, and exotic quality of the rain forests appeal to children and adults alike. The children are surprised and fascinated by the varied creatures and plants that live in rain forests. It is also important that we, as citizens of the world, learn about the many benefits of the rain forests and become aware of efforts to save them from destruction.

Concepts for the Rain Forest Unit

1. There are different types of rain forests: tropical rain forests, which include equatorial evergreen forests, tropical moist forests, and cloud forests; mangrove forests; and temperate rain forests.

    A. Tropical rain forests are warm, wet areas near the equator and include the Amazon Rain Forest and rain forests in Belize, Africa, South east Asia, and Australia.

    B. Cloud forests, located in the mountains near the equator, get their moisture from clouds rather than rain. They also tend to be cooler than tropical rain forests.

    C. Temperate rain forests are wet areas found in temperate climates—neither very hot nor very cold regions, such as the northwest coast of North America and the southwest coast of South America.

    D. Mangrove forests grow in warm tropical regions near the earth's equator. Mangrove trees, unlike most other trees, grow in shallow salt water. Their prop roots look like stilts and can support the trees in the ocean's waves and tides.

2. The rain forest is divided into layers. The top layer, called the pavilion, is where the emergent growth (crowns of trees) is located. The level below the pavilion is the canopy, which is the upper layer of foliage and is 60 to100 feet above the forest floor. The understory is the lower, relatively open area that is made up of mostly tree trunks and epiphytes. The lowest layer is the forest floor. This level is very shady. Because the forest floor is composed mostly of dead plant debris rather than soil, there are very few plants.

3. About one-half of all the world's plant and animal species live in tropical rain forests. Some of the rain forest plants are used to make medicines to fight diseases such as malaria and cancer.

4. Tropical rain forests are endangered because people are cutting down the trees and clearing the land for farming and housing. The destruction of the rain forests will mean the loss of important medicines and foods and could affect the world's climate. Because of their importance, there are many organizations that are working to preserve the rain forests.

Concept 1: Types of Rain Forests

Nature's Green Umbrella by G. Gibbons

A North American Rain Forest Scrapbook by V. Wright-Frierson

The Forest in the Clouds by S. Collard

The Most Beautiful Roof in the World by K. Lasky

Journey through the Northern Rainforest by K. Pandell

Concept 2: Rain Forest Layers

The Most Beautiful Roof in the World by K. Lasky

Tropical Rainforests by J. Hamilton

Rain Forest by F. MacDonald & P. Bull

Concept 3: Rain Forest Animals & Plants

Tropical Rain Forest by D. Stille

Animals of the Rain Forest by S. Savage

Tropical Rain Forests by D. Silver

A Rain Forest Tree by L. Kite

Plants of the Rain Forest by M. Woods

Plants and Planteaters by M. Chinery

Rain Forest by P. Clarke

Trees and Plants in the Rain Forest by S. Pirotta

Look Closer: Rain Forest by B. Taylor

Deep in the Rain Forest by G. Pascoe

Concept 4: Saving the Rain Forest

Why Save the Rain Forest? by D. Silver

Saving the Rain Forest by S. Morgan

Nature's Green Umbrella by G. Gibbons

Other Books

A Walk in the Rain Forest by K. J. Pratt

Here is the Tropical Rain Forest by M. Dunphy

Rainforest Wildlife by A. Cunningham (research)

· ~ **Figure 6.3** ~·

Children's Literature Selections for the Rain Forest Unit

We have provided a listing of suggested children's literature for the Rain Forest Unit in Figure 6.3. Most of the books selected are appropriate for reading aloud. Because of its length, *The Most Beautiful Roof in the World* by Kathryn Lasky may be read and discussed in sections rather than in one sitting. Many of the other books listed are short enough for a single session read-aloud. We have provided selections that should meet most reading levels within the classroom.

Sample Lessons

Rain Forests

Read aloud *Nature's Green Umbrella: Tropical Rain Forests* by Gail Gibbons.

Gail Gibbons has written and illustrated a vivid picture book about tropical rain forests. This is an excellent selection for introducing the unit. In this book, the author locates the world's rain

Nature's Green Umbrella

See expanded example below

A Walk in the Rain Forest

LA—Students create their own rain forest alphabet books

Art—Students illustrate alphabet books

Sci—Students research rain forest ecosystem to find ideas for each alphabet letter

A North American Rain Forest Scrapbook

Art—Students design a postcard depicting a scene from a rain forest

LA—Students write a message to someone about what they've learned about the rain forest (Writing for a Purpose; Grammar)

Sci—Discuss temperate rain forests—compare and contrast them with tropical rain forests

SS—Students research logging industry in NW United States; students prepare arguments for both sides (Economics and Conservation)

SS—Students research Olympic National Forest

RAIN FORESTS

A Forest in the Clouds

See expanded example below

Animals of the Rain Forest

Art—Students draw or make out of clay a rain forest animal of choice

LA—Students write a poem or story about their animal

Sci—Students research animal of choice

The Most Beautiful Roof in the World

Art—Create a rain forest plant

LA—Reader response—Would you like to be a research scientist like Meg Loman and work in the rain forest? Why or why not?

Sci—Students research epiphytes and bromeliads

SS—Students research the country of Belize

·⌐ Figure 6.4 ⌐·

Web of Children's Literature for the Rain Forest Unit

forests and helps the reader/listener to understand the rain forest ecosystem. We learn about the layers of the rain forest, the unique animals and plants that live in them, and why it is important that we preserve the remaining rain forests for the future. The last page of the book describes the different types of rain forests found around the world.

Preparation

1. Practice reading aloud *Nature's Green Umbrella,* planning where you will stop for questions or comments.
2. Have available a globe or world map for locating the equator, tropics, and the rain forests.
3. Have chart paper available for beginning the vocabulary word wall for the rain forest unit and for a K-W-L chart.
4. Locate pictures of the different types of rain forests for children to see as you discuss them.

Introduction

Begin with a K-W-L asking the students what they know and want to learn about rain forests. Give children ample time to think and talk. Open the book to the last page and read it first. If the children have identified only tropical rain forests, discuss with them the other types and show them the pictures you have gathered. Provide them with an opportunity to add what they want to learn about the other types of rain forests in the "W" column. Remind students to listen for answers to their questions as you read.

Reading the Book

As you read the book, pause when you and the students wish to point out places in the text where the class's questions are answered. At the end of the book, talk with children about what they have learned about rain forests. Add that information to the K-W-L chart. Ask children for suggestions for vocabulary words to place on the rain forest word wall. Remind the students that they may add words to the wall whenever they encounter a new word.

Curriculum Connections

Science

Discuss the tropical rain forest ecosystem. Define what an ecosystem is and begin to identify animals and plants that live in the tropical rain forest. (**Interpreting Data; Communication.**)

Art

Have students begin to turn the classroom into a tropical rain forest. They will need a large wall space and a variety of materials to construct their classroom rain forest. Talk with children about what the rain forest looks and feels like. Have them brainstorm what they want to include and what materials they want to use to construct it. The rain forest may be created with paint and/or three-dimensional materials. Before the students actually construct the mural, they need a way to figure out their ideas. Have them plan and sketch what the finished product is to look like. The entire project is likely to take several days to over a week to complete, depending on your students' levels of interest and creativity and available time. (**Media, Techniques, and Processes; Subject Matter, Symbols and Ideas.**)

Gail Gibbons illustrated the book using watercolors, colored pencils, and India ink. Another possible art project is to provide the students with these art materials and encourage them to draw/paint a picture of the rain forest. (**Media, Techniques, and Processes.**)

Language Arts

Students add new vocabulary words to the word wall as they encounter them in the read-alouds or independent reading. (**Vocabulary.**)

Invite the children to create questions and answers for a *Rain Forest Jeopardy!* game that the class will play at the end of the unit. Using categories such as Types of Rain Forests, Rain Forest Animals, Rain Forest Plants, Rain Forest Amphibians and Reptiles, Rain Forest Products, and Rain Forest Spelling, encourage students to write the questions and answers for each category. Talk with the class about how the *Jeopardy!* game is constructed. Contestants are given the answers, and they must come up with the correct questions. The total number of questions you will need depends on the number of students in your classroom. The more questions and

Connecting to Standards

Rain Forests

Science (Life Science): Students have knowledge of characteristics of organisms, life cycles, and environments (NRC, 1996).

Mathematics (Number & Operations): Students understand numbers, ways of representing numbers, relationships among numbers, and number systems. Students understand the meaning of operations and how they relate to one another. Students compute fluently and make reasonable estimates (NCTM, 2000).

Language Arts #8: Students use a variety of technological and informational resources to gather and synthesize information and to create and communicate knowledge.

Language Arts #12: Students use spoken, written, and visual language to accomplish their own purposes (NCTE & IRA, 1996).

Social Studies (People, Places, & Environments): Students can locate, compare, and contrast landforms and geographic features. Students will be able to explain the place each has in the ecosystem (NCSS, 1994).

The Arts (Visual Arts): Understanding and applying media, techniques, and processes. Making connections between visual arts and other disciplines (CNAEA, 1994).

answers written the better, so invite students to write as many as they wish. For the actual game, divide the class into teams, each team rotating a contestant to answer questions with you serving as moderator. Students select a category and amount and the game is played as it is on television except that you will need to have as many rounds as there are members in each group. For example, if you have five groups with five students in each, you will need to have five rounds of Rain Forest Jeopardy. In each round, include a "Double Jeopardy" question that you have written. It is also a good idea for you to write the "Final Jeopardy" questions for each round. At the end of the game, the team that has the most points gets to plan and host the class's Rain Forest Party. In essence, everyone wins. (**Vocabulary; Writing to Learn; Critical Thinking; Study Skills.**)

Social Studies

Using the globe and/or world maps, the students locate and identify the world's rain forests (tropical, temperate, and cloud), the equator, the tropics, and the continents. (**Geography.**)

Interdisciplinary (Mathematics, Social Studies, and Language Arts)

Students plan a simulated class trip to one of the world's rain forests. The class will need to review possible locations for the trip. The final destination may be decided through voting or consensus. Once a location is selected, the students will 1) research how they will get there, 2) plan sightseeing activities to do while in the rain forest, 3) plan where they will stay, 4) decide how long the trip will last, 5) decide what clothing and other items they will need to pack, and 6) determine the total cost and cost per student for the trip. (**Citizenship; Communication; Geography; Money.**)

Cloud Forests

Read aloud *The Forest in the Clouds* written by Sneed Collard and illustrated by Michael Rothman.

The Forest in the Clouds is a nonfiction book that explains what a cloud forest is and describes some of the interesting plants and animals that live in cloud forests. The cloud forest detailed in this book is the Monteverde Cloud Forest in Costa Rica. The author also discusses the environmental threats to this forest and what can be done to help. At the back of the book, the author includes a map of Costa Rica, a glossary, and Web sites for children to visit for more information on cloud forests.

Preparation

1. Practice reading aloud *The Forest in the Clouds,* determining when you will pause for comments and questions.
2. Have a map of Costa Rica and Central America available.
3. Also have chart paper for new vocabulary words to be added to the word wall.

Introduction

Ask children what they remember about rain forests from listening to *Nature's Green Umbrella* by Gail Gibbons. Refer to the K-W-L chart throughout the discussion. If no one voluntarily recalls the different types of rain forests, ask if anyone can name them. After the different types are listed, pose this question to children, "How might cloud forests be different from and the same as the tropical rain forests we have studied so far?" As children offer suggestions, write them down on the blackboard or chart paper with headings for similarities and differences. Tell the children you will be reading a book about the Monteverde Cloud Forest in Costa Rica. As you read, they should listen for the ways in which cloud forests are similar to and different from tropical rain forests.

Reading the Book

Read the book, pausing when students identify similarities and differences. When appropriate, make references to the students' prereading list of similarities and differences.

Curriculum Connections

Science

Students may access the Web sites listed in the back of the book and others of which you may know. Have the students report on the kind of information, activities, etc., available on the Web site and evaluate the Web site for its usefulness. (**Interpreting Data**; **Communication**.)

The author writes about the disappearance of the golden toads. In small groups, have the students research possible reasons for the extinction of this amphibian. They also may choose to research another rain forest animal that has become endangered. (**Inferring**; **Hypothesizing**.)

Connecting to Standards
Cloud Forests

Science (Inquiry): Students develop an understanding of and the abilities to do scientific inquiry (NRC, 1996).

Language Arts #5: Students employ a wide variety of strategies as they write and use different writing process elements appropriately to communicate with different audiences for a variety of purposes.

Language Arts #7: Students conduct research on issues and interests by generating ideas and questions, and by posing problems. They gather, evaluate, and synthesize data from a variety of sources to communicate their discoveries in ways that suit their purpose and audience.

Language Arts #11: Students participate as knowledgeable, reflective, creative, and critical members of a variety of literacy communities.

Language Arts #12: Students use spoken, written, and visual language to accomplish their own purposes (NCTE & IRA, 1996).

Social Studies (Culture): Students can explore the similar and diverse ways the world's cultures address human needs and concerns.

Social Studies (Global Connections): Students explore and discuss global issues (NCSS, 1994).

Interdisciplinary (Art and Language Arts)

As the children gain more knowledge about the importance of all kinds of rain forests, encourage them to design posters that address rain forest conservation. Before students begin designing their posters, revisit the illustrations in the book and discuss how the illustrations work with the text. Then have students analyze a variety of posters for how words and visual images go together. Remind students that illustrators and authors create rough drafts and sketches as part of the creative process. (**Writing Process; Informative Writing.**)

Language Arts

Students may communicate via the Internet with other students in the United States and/or globally to discuss rain forest conservation efforts. (**Critical Thinking; Communication.**)

Students should also continue to develop questions for the class *Rain Forest Jeopardy!* game using information they have learned about cloud forests. (**Vocabulary; Writing to Learn; Critical Thinking; Study Skills.**)

Social Studies

The Monteverde Cloud Forest is located in Costa Rica. The author also briefly mentions that the Aztecs used the feathers of the quetzals to decorate uniforms and costumes. You may have the students research the modern day country of Costa Rica and/or the ancient Aztec civilization. (**Culture; History; Geography.**)

Sample Unit for Intermediate Grades (Sixth Grade)

Weather

Children as well as adults are interested in the weather. How many of us remember as children listening for winter storm forecasts in hopes of a school cancellation? We watch daily weather reports on the television, listen to the radio for weather updates, or read the day's forecast in the newspaper. The weather impacts our activity plans for the day or week ahead, influences clothing choices, and is the topic of much discussion when a dramatic storm occurs. As teachers, we are able to capitalize on children's interest and teach about the predictable changes that occur in the weather. Nonfiction selections can be used to convey weather facts and dispel misconceptions about weather phenomena. Fictional selections may be used as vehicles for discussion of dangerous weather and responsible decision making.

The weather and seasonal changes may be studied for an entire school year. We present here a sixth-grade unit on weather that may last two or more weeks. As always, teachers should feel free to use the concepts and activities we have outlined below, or adapt them to meet the current interests and needs of their students.

Concepts for the Weather Unit

1. The earth's atmosphere is a system that interacts with the sun and the earth to produce weather. The earth's rotation and revolutions cause cycles of heating and cooling as well as seasonal weather changes.

2. Meteorology is the study of the atmosphere and the conditions and processes that cause weather. Meteorologists predict weather by studying the patterns of weather change that result from the interactions of atmospheric systems.

3. Weather systems form when atmospheric interactions result in changes in temperature and air pressure. These changes produce winds and affect the water cycle, which may produce clouds, rain, or snow.

4. Different atmospheric conditions produce different kinds of clouds. For example, cumulus clouds are fair-weather clouds, while stratus clouds are associated with stormy weather.

5. Warm, rising air creates low-pressure systems that become storm systems. These storm systems can develop into destructive tornadoes and hurricanes.

6. People in different areas around the world have created myths or folktales to explain weather phenomena.

A listing of suggested children's literature for the Weather Unit is provided in Figure 6.5. We have included both nonfiction and fiction selections.

Some of the books listed in Figure 6.5 for concept development are perfect for reading aloud. Seymour Simon's three books *Weather, Storms,* and *Tornadoes,* as well as *Cloud Dance* and *Water Dance* by Thomas Locker and *Hurricanes: Earth's Mightiest Storms* by Patricia Lauber make for good listening. In addition, *How the Cat Swallowed Thunder* by Lloyd Alexander is an amusing fictional book that may be used as a transitional activity or just for pure enjoyment. Other books listed in Figure 6.5 are more appropriately used for individual reading and student research. *The Science Book of Weather* by Neil Ardley is an example of a book that describes different science experiments students are able to carry out with adult supervision. We have suggested several of the experiments listed in this book as science projects to accompany the read-alouds for our Weather unit.

Concept 1: Earth's Atmosphere
Weather by S. Simon
The Weather Sky by B. McMillan
Weatherwise: Learning about the Weather by
  J. Kahl

Concept 2: Meteorology
Weather Watch: Forecasting the Weather by
  J. Kahl

Concept 3: Weather Systems
Water Dance by T. Locker
Weather by S. Simon
El Niño: Stormy Weather for People and Wildlife
  by C. Arnold
Weatherwise: Learning about the Weather by
  J. Kahl

Concept 4: Clouds
Cloud Dance by T. Locker
Clouds: From Mare's Tails to Thunderheads by S.
  Harper

Concept 5: Storms
Storms by S. Simon
Tornadoes by S. Simon
Lightning: Sheets, Streaks, Beads, and Balls by S.
  Harper
Thunderbolt: Learning about Lightning by J. Kahl
Hurricanes: Earth's Mightiest Storms by P. Lauber
*Eye of the Storm: Chasing Storms with Warren
  Faidley* by S. Kramer & W. Faidley
Hurricanes and Tornadoes by N. Morris
Hurricanes by D. Galiano
The Big Storm by B. Hiscock

Concept 6: Weather Myths & Folktales
Stolen Thunder: A Norse Myth by S. Climo
Tales of the Shimmering Sky retold by S. Milord

Other Books
How the Cat Swallowed Thunder by L. Alexander
The Rainbow and You by E. C. Krupp
Wild, Wet, and Windy by C. Llewellyn
The Science Book of Weather by N. Ardley
  (weather experiments)

Novels
The Silent Storm by S. Garland
Night of the Twisters by I. Ruckman

·～ **Figure 6.5** ～·

Children's Literature Selections for the Weather Unit

Sample Lessons

What's the Weather?

Read aloud *Weather* by Seymour Simon. In this nonfiction book, the author explains different weather phenomena, including how the weather is influenced by the earth's rotation and revolutions, and the development of winds, clouds, and weather fronts. Simon effectively uses pictures and illustrations to graphically represent these and other scientific concepts.

Preparation

1. Practice reading the book aloud. Plan where you will stop to ask questions or solicit comments from the students.
2. Have chart paper located close by for students to begin a list of weather vocabulary words.
3. Locate videotapes of movies that depict weather. Some good and obvious choices are *The Wizard of Oz, Twister,* and *The Perfect Storm.* Cue each of the videotapes to a segment that showcases the storms. Have a VCR and the videotapes ready for viewing.

Introduction

Ask the students if they have ever experienced severe weather such as a hurricane, tornado, or blizzard. Solicit several responses. Then tell the students they will be watching brief clips from videotapes of the selected movies. (Students most likely have seen them previously.) Show the clips, and ask the students if they think the videos depicted the storms accurately. Why or why not? Finally, ask the students if they know what causes the weather we experience daily. Again, allow students time to respond. Tell the students to listen for the author's explanations of weather phenomena.

Reading the Book

Read the book, stopping where you planned for questions or comments. You may suggest that students keep in mind vocabulary words with which they are unfamiliar as they listen to the book. Ask the students what they learned about weather. Revisit the text to check and explore answers.

Curriculum Connections

Science

Using Neil Ardley's *The Science Book of Weather,* have students work in small groups to conduct the experiment for Wind Speed. Each small group will make their own anemometer, test it outside, and record the data they collect on wind speed over the week. (**Experimenting; Communication.**)

Mathematics

Using the information Simon gives in the book *Weather* about temperature change per thousand feet of altitude, have students calculate temperatures at different altitudes given different temperatures at sea level. (**Computation with Whole Numbers and Decimals.**)

Ask the students to record the forecast from television, radio, and the newspapers each day on a poster chart in the classroom. They also record actual weather and temperature for each day. Over the course of the unit, the students will determine which source is most accurate. (**Interpreting Data; Measuring; Communication.**)

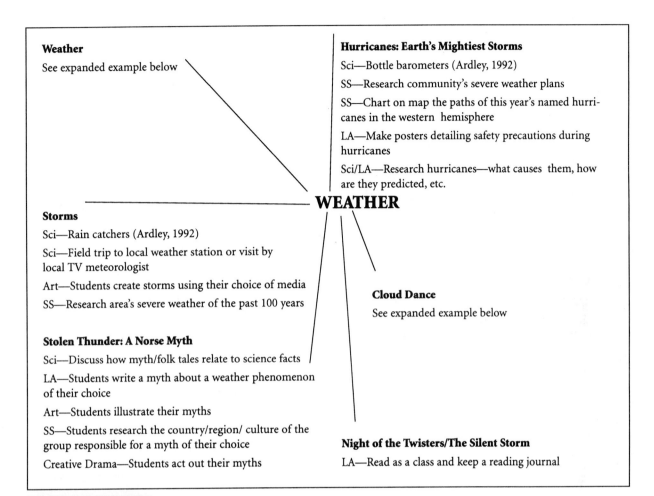

Weather

See expanded example below

Hurricanes: Earth's Mightiest Storms

Sci—Bottle barometers (Ardley, 1992)

SS—Research community's severe weather plans

SS—Chart on map the paths of this year's named hurricanes in the western hemisphere

LA—Make posters detailing safety precautions during hurricanes

Sci/LA—Research hurricanes—what causes them, how are they predicted, etc.

WEATHER

Storms

Sci—Rain catchers (Ardley, 1992)

Sci—Field trip to local weather station or visit by local TV meteorologist

Art—Students create storms using their choice of media

SS—Research area's severe weather of the past 100 years

Stolen Thunder: A Norse Myth

Sci—Discuss how myth/folk tales relate to science facts

LA—Students write a myth about a weather phenomenon of their choice

Art—Students illustrate their myths

SS—Students research the country/region/ culture of the group responsible for a myth of their choice

Creative Drama—Students act out their myths

Cloud Dance

See expanded example below

Night of the Twisters/The Silent Storm

LA—Read as a class and keep a reading journal

·◡ **Figure 6.6** ◡·

Web of Children's Literature for the Weather Unit

Language Arts

Students add words to a class chart of weather vocabulary as they encounter the words throughout the unit. (**Vocabulary.**)

Over the course of the unit, have students create crossword puzzles or other word puzzles using weather vocabulary. Puzzlemaker.com, an Internet site, is available for teachers and students to use for developing puzzles. Using the weather vocabulary chart, you and/or your students may construct and print word-search or crossword puzzles. (**Vocabulary; Thinking Skills.**)

Art

Talk with the students about the use of color to depict different types of weather. Explore how color influences the mood of a painting. For example, some pictures of rain create a gloomy feeling, whereas others convey feelings of happiness or relief. After this exploration, students paint pictures with weather as their subject. The paintings should be displayed; students should

Connecting to Standards
What's the Weather?

Science (Earth Science): Students develop an understanding of properties and changes of properties in matter, motions and forces, and transfer of energy. Students develop an understanding of science and technology (NRC, 1996).

Mathematics (Measurement): Students apply appropriate techniques, tools, and formulas to determine measurements.

Mathematics (Data Analysis & Probability): Students formulate questions that can be addressed with data and collect, organize, and display relevant data to answer them. Students develop and evaluate inferences and predictions that are based on data. Students understand and apply basic concepts of probability (NCTM, 2000).

Language Arts #3: Students use a variety of strategies to comprehend, interpret, and appreciate texts.

Language Arts #7: Students conduct research on issues and interests by generating ideas and questions, and by posing problems. They gather, evaluate, and synthesize data from a variety of sources to communicate their discoveries in ways that suit their purpose and audience (NCTE & IRA, 1996).

Social Studies (People, Places, & Environments): Students can describe weather patterns and phenomena in relation to geography (NCSS, 1994).

The Arts (Theater): Comparing and incorporating art forms by analyzing methods of presentation and audience response to theater, dramatic media, and other art forms

The Arts (Visual Arts): Using knowledge of structures and functions (CNAEA, 1994).

---

talk about the mood they were trying to create and how it influenced their choice of color. **(Structures and Functions in Visual Arts.)**

Social Studies

Students research and discuss how the geography of an area affects the weather. Depending on time constraints and interest, students may research the different regions of the United States or just the region in which they live. **(Geography.)**

Clouds

Read aloud *Cloud Dance* by Thomas Locker.

In lyrical text and captivating pictures, the author explores the many different kinds of clouds in our world. We are inspired not to stop and smell the roses, but instead to stop and look at the clouds. Factual information about the different types of clouds is presented at the end of the book.

Preparation

1. Practice reading aloud this short but wonderful book. We believe it is best to read this book in its entirety without stopping for questions or comments until the end.
2. Have pictures available of the different kinds of clouds.

Introduction

Ask the students if they have ever seen a cloud that looked like/reminded them of something else. Talk about their experiences. Ask the students to close their eyes and visualize the pictures that might go along with the text as you read.

Reading the Book

When you are finished reading, talk with the students about the images they visualized. Did the author's words make it easy for them to create their mental pictures? Reread the book, this time showing the students the illustrations. Ask the students if the pictures they visualized matched the pictures created by the artist. Allow time for students to respond.

Curriculum Connections

Science

Using Neil Ardley's *The Science Book of Weather,* have students work in small groups to complete the Cloud in the Bottle experiment. Students write reports on their construction of the cloud bottle and the results they achieved. (**Experimenting**; **Communication**.)

Students conduct independent research on the different kinds of clouds: how they are formed, what meteorologists can predict from the different kinds of clouds, and why clouds appear to be different colors. (**Library Research**; **Communication**.)

Art

Have students recall the pictures in the book *Cloud Dance.* Talk about the different kinds of clouds and the artist's depiction of them. Ask students which of the pictures they liked best. Provide stu-

---

Connecting to Standards
Clouds

Science (Earth Science): Students develop an understanding of properties and changes of properties in matter, motions and forces, and transfer of energy. Students develop an understanding of science and technology (NRC, 1996).

Language Arts #4: Students adjust their use of spoken, written, and visual language to communicate effectively with a variety of audiences and for different purposes.

Language Arts #5: Students employ a wide variety of strategies as they write and use different writing

process elements appropriately to communicate with different audiences for a variety of purposes.

Language Arts #6: Students apply knowledge of language structures, language conventions, media techniques, figurative language, and genre to create, critique, and discuss print and nonprint texts (NCTE & IRA, 1996).

The Arts (Visual Arts): Reflecting upon and assessing the characteristics and merits of their work and the work of others (CNAEA, 1994).

dents with paints and have them paint a picture of the sky with clouds. Have students share their pictures with classmates for critical review. (**Sharing and Critiquing Art Works**.)

Language Arts

After reading aloud *Cloud Dance*, hand copies of the poem to each student. Tell the students to read the poem silently and to circle several words or phrases that they feel are important to the meaning and feeling of the piece. Explain to the students that these words can be used to create a new poem. Have students take turns reading out loud one of their words or phrases. When everyone has had a turn, have students work in small groups to use their circled words to create a group response poem. (**Poetry**; **Writing Process**.)

CONCLUSION

In this chapter, we have demonstrated how to use children's literature effectively in the elementary science curriculum. Teachers can provide literature selections from all genres—nonfiction, contemporary and historical fiction, folk tales and myths, fantasy, poetry, and biography—to enhance and extend the information provided in textbooks. Well-written literature related to classroom topics brings science alive. Teachers who use literature wisely and effectively in curricular subjects such as science engage children in interesting and memorable learning experiences.

 Visit ChildLit at **www.mhhe.com/childlit** *for Web links related to this chapter.*

Children's Literature Cited in the Chapter

Allen, J., & Humphries, T. (2000). *Are You a Butterfly?* New York: Kingfisher.

Allen, J., & Humphries, T. (2000). *Are You a Ladybug?* New York: Kingfisher.

Carle, E. (1990). *The Very Quiet Cricket.* New York: Philomel.

Cole, J. (1990). *The Magic School Bus Lost in the Solar System.* Illustrated by B. Degen. New York: Scholastic.

Ehlert, L. (2001). *Waiting for Wings.* New York: Harcourt Brace.

Florian, D. (1998). *Insectlopedia: Poems and Paintings.* San Diego, CA: Harcourt Brace.

Gillette, J. L. (1996) *Dinosaur Ghosts: The Mystery of Coelophysis.* Pictures by D. Henderson. New York: Dial Books for Young Readers.

Hawes, J. (1991). *Fireflies in the Night.* Illustrated by E. Alexander. New York: HarperCollins Publishers.

Hehner, B. (1999). *First on the Moon: What It Was Like When Man Landed on the Moon.* Illustrated by G. Ruhl. New York: Hyperion Books for Children.

Himmelman, J. (1999). *A Monarch Butterfly's Life.* New York: Children's Press.

Hopkins, L. B. (1992). *Flit, Flutter, Fly! Poems about Bugs and Other Crawly Creatures.* Illustrated by P. Polagonia. New York: Doubleday Books for Young Readers.

Hopkinson, D. (1999). *Maria's Comet.* Illustrated by D. Lanino. New York: Atheneum Books for Young Readers.

Horner, J., & Lessem, D. (1992). *Digging Up Tyrannosaurus Rex.* New York: Crown.

Lauber, P. (1996). *You're Aboard Spaceship Earth.* Illustrated by H. Keller. New York: HarperCollins Publishers.

Llewellyn, C. (1997). *I Didn't Know That Some Bugs Glow in the Dark.* Brookfield, CT: Copper Beech Books.

Pringle, L. (1997). *An Extraordinary Life: The Story of a Monarch Butterfly.* Paintings by B. Marstall. New York: Orchard Books.

Ride, S., & Okie, S. (1986). *To Space and Back.* New York: Lothrop, Lee & Shepard.

Ride, S., & O'Shaughnessy, T. (1999). *The Mystery of Mars.* New York: Crown.

Sandved, K. B. (1996). *The Butterfly Alphabet.* New York: Scholastic.

Snedden, R. (1993). *What Is an Insect?* San Francisco, CA: Sierra Club Books for Children.

Simon, S. (2000). *Destination Mars.* New York: HarperCollins Publishers.

Simon, S. (1998). *Destination Jupiter.* New York: Morrow Junior Books.

Simon, S. (1994). *Comets, Meteors, and Asteroids.* New York: Morrow Junior Books.

Simon, S. (1986). *Stars.* New York: Morrow.

Swope, S. (2000). *Gotta Go! Gotta Go!* New York: Farrar, Straus & Giroux.

Children's Literature Cited for the Pond Unit

Fleischman, P. (1988). *Joyful Noise: Poems for Two Voices.* Illustrated by E. Beddows. New York: Harper & Row Publishers.

Fleming, D. (1993). *In the Small, Small Pond.* New York: Henry Holt.

Fowler, A. (1996). *Life in a Pond.* New York: Children's Press, Inc.

Fowler, A. (1992). *Frogs, Toads, and Tadpoles, Too.* New York: Children's Press.

French, V. (2000). *Growing Frogs.* Illustrated by A. Bartlett. Cambridge, MA: Candlewick Press.

George, W., & George, L. B. (1988). *Beaver at Long Pond.* Pictures by L. B. George. New York: Greenwillow.

George, W., & George, L. B. (1989). *Box Turtle at Long Pond.* New York: Greenwillow.

Graham, J. B. (1994). *Splish Splash.* Illustrated by S. Scott. New York: Ticknor & Fields.

Hibbert, A. (1999). *A Freshwater Pond.* New York: Crabtree Publishing Company.

Lasky, K. (1995). *Pond Year.* Illustrated by M. Bostock. Cambridge, MA: Candlewick Press.

London, J. (1996). *What Newt Could Do for Turtle.* Illustrated by L. Voce. Cambridge, MA: Candlewick Press.

Rosen, M. (1994). *All Eyes on the Pond.* Illustrated by T. Leonard. New York: Hyperion.

Schwartz, D. M. (1997). *At the Pond (Look Once, Look Again).* Cypress, CA: Creative Teaching Press.

Singer, M. (1989). *Turtle in July.* Illustrated by J. Pinkney. New York: Macmillan Publishing Co.

Children's Literature Cited for the Rain Forest Unit

Chinery, M. (2000). *Plants and Planteaters (Secrets of the Rain Forest).* New York: Crabtree Publishing Company.

Clarke, P. (1996). *Rain Forest.* Illustrated by C. Scrace. New York: Franklin Watts.

Collard, S. (2000). *The Forest in the Clouds.* Illustrated by M. Rothman. Watertown, MA: Charlesbridge Publishing.

Cunningham, A. (1993). *Rainforest Wildlife.* Illustrated by I. Jackson & D. Wright. London: Usborne Publishing Ltd.

Dunphy, M. (1994). *Here Is the Tropical Rain Forest.* Illustrated by M. Rothman. New York: Hyperion Books for Children.

Gibbons, G. (1994). *Nature's Green Umbrella: Tropical Rain Forests.* New York: Morrow Junior Books.

Hamilton, J. (1990). *Tropical Rainforests.* San Luis Obispo, CA: Blake Publishing.

Kite, L. (1999). *A Rain Forest Tree (Small Worlds).* New York: Crabtree Publishing Company.

Lasky, K. (1997). *The Most Beautiful Roof in the World.* Photographs by C. G. Knight. San Diego, CA: Harcourt Brace & Company.

MacDonald, F., & Bull, P. (2000). *Rain Forest.* New York: Franklin Watts.

Morgan, S. (1999). *Saving the Rain Forest.* New York: Franklin Watts.

Pandell, K. (1999). *Journey through the Northern Rainforest.* Photographs by A. Wolfe. Illustrations by D. V. Takahashi. New York: Dutton Children's Books.

Pascoe, G. (1999). *Deep in a Rain Forest.* Illustrated by V. Jefferis. Milwaukee, WI: Gareth Stevens.

Pirotta, S. (1998). *Trees and Plants in the Rain Forest (Deep in the Rain Forest).* Austin, TX: Raintree Steck-Vaughn.

Pratt, K. J. (1992). *A Walk in the Rain Forest.* Nevada City, CA: Dawn Publications.

Savage, S. (1997). *Animals of the Rain Forest.* Austin, TX: Raintree Steck-Vaughn.

Silver, D. M. (1998). *Tropical Rain Forests.* Boston: McGraw-Hill.

Silver, D. M. (1993). *Why Save the Rain Forest?* Illustrated by P. J. Wynne. New York: Julian Messner.

Stille, D. R. (1999). *Tropical Rain Forest.* New York: Children's Press.

Taylor, B. (1998). *Look Closer: Rain Forest.* Photographs by F. Greenaway. New York: DK Publishing.

Woods, M. (2000). *Plants of the Rain Forest.* Minneapolis, MN: Abdo & Daughters.

Wright-Frierson, V. (1999). *A North American Rain Forest Scrapbook.* New York: Walker & Company.

Children's Literature Cited for the Weather Unit

Alexander, L. (2000). *How the Cat Swallowed Thunder.* Illustrated by J. B Schachner. New York: Dutton Children's Books.

Ardley, N. (1992). *The Science Book of Weather.* Orlando, FL: Harcourt Brace Jovanovich Publishers.

Arnold, C. (1998). *El Niño: Stormy Weather for People and Wildlife.* New York: Clarion Books.

Climo, S. (1994). *Stolen Thunder: A Norse Myth.* Illustrated by A. Koshkin. New York: Clarion Books.

Galiano, D. (2000). *Hurricanes.* New York: The Rosen Publishing Group Inc.

Garland, S. (1993). *The Silent Storm.* San Diego, CA: Harcourt Brace Jovanovich.

Harper, S. (1997). *Clouds: From Mare's Tails to Thunderheads.* New York: Franklin Watts.

Harper, S. (1997). *Lightning: Sheets, Streaks, Beads, and Balls.* New York: Franklin Watts.

Hiscock, B. (1993). *The Big Storm.* New York: Atheneum Books for Young Readers.

Kahl, J. (1996). *Weather Watch: Forecasting the Weather.* Minneapolis, MN: Lerner Publications Company.

Kahl, J. (1993). *Thunderbolt: Learning about Lightning.* Minneapolis, MN: Lerner Publications Company.

Kahl, J. (1992). *Weatherwise: Learning about the Weather.* Minneapolis, MN: Lerner Publications Company.

Kramer, S., & Faidley, W. (1997). *Eye of the Storm: Chasing Storms with Warren Faidley.* New York: G. P. Putnam's Sons.

Krupp, E. C. (2000). *The Rainbow and You.* Illustrated by R. R. Krupp. New York: HarperCollins Publishers.

Lauber, P. (1996). *Hurricanes: Earth's Mightiest Storms.* New York: Scholastic.

Llewellyn, C. (1997). *Wild, Wet, and Windy.* Cambridge, MA: Candlewick Press.

Locker, T. (2000). *Cloud Dance.* San Diego, CA: Silver Whistle Harcourt, Inc.

Locker, T. (1997). *Water Dance.* San Diego, CA: Harcourt Brace & Company.

McMillan, B. (1991). *The Weather Sky.* New York: Farrar, Straus & Giroux.

Milord, S. (1996). *Tales of the Shimmering Sky.* Paintings by J. E. Kitchel. Charlotte, VT: Williamsburg Publishing.

Morris, N. (1998). *Hurricanes and Tornadoes.* New York: Crabtree Publishing Company.

Ruckman, I. (1994). *Night of the Twisters.* New York: Harper.

Simon, S. (1999). *Tornadoes.* New York: Morrow Junior Books.

Simon, S. (1993). *Weather.* New York: HarperCollins Publishers.

Simon, S. (1989). *Storms.* New York: Mulberry Books.

Videos Cited for the Weather Unit

Kennedy, K., Bryce, I., & Crichton, M. (Producers), & De Bont, J. (Director). (1996). *Twister* [Film]. (Available from Warner Home Video.)

LeRoy, M. (Producer), & Fleming, V. (Director). (1939). *The Wizard of Oz* [Film]. (Available from MGM/UA.)

Petersen, W., Weinstein, P., & Katz, G. (Producers), & Petersen, W. (Director). (2000). *The Perfect Storm.* [Film]. (Available from Warner Brothers.)

References

Armbruster, B. (1993). Science and reading. *The Reading Teacher, 46*(4), 346–347.

Austin, P., & Buxton, C. (2000). Science as inquiry. *Book Links, 10*(2), 10–15.

Cerullo, M. M. (1997). *Reading the Environment: Children's Literature in the Science Classroom.* Portsmouth, NH: Heinemann.

Gallagher, J. J. (2000). Teaching for understanding and application of science knowledge. *School Science and Math, 100*(6), 310–318.

Miller, J. D. (1996). Scientific Literacy for Effective Citizenship. In R. E. Yager (Ed.), *Science/Technology/Society as Reform in Science Education* (pp. 185–204). Albany, NY: State University of New York Press.

National Research Council. (1996). *National Science Education Standards.* Washington, D.C.: National Academy Press.

Savage, J. F. (2000). *For the Love of Literature: Children & Books in the Elementary Years.* Boston: McGraw-Hill.

Yager, R. E. (2000). A vision for what science education should be like for the first 25 years of a new millennium. *School Science and Math, 100*(6), 327–341

CHAPTER 7

Books That Bring Out the Social Scientists in Us

Children's daily lives are filled with interactions. When we stop and analyze these interactions, many can be viewed as lessons in the social sciences and history. When Anisha's scout troop sells cookies to finance their annual camping trip, she is learning about buying and selling and the rewards of work. When Joey realizes that not everyone celebrates Christmas Eve by going to his or her Noni's for the dinner of the seven fishes, he is learning about culture and cultural differences. When Katie's dad explains that even though they are wearing snow suits at home, they need to pack shorts and T-shirts for a winter vacation in Florida, Katie is learning about geography. And when William's grandmother tells him stories about an ancestor who was a conductor on the Underground Railroad in Philadelphia, he is learning history. Both informal learning experiences and formal study of history and the social sciences can help us to understand ourselves, others, and the world we share.

The content area we call Social Studies is all about people, about us. People individually and collectively are complex. Many things, including where we live, what we value and believe, what we have experienced, and what others believe about us, shape us and the societies in which we live. Because of this complexity, we rely on not one but many disciplines to help us understand ourselves and others. The National Council for the Social Studies (NCSS) defines social studies as the "integrated study of the social sciences and the humanities to promote civic competence" (NCSS, 1994, p.3). The many individual disciplines included in the definition may surprise us: anthropology, archaeology, economics, geography, history, law, philosophy, political science, psychology, religion, and sociology. The definition goes on to state that content from the humanities, mathematics, and the natural sciences is also considered to be a part of the social studies curriculum when appropriate. Because the social studies utilize the knowledge and expertise of so many different disciplines, it is no wonder that Pappas, Kiefer, and Levstik (1999) believe that social studies is often at the heart of the elementary school curriculum.

Prominent educators in the field agree that studying social studies has the potential to help students develop the social, intellectual, and critical thinking skills they will need to lead lives worth living—lives that can help create a compassionate and just world (Banks, 1987; Houser, 1999; Levstik & Barton, 2001; Pappas, Kiefer, & Levstik, 1999; Weinberg, 1999; Zarillo, 2000). In her address at a NCSS's annual conference, Susan Adler, NCSS President, reminded the association's members that "Citizenship is more than compliance. It involves thought and deliberation. It means thinking critically, participating thoughtfully, interacting with others respectfully, accepting our differences, and stepping outside of our comfortable boundaries." She challenged teachers to create "educative, caring, participatory, and socially just classrooms" (Adler, 2000).

How, we ask, can a school subject accomplish such lofty goals? Content is certainly important, but how we teach that content is equally important. Social studies at its best engages students in grand conversations. By grand conversations, we mean conversations that are both thought-provoking and relevant. Our use of the word conversation is no accident. Conversation requires the active participation of two or more people. Peterson and Eeds (1990) in their book *Grand Conversations: Literature Groups in Action* remind us that conversations are how people tend to learn things. When we engage in a conversation or dialogue, we are active participants who ask questions, gain exposure to new information and ideas, help the conversation move ahead, challenge the ideas of others, rethink our own ideas, and begin to formulate solutions. As teachers, we can structure these conversations so that students learn to collect, interpret, and evaluate data; consider multiple perspectives; ask interesting and important questions; and make decisions based on information and reason rather than emotion and tradition (Houser, 1999; Levstik & Barton, 2001; Pappas, Kiefer, & Levstik, 1999; Weinberg, 1999).

Those who examine social studies curricula believe that by its very nature social studies is controversial. If we choose to shy away from or ignore this aspect, we drain the life from this fascinating subject. Social studies becomes a deadly dull recitation of dates, events, people, and places. Yes, conversations about race, gender, class, and the distribution of wealth and power in societies are controversial. However, they are also interesting (Pappas, Kiefer, & Levstik, 1999) and, we would add, important. What better place to talk about these issues than in school? Imagine learning about citizenship by researching and then debating whether or not John Brown, Margaret Sanger, Russell Means, or Malcolm X was a good citizen? Such an assignment takes students beyond a rote recitation of dates, people, and places. It requires them to think and deliberate, to examine the evidence, to consider multiple perspectives, to step outside their worlds, to interact respectfully with others, and perhaps most importantly to care. As citizens of a global society, knowing how to do these things will help students meet the challenges that lie ahead.

National Council for the Social Studies Standards

In 1994, the National Council for the Social Studies (NCSS) published *Expectations of Excellence: Curriculum Standards for the Social Studies*. These standards are unique because instead of addressing standards for the individual disciplines that make up the social studies, they center around ten themes, which are interdisciplinary in nature. The NCSS envisioned these themes as a framework for social studies curricula and instruction. The ten themes are Culture; Time, Continuity, and Change; People, Places, and Environments; Individual Development and Identity; Individuals, Groups, and Institutions; Power, Authority, and Governance; Production, Distribution, and Consumption; Science, Technology, and Society; Global Connections; and Civic Ideals and Practices. Each theme contains increasingly sophisticated

performance standards for the primary, middle school, and high school levels. Included in the discussion of each theme are classroom examples of best practices at all levels. A listing of the Social Studies Standards for elementary grades may be found in the appendix.

Let's go back and look at our example of debating the merits of John Brown, Margaret Sanger, Russell Means, or Malcolm X as good citizens. The themes that come to mind at first are Civic Ideals and Practices, and Power, Authority, and Governance. A closer look suggests that students will also be working with the themes of Time, Continuity, and Change, as well as Individuals, Groups, and Institutions.

Textbooks, Primary Sources, and Literature

Everyone from researchers to classroom teachers seems to agree that social studies instruction is woefully inadequate if the textbook is the only source of information available to students (Dunn, 2000; Levstik & Barton, 2001; Loewen, 1994; Maxim, 1999; Wasta & Lott, 2000; Zarillo, 2000). Even textbook publishers acknowledge that the nature of the social studies demands the use of multiple sources. They encourage teachers to go beyond the textbook when developing curricula. For example, the teachers' editions for the Macmillan/McGraw-Hill social studies series, "Adventures in Time and Place," include annotated bibliographies of adult sources, children's books, computer software, and videos for each unit of study.

Along with the NCSS, researchers and teachers are particularly enthusiastic about using literature published for children and young adults in the social studies curriculum (George & Stix, 2000; Levstik & Barton, 2001; Maxim, 1999; Stix, 2000; Zarillo, 2000). Since the 1970s, the National Council for the Social Studies has given the Carter G. Woodson Awards annually. These awards recognize children's books that do an outstanding job of depicting ethnicity and race relations. Additionally, each year the organization, in conjunction with the

Children's Book Council, chooses books that they feel are outstanding social studies trade books for children. An annotated list of the Woodson award winners and the selected outstanding trade books is published in the May/June issue of *Social Education.*

The titles in the lists are arranged by broad categories such as Biography, Folk Tales, Contemporary Issues, etc. Each annotation includes a description of the book, the book's reading level, and the thematic stands of the social studies curriculum standards that relate to the text. These lists along with textbook publishers' suggestions are valuable resources for teachers as they work to incorporate literature into the curriculum.

Primary Sources

Historians and social scientists rely first and foremost on primary sources as they try to make meaning of both the past and the present. Zarillo (2000) defines a primary source as a "document, work of art, or artifact produced during the period being studied" (p. 287). While many historical documents are too difficult for elementary students to read and understand, some are not. For example, Julius Lester's *To Be a Slave* contains excerpts from slave narratives that make compelling reading for upper elementary school students. The excerpts are generally short, and teachers and students can pick and choose which to read. An illustrated version of Dr. Martin Luther King's speech "I Have a Dream" was published specifically for children by Scholastic in 1997. The 15 artists chosen to illustrate the book are all highly respected for their work in the field of children's book art. Teachers with whom we've shared the book have suggested that while the entire text is suitable for older children, younger children can easily be introduced to parts of the text.

Songs are also considered to be primary sources. There are a number of fine folk song collections and picture books devoted to individual songs available for children. One of our favorite collections is *Walk Together Children: Black American Spirituals* by Ashley Bryant. We have found the book especially helpful in explaining the role song played in the lives of enslaved African-Americans. Two recent collections, *In the Hollow of Your Hand: Slave Lullabies* by Alice McGill and *Hush Songs: African American Lullabies* by Joyce Carol Thomas are appropriate for use with both primary and upper-elementary students.

A picture book version of Woody Guthrie's song *This Land Is Your Land* with paintings by folk artist Kathy Jakobsen helps students gain a deeper understanding of a song often taught in school or at summer camp. Many of the children we have talked with about this song know the first two or three verses. When we ask them why they think Woody Guthrie wrote the song or what the song is about, they tell us that the song is about how beautiful or great America is and how America belongs to all of us. When we read or sing only the first several verses, the children's interpretations make sense. But of course, if we sing the entire song, a very different meaning emerges. We discover that in fact Guthrie was writing about what he and others experienced during the Great Depression of the 1930s. Children are often surprised to find that the song is one of protest rather than glorification. Guthrie's words have prompted students we know to explore social justice concerns facing the United States today and to consider how music can be used to promote social change.

Many works of nonfiction make use of primary documents such as letters, diaries, newspaper advertisements, and photographs. A powerful book that contains replicas of both primary documents and artifacts is *Lest We Forget: The Passage from Africa to Slavery and Emancipation* by Velma Maia Thomas. The book has an interactive format that invites us to learn about the time period in a very concrete way. Students can "open" the hold of a ship and see how Africans were stacked like cargo during the middle passage. Through facsimiles of an insurance policy for a slave ship, advertisements for runaway slaves, and a paper replica of a tobacco can that when opened reveals a slave's manumission document, we are able to explore this topic in a very tangible way. Other authors who make use of reproductions of primary documents, artifacts, and photographs include Jerry Stanley, Milton Meltzer, and Russell Freedman. Because students feel that they are experiencing the event or events firsthand, using primary documents makes for powerful and authentic learning.

In studying social studies, a picture is often worth a thousand words. Photographs offer us a window into both the wider world and the past. Just as with primary documents and artifacts, photographs can prompt us to ask questions, search for more information, see a variety of perspectives, draw conclusions, and make judgments based on the evidence at hand. The book *Century Farm: One Hundred Years on a Family Farm* by Cris Peterson relies on archival and contemporary photographs to help us gain an understanding of how farming has both changed and stayed the same over 100 years. In a similar vein, Ann Morris introduces young students to cultural universals, basic human needs, and living patterns in her photographic explorations of daily life around the world. In her books *Hats, Hats, Hats* and *Loving*, Morris uses simple text and pictures to teach about the unity and diversity found in human societies and cultures, and students see people who may or may not look like them doing things and enjoying life in ways that are both familiar and unfamiliar.

We said before that history and the social sciences deal primarily with people. Children tend to be interested in how other people live and lived especially if those people are children their own age. Jerry Stanley's *Children of the Dust Bowl: The Story of the School at Weedpatch Camp* and Russell Freedman's *Immigrant Kids* and *Kids at Work: Lewis Hine and the Crusade against Child Labor* help students understand what their lives might have been like during a particular time in history. In a similar vein, Susan Kuklin's *How My Family Lives in America* for primary students and *Voices from the Fields: Children of Migrant Farmworkers Tell Their Stories* by S. Beth Atkins for older students use interviews with children and young adults to explore contemporary life.

Biography and Autobiography

Full-length biographies, such as *Ida B. Wells: Mother of the Civil Rights Movement* by Judith Bloom Fradin and Dennis Brindell Fradin, *Always Inventing: A Photobiography of Alexander Graham Bell* by Tom L. Mathews, *Carl Sandburg: A Biography* by Milton Meltzer, and *At Her Majesty's Request: An African Princess in Victorian England* by Walter Dean Myers offer complete and complex treatments of their subjects. Autobiographies and biographies can be particularly powerful because they allow us to feel as though we have met and come to know the person about whom we are reading. We often feel as though we are reliving the person's life. A student of ours reported that when she read about Frederick Douglass, she felt as if she were in the story experiencing Douglass's triumphs and challenges along with him. Becoming part of the story is part of the power of autobiography and biography.

A recent trend in biographical writing for children, known as fictionalized biography (Huck, Hepler, Hickman, & Kiefer, 2001), takes a particular incident from a person's life and creates a story around the facts. *Freedom River*, a 2000 Coretta Scott King Honor Book by Doreen Rappaport, is based on an incident in the life of John Parker, a man who bought his freedom and then helped others escape from slavery. The book begins with an explanation of who John Parker was and then goes on to relay a particularly compelling rescue. A historical note at the end provides us with more information about Parker as well as an explanation of the primary sources used by the author. Rappaport also tells us that she invented certain details (the name of the escaping family and the month of the escape) because the primary sources made no mention of these facts.

Selecting Nonfiction

Using trade books as part of the curriculum allows us to delve into subjects more deeply, offer students an opportunity to choose books that interest them, provide materials written at students' individual reading levels, and furnish students with a variety of perspectives on a given topic. In order to ensure that we provide students with first-rate nonfiction books, we must be concerned with both the accuracy and quality of the writing and illustrations of the books. First and foremost, the writing and illustration must attract and keep students' attention. In addition, the book's facts must be current, accurate, and as complete as possible. For example, rather than present a glorified version of a person, excellent biography shares an individual's shortcomings as well as her virtues; her struggles as well as her achievements. In *Alice Ramsey's Grand Adventure* by Don Brown, we experience Ramsey's triumphs and travails as she becomes the first woman to drive across the United States. Levstik and Barton (2000) also remind us that the author should share with the reader what is fact and what is supposition, as Rappaport does in *Freedom River*. Finally, we must consider a book's organization. Works of nonfiction are not always read cover-to-cover. This means that the table of contents, index, chapter headings, and subheadings should aid us in locating information. We also think that excellent informational books provide the reader with a bibliography of the author's sources as well as a list of additional sources, for those who want to explore the topic further.

POETRY AND PROSE

Through beautiful language and compelling stories, poetry and prose have the power to capture our attention and entice us into wanting to know more. When we study regions of North America with our fourth-graders, the poems in books such as *If You're Not from the Prairie* by Dave Bouchard, *Heartland* and *Mojave* by Diane Siebert, and *Desert Voices* by Byrd Baylor introduce us to the uniqueness and beauty of each region in very lyrical ways. Similarly, history can also be the subject of a poem. Beginning with the musings of an indigenous person in 1500 and ending with the thoughts of a child today, Sherry Garland's *Voices of the Alamo* provides us with varying perspectives on the place that we know as the Alamo. Reading this poem helps reinforce how important it is to consider everyone's story when we study history and the social sciences. *Out of the Dust*, a book-length poem by Karen Hesse, helps us understand what life was like for farmers trying to hold onto their land in the 1930s. We internalize the characters' dreams, determination, anger, and sorrow. We wonder how we would have felt and what we might have done in the face of such daunting circumstances.

Like poetry, folk tales can also help us gain an understanding of the world around us. The particular strength of this genre is that the stories impart cultural information in very entertaining ways.

Moreover, these stories help us see how people are at the same time alike and different. A current favorite of ours, *The Hatseller and the Monkeys* by Baba Wagué Diakité, is a variant from Mali of the tale we know as Esphyr Slobodkina's *Caps for Sale*. Through his use of Bambara words and phrases, the cadence of the text, and stunning illustrations, Diakité transports us to a West African village where we find ourselves listening to a storyteller. As we listen to the words and enjoy the pictures, we learn much about the culture of Mali. We learn that in some families occupations are passed down from one generation to the next. We learn about two types of hats made and worn in West Africa. We also learn about the landscape of Diakité's homeland. Most importantly, we learn that the society values hard work, learning from adversity, and good will towards others.

While this story has a fairly modern feel to it, Zarillo (2000) reminds us that many folk tales are depicted in preindustrial settings. Because of this, we need to make sure books set in the present are also part of the curriculum. Books that can be used to depict life in contemporary Africa include Maya Angelou's *My Painted House, My Friendly Chicken, and Me* and Ifeoma Onyefulu's *Emeka's Gift: An African Counting Story*.

Both historical fiction and contemporary fiction have the ability to bring the past and present to life. In addition to providing relevant information, fiction also has the potential to help us to develop empathy (Zarillo, 2000). Books such as *Roll of Thunder, Hear My Cry* by Mildred Taylor, *Fever 1793* by Laurie Halse Anderson, and *The Birchbark House* by Louise Erdrich enable us to experience life as it was lived by a child or young adult long ago. We find ourselves laughing and crying with the protagonists in these books, and we often become part of the story. When we share *Fly Away Home* by Eve Bunting or *Miracle's Boys* by Jacqueline Woodson with the students, social concerns such as hunger, homelessness, and other pressures facing many families today become more concrete and personal. *My Rows and Piles of Coins* by Tololwa Mollel, *Shabanu: Daughter of the Wind* by Susan Fisher Staples, and *Kit's Wilderness* by David Almond allow us to experience life as it is lived in other parts of the world today.

Selecting Poetry and Prose

Naturally, the guidelines we use for selecting quality children's literature also apply to the poetry and prose we use for teaching social studies. In addition, special care should be taken to ensure that the historical, cultural, and geographic information presented is sound and current. Dialogue should use language that accurately reflects the setting and the time period. We also need to ask ourselves whose story is being told, and we need to be mindful of who or what is being left out. It is also important that the books we choose help our students navigate the present and prepare for the future as well as understand the past (Levstik & Barton, 2001).

The remainder of this chapter explores how children's literature can be used to create cross-curricular thematic units. While our emphasis will be on the social studies, we will also suggest how each unit lends itself to studying the language arts, math, science, and the arts. As in Chapter 6, we will identify key concepts, suggest a variety of appropriate trade books, and offer learning activities based on several of the children's literature selections. The first unit is entitled "Places We Call Home" and is designed for primary students. The second, for upper-elementary students, is "Community, Culture, and Resistance."

Sample Unit for Primary Grades

Places We Call Home

Most social studies curricula are still influenced by an approach known as expanding environments. This approach suggests that young children need to first study topics with which they have personal connections. For instance, topics such as self, family, friends, school, neighborhoods, and community are often studied in grades K–3. Unfortunately, the teaching that has resulted from this approach is often very narrow in its scope and somewhat superficial in its treatment of the various topics. Today, leading social studies educators suggest that while the approach is still relevant, topics need to include a global perspective so that children early on are cognizant of the wider world. They also believe that treatment of each topic should be more substantive. One way to do this is to study cultural universals, those institutions and living patterns that all cultures share. For example, primary children should learn not only about the houses found in their immediate environment, but also about those in the larger world. They need to learn about the different kinds of dwellings in the world and the reasons for the differences (Banks, 2000; Brophy; 2000; Zarillo, 2000).

Our unit "The Places We Call Home" addresses four of the NCSS strands: Culture; Time, Continuity, and Change; People, Places, and Environments; and Science, Technology, and Society. The following is a list of suggested concepts that are appropriate for this unit. We have noted the social studies disciplines that relate to each concept. You may choose to use these concepts or refine them to meet the needs and interests of the children in your classroom.

Concepts for the Places We Call Home Unit

1. Homes take many forms. They may be one or more rooms. They may house one or more families. They may be portable. They may be made of straw, canvas, skin, wood, snow, brick, aluminum, cardboard, etc. They may be square, circular, rectangular, cylindrical, or triangular in shape. They may or may not have walls, doors, windows, etc. (**Geography; Anthropology.**)

2. The kind of houses people live in is determined by physical needs. People need their homes to keep them warm, dry, and/or cool. Homes provide protection from animals and other people.

Some people need houses that can be built quickly. Other people move often and may need to take their homes with them. (**Geography**; **History**.)

3. Available materials often determine the type of house in which people live. (**Geography**.)

4. Culture influences the type of house in which people live. (**Anthropology**; **History**.)

5. Homes of the past and the artifacts left behind have much to tell us about how people in the past lived. (**Archaeology**; **History**.)

6. The development of tools, machines, and materials has changed the types of homes in which people live. (**Science and Technology**; **History**.)

7. The people who live in a house make the dwelling a home. (**Sociology**.)

8. All forms of houses can be happy homes. (**Sociology**.)

9. Some people in the world are homeless. (**Sociology**.)

As you consider the above concepts, the literature that we have chosen, and the sample lessons, think about the way other curricular areas relate to this topic. You can easily see the connections with science (e.g., the study of climates).

Language Arts brings to mind stories that are told and read at home such as folk and fairy tales, memorats, circle stories, and contemporary fiction. In math, the topic lends itself to a study of shapes and geometry or measurements used in building, and the ways in which we use mathematics in our daily lives. Lullabies, folk songs, spirituals, songs sung at celebrations, and popular songs are songs we sing at home. Art immediately brings to mind an investigation of architecture. Figure 7.1 offers a suggested list of children's literature for the Homes unit.

Geography: Concepts 1-3

Someplace Else by C. P. Saul

This Is My House by A. Dorros

Homes around the World by B. Kalman

Shelters: From Tepee to Igloo by H. Weiss

The Someday House by A. Sibley

Houses of Hide and Earth by B. Shemie

Houses of Adobe by B. Shemie

Houses of Snow, Skin, and Bones by B. Shemie

Houses and Homes by A. Morris

Anthropology/Archaeology: Concepts 4-5

This House Is Made of Mud by K. Buchanan

The Village of Round and Square Houses by A. Grifalconi

Homeplace by C. Dragonwagon

Houses and Homes by T. Wood

My House Has Stars by M. McDonald

Science & Technology: Concept 6

Building a House by B. Barton

How a House Is Built by G. Gibbons

Sociology: Concepts 7-9

Hush: A Thai Lullaby by M. Ho

Nana Upstairs and Nana Downstairs by T. DePaola

Kele's Secret by T. Mollel

Homeplace by A. Sibley

Fly Away Home by E. Bunting

Going Home by E. Bunting

Sam and the Lucky Money by K. Chin

The Lady in the Box by A. McGovern

History: Concepts 2, 4, 5, & 6

Town Mouse House by N. Brooks & A. Horner

Country Mouse Cottage by N. Brooks & A. Horner

·꙲ **Figure 7.1** ꙴ·

Children's Literature Selections for the Homes Unit

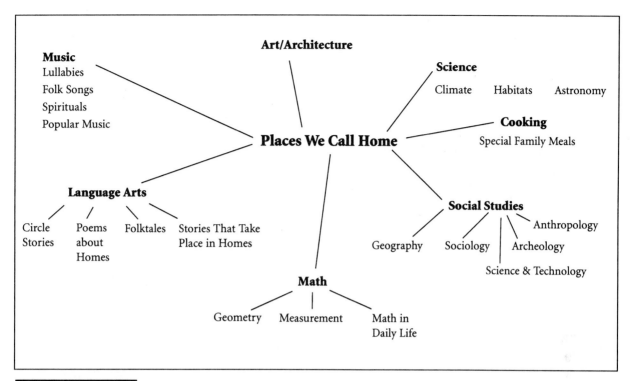

·ᴗ Figure 7.2 ᴗ·

Web for Places We Call Home Unit

Sample Lessons

Different Homes for Different People and Places

Read Aloud *Someplace Else* by Carol P. Saul and illustrated by Barry Root. This book is a work of fiction that follows a woman's search for the "perfect" place to live. Mrs. Tilby has spent her entire life living in the same place. It is a very nice place, but she wonders what it would be like to live somewhere else. So one day, she decides to find out. Will she like the city better? The seashore? Will she decide to stay in the mountains? Or is it true that there is no place like home? Her solution is an ingenious one that is both sensible and surprising.

Preparation

1. Practice reading the story. You will want to choose one or two stopping points to solicit student responses and predictions. For example, you might ask, "What do you think Mrs. Tilby will like about the mountains?" or "What would you like about the city?" A good place for predictions comes toward the end when Mrs. Tilby has just about given up on finding a perfect place for herself.
2. Have available an easel and chart paper for the introductory brainstorming activity.
3. Create or assemble felt- or velcro-backed pictures that depict the places and homes visited by Mrs. Tilby.

Introduction

Ask your students if they have ever wished they could live somewhere else. Spend several minutes talking about where that was and why they thought they might like to live there. Then ask them to spend a minute thinking about the different kinds of places in which people live. Record their responses on chart paper. Show students the cover of the book and read the title. What do they suppose the story is about? Explain that Mrs. Tilby, the woman in the story, is looking for a new place to live. Ask them to listen for the places that Mrs. Tilby visits and how she makes her decision about where to live.

Reading the Book

Read the story, stopping briefly to encourage students to share their reactions to the different places Mrs. Tilby visits. Would they have chosen to stay? Why or why not? When finished, solicit comments about what they think about Mrs. Tilby's solution. What would they have done in her place? Go back to the chart paper. Circle those places mentioned in the book and add those in the book that are not on the list. Spend a minute or two talking with the children about all the interesting places and homes there are in the world.

Curriculum Connections

Social Studies

Revisit the text. Look at the illustrations of the homes in the various places. Ask students to put on their "observation caps." Direct their attention to the 40-story apartment building in the city, then the house on stilts at the seashore, the fireplace in the house in the mountains, and so on. Explore with students the reasons why the houses in each place are built in a certain way. Then talk about homes in the book that move. Why might some people need homes that move? Help students make the connection that the kinds of homes we live in are often determined by the places in which we live. (**Geography; Making Hypotheses**.)

As a follow-up activity for the Social Studies Center, ask children to bring in pictures of their homes or collect pictures of a variety of homes from a realtor and/or magazines. Display all of the pictures. Make individual charts for the children that contain two columns: one for how the houses are the same, the other for how the houses are different. While at the Center, the children record their observations. When all children have visited the Center, you and the class can compile and interpret the data. For the individual charts, simply draw a large capital T so that there are two columns in which students can record their observations. Label one side of the T "same" and the other "different." Have a larger copy of the chart for compiling the data. Use the chart to engage the children in a discussion about the ways in which the houses are similar and different. (**Collecting and Analyzing Data.**)

Art

Provide children with art supplies, natural materials, and a collection of recyclables. Using these materials and their creativity, the children may construct homes in which they might choose to live. (**Media, Techniques, and Processes.**)

Interdisciplinary (Cooking, Social Studies, and Language Arts)

Mrs. Tilby helps to make fish chowder while she is visiting her daughter's house at the beach. Chowders were originally regional dishes that used ingredients that were plentiful and inexpensive. In some parts of the United States this meant fish, while in others it meant potato or corn. Prepare a chowder or other regional soup with your class. As you cook and later enjoy the soup, share the idea that in the past people cooked and ate things that were available where they lived. (**Culture; Production, Distribution, and Consumption.**)

Students may also want to write about either their cooking or eating experience or the origin of the dish they prepared. (**Writing Process.**)

Language Arts

Many stories in first grade are circle stories; at the end of these kinds of stories we find ourselves right back at the beginning. *Someplace Else* is a circle story; Mrs. Tilby begins at the orchard, and she decides she will return to the apple orchard every fall. Show the class feltboard pictures of the places Mrs. Tilby visited. Have the class identify the various pictures. As children relate where Mrs. Tilby went in the story, arrange the pictures in a circle on the feltboard. Point out that at the end, Mrs. Tilby is where she was at the beginning. Do the children know other stories where the reader is back at the beginning when the story ends? (**Retelling; Story Sequence; Story Structure.**)

Interdisciplinary (Language Arts and Art)

You may wish to write a circle story with the class. Discuss with the children the various circle experiences in their daily lives: waking up, going to sleep, and then waking up the next morning; going to and from school or a friend or relative's home; going on vacation and then returning home. Could a circle story be about a house? Share *My House* by Lisa Desimini with the class. The house wakes up in the morning and goes to sleep at night experiencing many different changes throughout the day. Help the class brainstorm the many different things that might happen to a house throughout a 24-hour period or the seasons of the year. Plot out the events on the board or chart paper so that students visually see the circular structure of the story. Assign pairs of students different events about which to write. The finished product may be an illustrated big book. Desimini's illustrations suggest collage, so you and your students may want to gather a variety of materials to use in illustrating the book. Upon completion of the book, spend some time as a class reading the story together and admiring the writing and illustrations. (**Writing Process; Story Structure; Creative Thinking; Media, Techniques, and Processes.**)

Mathematics

Place the house pictures gathered for the social studies lesson in the Math Center. Have the students sort and classify the houses by different attributes. The children will need to determine the attributes for sorting. (**Sorting and Classifying.**)

Investigate circles. Have the children find circles that are a part of or within objects in their environment. For example, they might suggest dishes, the inside rims of nuts that secure bolts, snaps, the tops of new erasers on pencils, etc. Students may work in pairs to list all the circular objects they can find. They then report to the class the items on their lists. As students name their objects, list them on chart paper. Have the class count how many they found and discuss which

Connecting to Standards

Different Homes for Different People and Places

Social Studies (People, Places, & Environments): Students can describe and compare how people create homes that fit their culture and environment (NCSS, 1994).

Language Arts #5: Students employ a wide variety of strategies as they write and use different writing process elements appropriately to communicate with different audiences for a variety of purposes.

Language Arts #11: Students participate as knowledgeable, reflective, creative, and critical members of a variety of literacy communities.

Language Arts #12: Students use spoken, written, and visual language to accomplish their own purposes (NCTE & IRA, 1996).

Mathematics (Geometry): Students analyze properties of two- and three-dimensional geometric shapes.

Mathematics (Communication): Students communicate their mathematical thinking coherently and clearly to peers, teachers, and others (NCTM, 2000).

The Arts (Music): Singing, alone and with others, a varied repertoire of music (CNAEA, 1994).

were the most unusual. If the children are interested, you may suggest they search for more circles on the playground or at home and report back to the class. (**Geometry**; **Communication**.)

Music and Movement

Share with students that just like the story *Someplace Else* there are songs that end in the same place in which they began. These songs are called rounds. Teach the children some simple rounds. Margaret Read MacDonald and Winifred Jaeger's *The Round Book: Rounds Kids Love to Sing* is an excellent resource. You may also want to play circle games with the children. These can be contrasted with games that take place in a line or in a square. (**Singing with Others**.)

A Roof over Our Heads

Read aloud *This Is My House* by Arthur Dorros.

This engaging informational book uses simple text to explore the different kinds of houses in the world and the types of materials used to build them. As we meet the diverse children in the book, we also learn how to say "This is my house" in 14 different languages.

Preparation

1. Practice reading *This Is My House,* planning where you will stop to ask questions or solicit children's comments. It will be particularly important to feel comfortable pronouncing "This is my house" in the different languages.
2. Prepare a K-W-L chart.
3. Prepare a Venn diagram.

Introduction

Begin by showing students the cover of the book and reading the title. Ask students what they think the book will be about. Have children share their predictions and explain their thinking. After listening to several answers, affirm that this book is about children from all over the world and the types of houses in which they live. Direct everyone's attention to the K-W-L chart. Record student answers in the "K" column as they share what they know about houses. Then ask students what they would like to learn about houses found in different parts of the world. Record these questions in the "W" column. Remind children to listen carefully for answers to their questions as well as for any other interesting or important information about the kinds of houses there are in the world.

Reading the Book

Read the book, stopping along the way for children to point out information that provides answers to their questions. When finished, ask students what they have learned. Record their responses in the "L" column. Reevaluate and revise the "W" column with the children. Has this book raised any new questions? Talk with children about the different materials used for building houses and why houses are different in different places.

Curriculum Connections

Social Studies

Using the information on the K-W-L chart, have students create a bulletin board that explains what they have learned about homes. As the unit proceeds, they should add new information to the board. (**Geography**; **Culture.**)

On a map or globe, locate the various countries in which the children in the book live. Attach a replica of the flag and the name of the child to the map or globe. (**Map Skills.**)

If your school is near a historic restoration site, you may want to arrange a field trip for students to learn about houses of the past. If you know someone who lives on a boat or in a mobile home, you might ask them to come visit the classroom and share what it is like to live in a movable home. (**Culture**; **Geography.**)

Language Arts

Revisit the book. Choose two homes that can be easily compared. The home in Mexico and the home in Mali, or the home in Saudi Arabia and the home in Thailand are good choices. Tell students that you are going to read about two homes that are both alike and different. Ask them to listen for the ways in which the houses are alike and the ways in which they are different. As children discuss the ways the houses are the same and different, record their responses in a Venn diagram. A Venn diagram is a pair of intersecting circles that provides a way to visually compare two things. See Figure 7.3 for an example of a possible Venn diagram. (**Listening for a Purpose**; **Comparing and Contrasting.**)

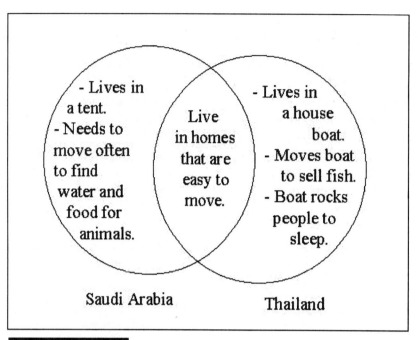

Saudi Arabia

Thailand

· Figure 7.3 ·

***Example of Venn diagram for** This Is My House*

Mathematics

Show children the cover of the book. Ask them what shapes they can identify on the cover (circle, rectangle, square, and triangle). Choose a page or two in the book and have students identify the shapes of several different houses as well as shapes contained within the houses. At the math center, have copies of *This Is My House* and *Homes around the World* by Bobbie Kalman and/or selected copies of *World* or *National Geographic* magazine for students to look for house shapes. If you have enough magazines, have a piece of posterboard labeled for each shape. Have students paste houses onto the correct poster. You can also make a sorting game by cutting out and laminating various houses or architectural details and having children sort by shape. (**Geometry; Problem Solving.**)

Science

This topic leads naturally into an investigation of climate. Share with children the sections in *Homes around the World* by Kalman entitled: Mountain Homes, Tropical Homes, Arctic Homes, and Desert Homes. Refer back to the K-W-L chart and record what students have learned about the homes in different climates. (**Interpreting Data; Communication.**)

A sorting activity with pictures of homes from different climates will help younger children apply what they have been learning. (**Classifying.**)

Art

Gather reproductions of famous artworks that include houses or domestic scenes. Horace Pippin, Charles Wysocki, Simón Silva, Pablo Picasso, and Grandma Moses are some artists to consider.

Connecting to Standards

A Roof over Our Heads

Social Studies (People, Places, & Environments): Students can construct mental maps that demonstrate understanding of geography (NCSS, 1994).

Language Arts #1: Students read a wide range of print and nonprint texts to build an understanding of texts, of themselves, and of the cultures of the United States and the world.

Language Arts #3: Students use a variety of strategies to comprehend, interpret, and appreciate texts (NCTE & IRA, 1996).

Mathematics (Geometry): Students analyze properties of two- and three-dimensional geometric shapes and develop mathematical arguments about geometric relationships.

Mathematics (Problem Solving): Students build new mathematical knowledge through problem solving. Students apply and adapt a variety of appropriate strategies to solve problems.

Mathematics (Communication): Students organize and consolidate their mathematical thinking through communication (NCTM, 2000).

Science (Earth Science): Students have knowledge of environments and climates (NRC, 1996).

The Arts (Visual Arts): Using knowledge of structures and functions (CNAEA, 1994).

Have students look closely at the reproductions to identify geometric shapes found in each. Students place tracing paper over the reproductions and then trace the shapes. This activity helps children begin to develop an understanding of composition. (**Structures and Functions.**)

Many Stars, One Sky

Read aloud *My House Has Stars* by Megan McDonald.

A young girl and her mother meet children from other countries as they contemplate the stars. Each of the eight children shares physical and cultural information about his/her home as well as experiences and feelings about the stars. The text and illustrations share a poetic quality that makes this beautiful book perfect for reading aloud. Depending upon grade and attention span, you may choose to read the entire book, several selected pages, or a single page at a time.

Preparation

1. Practice reading the book aloud.
2. Have the K-W-L chart within reach of where you will read the story.
3. Locate a world map large enough for all to see.

Introduction

Begin by saying something like "We've been reading and learning about the many different kinds of houses in the world. We've learned about why people build houses and the materials they use. Let's spend a minute reviewing what we now know." After soliciting comments, explain that the book you are about to read tells about the people who live in different kinds of houses. Instruct students to listen for things that are special about the children they meet and their homes.

Reading the Book

Read the book, stopping periodically for questions and comments. Upon finishing, ask students to tell a partner which of the homes they would like to visit. Have several students share their thoughts. Ask each to explain why the particular home and family appeals to him. Share a home you would like to visit and explain why that particular place appeals to you. Show students the map on the endpapers. Place a dot or a pushpin on a larger map to indicate the country where the class lives, and then point out the countries where the students' choices are located. Use different colors on the map for their choices. Discuss with the children what they learned about these homes and families. Record new information on the K-W-L chart as the students explain their answers. Explore the meaning of the last sentence of the book with the children. What do they think the author is trying to tell us?

Curriculum Connections

Social Studies

In addition to the work with the K-W-L chart, you may want to read and discuss several folktales from the cultures in the book. Gerald McDermott has written many books that retell tales from around the world. Reading various legends about the stars, for example Joseph Bruchac and Gayle Ross's *The Story of the Milky Way* also helps children to make connections between culture and the physical world. (**Culture; Geography**.)

Art

Show children a reproduction of Van Gogh's painting *Starry Night*. Talk with the students about the artist's style of painting. Point out the use of circles in the painting. Provide the children with art materials to create their own version of *Starry Night*. (**Media, Techniques, and Processes**.)

Creative Movement

Play a game or games from one of the countries in this book. Rice University publishes an online magazine entitled *Topics: Online Magazine for Learners of English,* edited by Peters and Peters. Issue 11 contains descriptions of and directions for numerous games played around the world. (**Physical Activity**.)

Language Arts

Write a class poem about houses. Use the K-W-L chart to compile a list of important characteristics of houses. Then begin with a question like, "What is a house?" Have children add lines that either answer the question or tell something about houses. Another way to approach the poem is to have the children write sentences about houses and then periodically add an agreed-upon phrase like "A house has love," "A house keeps us safe," or "All different, yet all the same." Work

---

Connecting to Standards

Many Stars, One Sky

Social Studies (Culture): Students understand both the unity and diversity found in cultures throughout the world. Students explore how common experiences can be interpreted from different cultural perspectives.

Social Studies (People, Places, & Environments): Students investigate and draw conclusions about physical and cultural patterns (NCSS, 1996).

Language Arts #2: Students read a wide variety of literature from many periods and many genres to build an understanding of human experience (NCTE & IRA, 1996).

The Arts (Music): Singing, alone and with others, a varied repertoire of music (CNAEA, 1994).

---

with the children to arrange the sentences in a pleasing order. Copy the poem on chart paper or on individual sheets of paper. Read the poem chorally or let children read their lines with everyone joining in on the repetitive phrase. (**Writing Process**; **Communicating Ideas**; **Oral Reading**.)

Music

Learn a song from another country. Enlist the help of your school's music teacher or obtain a children's tape of international music from your public library. Putumayo's *World Playground* is a tape we especially like, but there are many others as well.

Sample Unit for the Upper Elementary Grades

Community, Culture, and Resistance

Imagine living in a society that denies your humanity. Yet you and those around you have the strength and determination to create communities. You dare to care for others, to love and be loved, to marry, to have children. Imagine living in circumstances that deny you the most basic human rights. Yet you and others have the desire to create songs and stories that are sung, told, and admired more than 150 years later. Imagine living in such a time and still having the courage to resist and rebel against your oppressors.

In addition to learning about the exploitation and cruelty of slavery, students should understand that enslaved Africans and African-Americans fought against their oppressors and lived lives that had meaning and contained hope. Levstik and Barton (2001) believe that the study of slavery in America must include the ways in which the enslaved were able to create a "vibrant and meaningful culture" (p. 159). They go on to say that this aspect is most often ignored in the curriculum. The unit that follows assumes that your curriculum includes the history, economics, and politics of slavery in America. This unit explores the community, culture, and resistance of enslaved Africans and African-Americans. A list of suggested concepts that are appropriate for a unit on "Community, Culture, and Resistance" includes information from four themes: Culture; Time, Continuity, and Change; People, Places and Environments; and Power, Authority, and Governance. You may choose to use these concepts or refine them to meet the needs and interests of the children in your classroom.

Concepts for the Community, Culture, and Resistance Unit

1. In spite of the dehumanizing conditions in which slaves lived, they created functioning communities in which people cared for each other, celebrated together, suffered, and mourned together.

2. Slaves created stories and songs that served various functions. These songs and stories taught lessons, carried messages, protested against the institution of slavery, entertained, and gave hope and comfort.

3. Slaves resisted by learning to read and write despite laws that prohibited the acquisition of literacy.

4. Slaves resisted on a daily basis in various ways, for example: feigning disability, breaking tools and equipment, pretending not to understand, and outsmarting overseers and masters.

5. Even though escaping was a dangerous proposition, slaves resisted by attempting to escape.

6. Free African-Americans and others also protested slavery through participation in abolition efforts and the Underground Railroad.

7. The Fugitive Slave Law of 1793 allowed slave holders to pursue runaway slaves. The Fugitive Slave Law of 1850 made it a federal offense to shelter or aid a runaway slave. The penalty for aiding runaways was a fine and time in jail. Local law enforcement officials were expected to help owners find and arrest runaways. Moreover, the law stated that it was the duty of all citizens to identify and capture fleeing slaves.

8. Slaves resisted through organized rebellions.

We said earlier that social studies was by its very nature interdisciplinary. This particular unit relies on information not only from history, anthropology, and sociology but also literature, law, music, dance, and art. These disciplines help us understand the rich and vibrant culture created by people who were enslaved. To a lesser extent, science and technology also help us understand the time period and the contributions made by Africans and African-Americans. Many of the books we have chosen include more than one concept and often use the expertise of several disciplines. Figure 7.4 presents literature selections for Community, Culture, and Resistance.

Sample Lessons

Escape!

Read aloud *Freedom River,* a picture book written by Doreen Rappaport and illustrated by Bryan Collier.

This well-researched account of an incident in the life of John Parker provides us with a starting point for discussing the factors slaves faced in deciding whether or not to attempt an escape. The first page of the book contains two paragraphs of background information that help to set the stage for the story. The story is dramatic and captivating. Moreover, there are several points in which decisions about whether or not to escape are made. Students should be encouraged to weigh the pros and cons involved in each decision. A historical note at the end of the book provides the reader with further information about Parker, describes the author's research, and lists additional sources for learning more about the Underground Railroad.

History (Concepts 1, 4, 5, 6, 7, 8)
Bound for the North Star by D. B. Fradin
If You Traveled on the Underground Railroad by E. Levine
Long Journey Home by J. Lester
Many Thousands Gone by V. Hamilton
Freedom River by D. Rappaport
Escape from Slavery by D. Rappaport
Lest We Forget by V. Thomas
Black Hands, White Sails by P. McKissack & F. McKissack
Rebels against Slavery: American Slave Revolts by P. McKissack & F. McKissack

Anthropology & Archaeology (Concepts 1, 2, 4, 5, 6)
The Strength of These Arms by R. Bial
The Underground Railroad by R. Bial

Sociology (Concepts 1, 2, 4, 5)
Christmas in the Big House, Christmas in the Quarters by P. McKissack & F. McKissack

Primary Sources (Concepts 1, 2, 3, 4, 5)
To Be a Slave by J. Lester
Frederick Douglass: In His Own Words ed. by M. Meltzer
Our Song, Our Toil: The Story of American Slavery as Told by Slaves ed. by M. Steptoe

Autobiography and Biography (Concepts 1, 3, 4, 5, 6)
Sojourner Truth: Ain't I a Woman? by P. McKissack & F. McKissack
Harriet and the Promised Land by J. Lawrence
Escape from Slavery: The Boyhood of Frederick Douglass in His Own Words ed. by M. McCurdy
My Family Shall Be Free: The Life of Peter Still by D. B. Fradin
Sisters against Slavery: A Story about Sarah and Angelina Grimke by S. M. McPherson
Only Passing Through: The Story of Sojourner Truth by A. Rockwell

Historical Fiction (Concepts 1, 2, 3, 4, 5, 6)
Dancing with the Indians by A. S. Meaderis
Minty: A Story of Young Harriet Tubman by A. Schroeder
Come Morning by L. D. Guccione
Send One Angel Down by V. F. Schwartz
Dear Austin: Letters from the Underground Railroad by E. Woodruff
Stealing Freedom by E. Carbone
The Second Escape of Arthur Cooper by C. M. Stowe
North by Night by K. Ayres

Folk Tales (Concepts 1, 2, 4)
From Sea to Shining Sea compiled by A. L. Cohen
The People Could Fly told by V. Hamilton
Big Jabe by J. Nolen
In the Time of the Drums by K. L. Siegelson
A Ring of Tricksters by V. Hamilton

Poetry (1, 2, 5, 6)
i see the rhythm by T. Igus
Freedom Like Sunlight: Praisesongs for Black Americans by J. P. Lewis
Words with Wings: A Treasury of African American Poetry and Art compiled by B. Rochelle

Music (Concepts 1, 2, 4)
In the Hollow of Your Hand: Slave Lullabies collected by A. McGill
Walk Together Children collected by A. Bryant
How Sweet the Sound: African American Songs for Children selected by W. & C. Hudson
From Sea to Shining Sea compiled by A. L. Cohen
Hush Songs: African American Lullabies by J. C. Thomas

Art (Concept 1)
Stitching the Stars: The Story Quilts of Harriet Powers by M. E. Lyons
African American Quilting: The Warmth of Tradition by S. G. Wilson

·⌐ **Figure 7.4** ⌐·

Children's Literature Selections for Community, Culture, and Resistance

Preparation

1. Practice reading the book aloud. Plan to stop and talk about why Sarah and Isaac aren't sure running away is a good idea. Ask what they think of Parker's plan. Why do they think Parker is so emphatic about the escape?
2. Create a story box. The one we use for this story is actually a bundle made of cloth. Inside the bundle are: a baby shirt or cloth diaper, a candle, a map, a horseshoe, a picture of a river, and a work boot.

Introduction

Place the story bundle in front of the students. Tell students that the bundle and its contents provide clues about the story. Take one item out at a time, and solicit ideas and predictions. The predictions will change as items are removed. Once all the items have been discussed, show students the cover and read the title. Spend a minute discussing whether the cover and title confirm or cause us to change our predictions.

Reading the Book

Read the story, stopping before the historical note. Make sure that at some point in the story students have an opportunity to comment on the decisions that are being made. Once you finish the story solicit students' reactions. Do they think John Parker was brave or reckless? What would they have done in his place? What would they have done if they had been Sarah or Isaac? Ask students to explain and justify their answers. Tell students that the author has written a note that gives us more information about Parker. They should listen for information that might explain why he acted the way he did. Read the historical note. Discuss what insights the note provides. Also discuss Rappaport's research methods. Point out that she tells us what details she added to the story. Discuss why this is important information for readers to know.

Curriculum Connections

Social Studies

Use individual K-W-L charts for students to record what they know about runaway slaves and the Underground Railroad. After the class discusses and records on a large chart what they know and would like to know about these topics, have students choose a question or questions that they want to research. Have a variety of books available for students to use. See the list of suggested books in this chapter. When students have found the answers to their questions, they record them. Provide a time for students to share what they learned with the class. Teach students how to use the table of contents and index if they have not learned these research skills. (**Research Skills; Communicating Research Findings.**)

National Geographic's Web site has a link that allows students to experience what it might have been like to be a runaway slave. Students may want to visit and explore this site: *www.nationalgeographic.com/99/railroad.* (**Individuals, Groups, and Institutions**.)

Connecting to Standards

Escape!

Social Studies (Time, Continuity, & Change): Students locate and employ processes that allow them to accurately examine historical figures and events. Students develop an understanding of historical context as they study mores and actions of people in the past (NCSS, 1994).

Language Arts #7: Students conduct research on issues and interests by generating ideas and questions, and by posing problems. They gather, evaluate, and synthesize data from a variety of sources to communicate their discoveries in ways that suit their purpose and audience (NCTE & IRA, 1996).

The Arts (Music): Understanding music in relation to history and culture.

The Arts (Visual Arts): Understanding the visual arts in relation to history and cultures (CNAEA, 1994).

Art

In a note at the front of the book, Bryan Collier relays that in several illustrations he has included the likenesses of people who have guided him. Revisit the text and examine these illustrations with students. Then share several of the selections in *Honoring Our Ancestors* edited by Harriet Rohmer. Through artwork, 14 artists describe relatives and "relatives in spirit" who have influenced and guided them. Ask the students to think about who has guided them. Supply students with a variety of art materials so that they are able to create their own spirit/guide portraits. Install portraits in a portrait gallery. Make sure students have an opportunity to share their work with the class. **(Media, Techniques, and Processes.)**

Language Arts

Freedom River is told primarily from John Parker's point of view. How would Mr. Shrofe, Sarah, Isaac, or the baby tell the story? Have the class choose one viewpoint and do a group write. This strategy is a collaborative activity in which a group brainstorms ideas, creates, and revises a piece of writing. Afterward, you may want students to write individual pieces from another person's point of view. Make sure students have an opportunity to share their work with the class. **(Point of View; Writing Process.)**

Music

Read the introduction to Ashley Bryan's *Walk Together Children*. Discuss the role song played in the lives of Africans and African-Americans who were enslaved. Then play the song "Deep River" for the class. We particularly like the rendition on the CD *Jubilant* by Jubilant Sykes, but there are many others available as well. Discuss how the song relates to the book. **(Relating Music and Culture/History.)**

The Rest of the Story

For this lesson, we are pairing selections from Dennis Brindel Fradin's book *Bound for the North Star: True Stories of Fugitive Slaves* and *Escape from Slavery: Five Journeys to Freedom* by Doreen Rappaport.

Both books make for compelling reading. Rappaport's consists of five individual accounts of people fleeing slavery and those who helped them. The accounts are written as narratives and vary in length from 10 to 20 pages. Fradin's accounts are expository in form, more detailed, and provide additional political and historical information.

While all of the stories in *Escape from Slavery* are suitable reading for the intermediate grades, some of the accounts in Fradin's book may not be. Choose selections based on the age and the developmental level of your students. We have paired Rappaport's "The River of Ice" with Chapter 3 in *Bound for the North Star*. Both selections deal with the daring and desperate escape of Eliza Harris.

Preparation

1. Read both pieces.
2. Prepare an overhead that outlines the Fugitive Slave Acts.

Introduction

Begin by sharing the title of "The River of Ice." Ask students to predict how someone might escape across a frozen river. What might the pros and cons to such a plan be?

Reading the Book

Read the story. Solicit reactions during and at the end. What words would students use to describe Eliza? Possible responses include courageous, foolish, desperate, and lucky. Ask students to explain their thinking. Tell students that they will hear the rest of Eliza's story during social studies or later in the day.

Curriculum Connections

Social Studies

Have students briefly retell Eliza's story. Read the rest of her story from Chapter 3 in Fradin. Tell students that as they listen they will learn how the Underground Railroad got its name, as well as the secret codes used by those working in the Underground Railroad. After you have finished reading, talk with students about Eliza and Levi and Katie Coffin. Make a web of Underground Railroad terminology with the students. **(History.)**

On an overhead, project the outlines of the Fugitive Slave Law of 1793 and the Fugitive Slave Law of 1850. Read the outlines with the students. Discuss what each law meant for slaves, slave owners, and people who worked on the Underground Railroad. How was each group affected by the laws? How did each group feel about the laws? Point out that different groups

Connecting to Standards
The Rest of the Story

Social Studies (Culture): Students understand how shared assumptions, values, and beliefs affect how people react to their physical and social environments.

Social Studies (Time, Continuity, & Change): Students use appropriate terminology to make connections over historical time and events.

Social Studies (Individual, Groups, & Institutions): Students understand specific sociological terms such as role or status. Students can explain the influence of groups and institutions on individuals' behavior. Students can illustrate the conflicts experienced when individual belief systems differ from governmental policies or law.

Social Studies (Power, Authority, & Governance): Students explore the issues of individual rights and collective welfare. Students examine the workings of governments and organizations (NCSS, 1994).

Mathematics (Measurement): Students apply appropriate techniques, tools, and formulas to determine measurements (NCTM, 2000).

Language Arts #12: Students use spoken, written, and visual language to accomplish their own purposes (NCTE & IRA, 1996).

had different perspectives about the laws. Create a different perspectives chart or a graphic organizer with the class. (**Political Science.**)

Language Arts

Have students choose one of the remaining stories in *Escape from Slavery: Five Journeys to Freedom* to read with a small group. After reading, students will create story boxes for the stories they read. Groups should present their boxes to each other and then act out or tell their stories. When all stories have been presented, the class can create a list of the similarities found in each story. As they analyze the list, ask what conclusions they can draw about people who escaped and those who helped them. (**Retelling**; **Drawing Conclusions**; **Comparing.**)

Harriet Beecher Stowe's novel *Uncle Tom's Cabin* is based on Eliza Harris's life story. You may want to share with the students Stowe's description of Eliza's flight across the river. Have students compare each book's use of language, illustrations, and writing style. (**Author's Craft.**)

Mathematics

Have students investigate routes of the Underground Railroad. Once routes have been identified, have the students calculate the distances runaways traveled to freedom. (**Measurement.**)

Building a Life, Hoping for Freedom

Raymond Bial's *The Strength of These Arms* chronicles how, against great odds, enslaved Africans and African-Americans both preserved African traditions and created a vibrant and rich culture in

America. Archival photographs that document life in the quarters along with contemporary photographs of excavated plantation sites help bring the text to life. Because the book contains a good deal of unfamiliar information, we suggest teaching the text over several days. The text contains several natural stopping points:

- General background information on slavery
- A description of daily life in the quarters
- An explanation of the work done by slaves
- The various methods used by owners to control those they enslaved

The book lends itself to partner reading, but can easily be read aloud as well.

Preparation

1. Divide the book into logical and manageable sections.
2. Collect contemporary photographs of African village life. The photographs chosen should help students make connections between the characteristics mentioned in Bial: clothing, jewelry, style of baskets, shapes of fences, etc. You may want to collect additional archival photographs of life in the quarters to supplement those found in the book.
3. Decide on student pairs for partner reading.

Introduction

Have students do a quickwrite on what they know about the lives of slaves. As students share what they have written, list their ideas on chart paper. Share the title of the book. Have students spend a minute discussing with their partners why Bial may have chosen such a title. Ask several pairs to share their ideas with the class. Ask students to listen for information that confirms or changes what they wrote in their quickwrites.

Reading the Book

Read aloud the first section of the book. We chose pages 5–13, which contain background information on what it meant to be enslaved. Students should listen for information that might explain the title as well as new information about the institution of slavery. Stop periodically for partners to share ideas with each other about what they have just heard, and then ask several pairs to share their thinking. Upon finishing, ask students to share with their partner the most important thing they learned. As pairs report back to the group, record their answers on chart paper. Share your ideas and thinking as the students are reporting. Return to the title and ask for students' thoughts. Over the next several days, continue reading the book in this manner.

Curriculum Connections

Social Studies

Have students examine an archival photograph such as the one found at the beginning of *The Strength of These Arms*. At first, solicit comments about what students observe in the photograph.

In this case there are two boys standing side by side wearing worn clothing. As the students comment, record their statements on chart paper or an overhead transparency. Students will most likely include inferences as part of their observations; for example, the boys are slaves, solemn, unhappy, and so on. Discuss the differences between observation and inference. Observation is objective, while inferencing is subjective. Then revisit the list, deciding with students which points are observations and which are inferences. Have students explain and justify their answers. In the Social Studies Center, place photographs of contemporary life in African villages. Have pairs compare these photographs with those found in Bial's book. To help students with this task, you may want to group the photographs according to subject matter: dress, fences, baskets, and the like. (**Anthropology**.)

Language Arts

Over several days read *Christmas in the Big House, Christmas in the Quarters* by Patricia and Frederick McKissack. After each section, have students compare life in the Quarters to life in the Big House. A simple chart or Venn diagram can help students organize the information they are learning.

Discuss the McKissacks' decision to tell about life in the Quarters and life in the Big House simultaneously. Why might the authors have chosen to do this? As readers, would we have had a different experience if the book were about just one group of people? How is this book different from *The Strength of These Arms*? Which book do we prefer? Is it the book's information or style that influenced our choices? At this point, you may wish to explore the differences between expository and narrative texts.

A writing assignment that relates to both books asks students to use information from Bial to write a narrative about life in the Quarters from either the slaves' or the owners' perspectives. For example, slaves and owners had different feelings about the proximity of the Quarters to the Big House. (**Considering Different Perspectives**; **Writing Style**; **Writing Process**.)

Music and Dance

Both *The Strength of These Arms* and *Christmas in the Big House, Christmas in the Quarters* describe the singing and dancing that took place in the Quarters. The McKissacks tell us that the Cakewalk was a popular dance created in the Quarters. Teach students this dance using the words and music found in Cheryl and Wade Hudson's *How Sweet the Sound: African American Songs for Children*.

A recent collection of slave lullabies, *In the Hollow of Your Hand*, can be used to reinforce the idea of the value slaves placed on children and family. Included with the book is a CD, which contains both the songs and a narration by the collector of the lullabies, Alice McGill. Students may both learn the lullabies and/or analyze them for information about life in the Quarters. (**Relating Music to History and Culture**.)

Cooking

We enjoy foods like barbecue and gumbo today because slaves took local ingredients and fashioned them into familiar dishes from Africa. A recipe for sweet potato pie is included in *Christmas*

Connecting to Standards

Building a Life, Hoping for Freedom

Social Studies (Culture): Students can explain the influence of culture by how people address their needs, interpret experiences, and respond to their physical and social environments.

Social Studies (Individual Development & Identity): Students can explain the influence of family, gender, ethnicity, nationality, and institutional associations on an individual's identity and daily life (NCSS, 1994).

Language Arts #3: Students use a variety of strategies to comprehend, interpret, and appreciate texts.

Language Arts #4: Students adjust their use of spoken, written, and visual language to communicate effectively with a variety of audiences and for different purposes (NCTE & IRA, 1996).

The Arts (Dance): Identifying and demonstrating movement elements and skills in performing dance. Demonstrating and understanding dance in various cultures and historical periods.

The Arts (Visual Arts): Understanding the visual arts in relation to history and cultures (CNAEA, 1994).

---

in the *Big House, Christmas in the Quarters*, and students may enjoy baking this dessert. A traditional West African dish such as Groundnut Stew is simple enough to be made by students with supervision. A more ambitious project is preparing gumbo.

Art

Bial points out that many slaves were highly skilled craftspeople who provided the plantations with items such as pottery, baskets, furniture, and needlework that were needed for daily life and commerce. These objects were functional and often very beautiful. For example, Winterthur Museum recently hosted an exhibition of the pottery made by a slave we know only as Dave. His pottery is remarkable for both its size and the lyrical inscriptions found on many of the pieces. Similarly, the sea grass baskets first made by slaves living in the coastal region of South Carolina are still being made today. They, too, are highly prized for their beauty and utility. In addition, the quilts of Harriet Powers can be found in private and museum collections. You and your students may wish to learn more about pottery, basketry, and quilting through research or by visiting a museum. Learning how to make pots, baskets, or quilts will also help students appreciate the creative powers and skills of those who lived in slavery. (**Visual Arts; History and Culture.**)

Mother Wit

Read aloud the story "High John the Conqueror" by Steve Stanfield in Cohen's *From Sea to Shining Sea: A Treasury of American Folklore and Folksongs*

Many of the tales told by slaves served as a form of resistance as well as a form of entertainment and instruction. A popular theme of these stories centers around a smaller, more vulnerable animal or person outwitting another who was larger or more powerful. Br'er Rabbit is perhaps the best known example of a character who thinks on his feet and who at times courts trouble, but there are others as well. High John, a well known figure in African-American folk tales, is valued not only for his quick thinking but also his ability for living.

Preparation

1. Practice reading "High John the Conqueror" aloud.
2. Collect a variety of African-American stories that teach as well as entertain. (See the list included at the beginning of this unit.)

Introduction

Write the word "conqueror" on the board. Ask students what the word means. If necessary, provide students with a definition. Read the title of the story. Explain that the story is about a slave named High John. Why do they suppose he is called a conqueror? List responses on the board or chart paper. Instruct students to listen for information that supports the notion of High John as a conqueror.

Reading the Story

This is a short piece, so unless students comment, read the story without stopping. At the conclusion of the story, return to the idea of conqueror. Do they think the title is accurate? Why or why not? How does High John resist his enslavement? Explore the idea that High John is able to think on his feet and solve problems creatively. Discuss why this story may have been created and told.

Curriculum Connections

Social Studies

Have available a variety of African-American tales that teach as well as entertain for students to read in pairs or small groups. After reading and sharing personal responses within their pairs, students practice retelling their stories to their partners. Pairs then take turns sharing their stories with a larger group. After each retelling, the groups discuss and record what they think each story tries to teach. After all stories have been discussed, have students think about why the lessons they listed would be important for slaves to learn. Are they important for us today? Have students explain and support their answers. (**Culture**.)

Language Arts

Big Jabe, an original tall tale by Jerdine Nolen, is written in the High John tradition. Read the story aloud to students and have them compare it to "High John the Conqueror." A Venn diagram may be used after brainstorming and discussion. If you and your class are interested in how oral tales influence writers today, you may also want to examine Faith Ringgold's use of flight in *Tar Beach* and *Aunt Harriet's Underground Railroad in the Sky* with the traditional story "The People Could Fly." Students may also want to try their hands at writing a modern version of the tale they read

---

Connecting to Standards
Mother Wit

Social Studies (Culture): Students will learn how stories are used to pass down culture from one generation to the next (NCSS, 1994).

Language Arts #2: Students read a wide range of literature from many periods in many genres to build an understanding of human experience (NCTE & IRA, 1996).

Science (Life Science): Students have knowledge of characteristics of organisms, life cycles, and environments (NRC, 1996).

The Arts (Music): Singing, alone and with others, a varied repertoire of music.

The Arts (Music): Understanding music in relation to history and culture (CNAEA, 1994).

---

in social studies. Using a group-write, have the class create a modern variant. (**Investigating Literary Themes and Motifs**.)

Science

The profitability of cotton was directly related to the growth of slavery in the United States. Have students research how the plant develops, the conditions needed for growing cotton, and the natural enemies of cotton. Compare the technology of the 19th century with the technological advances of the 20th and 21st centuries. Explore how these advances affected humans. If you live in an area of the country where cotton is grown or processed, arrange a class trip so that students can experience these processes first hand. If not, share the book *Working Cotton* by Sherley Anne Williams. (**Interpreting Data; Technology**.)

Music

Teach students a work song like "Long John" or the rhythmic pats (claps/patterns) that go with songs like "Hambone" or "Juba This and Juba That." Music, lyrics, and pats for these songs can be found in *From Sea to Shining Sea* by Amy L. Cohen. (**Singing; Music and Culture**.)

CONCLUSION

Social studies tells the story of humankind's life on earth. It is, in fact, our story. Because we are part of the story, what we do individually and collectively influences the story and may even change it. How the story unfolds is really up to us. It is important that we use what we know about history, economics, geography, and sociology as we create our story.

In this chapter, we have demonstrated the ways in which literature may be used to enhance the teaching and learning of social studies. We also have investigated how the stories of others may teach us about ourselves as well as about them. We hope that our explorations will help you as you create classrooms that prepare children to write the world's story.

Visit ChildLit at **www.mhhe.com/childlit** *for Web links related to this chapter.*

Children's Literature Cited in the Chapter

Almond, D. (2000). *Kit's World.* NY: Delacorte Press.

Anderson, L. H. (2000). *Fever 1793.* NY: Simon & Schuster Books for Young Readers.

Angelou, M. (1994). *My Painted House, My Friendly Chicken, and Me.* Illustrated by M. Courtney-Clarke. NY: Clarkson Potter.

Atkins, S. B. (1993). *Voices from the Fields: Children of Migrant Farmworkers Tell Their Stories.* Boston: Little, Brown & Company.

Baylor, B. (1981). *Desert Voices.* Illustrated by P. Parnall. NY: Charles Scribner.

Bouchard, D. (1995). *If You're Not from the Prairie.* Illustrated by H. Ripplinger. NY: Atheneum.

Brown, D. (1997). *Alice Ramsey's Grand Adventure.* NY: Houghton Mifflin Co.

Bryan, A. (1974). *Walk Together Children.* NY: Atheneum.

Bunting, E. (1991). *Fly Away Home.* Illustrated by R. Himler. NY: Clarion Books.

Diakite, B. W. (1999). *The Hatseller and the Monkeys.* NY: Scholastic Press.

Erdrich, L. (1999). *The Birchbark House.* NY: Hyperion Books.

Fradin, D. B., & Fradin, J. B. (2000). *Ida B. Wells: Mother of the Civil Rights Movement.* NY: Clarion Books.

Freedman, R. (1994). *Kids at Work: Lewis Hine and the Crusade against Child Labor.* NY: Clarion Books.

Freedman, R. (1980). *Immigrant Kids.* NY: Dutton.

Garland, S. (2000). *Voices of the Alamo.* Illustrated by R. Himler. NY: Scholastic Press.

Guthrie, W. (1998). *This Land Is Your Land.* Paintings by K. Jakobsen. Boston: Little, Brown & Company.

Hesse, K. (1997). *Out of the Dust.* NY: Scholastic Press.

King, M. L. (1997). *I Have a Dream.* Paintings by 15 Coretta Scott King Award and Honor Book Artists. NY: Scholastic Inc.

Kuklin, S. (1992). *How My Family Lives in America.* NY: Bradbury Press.

Lester, J. (1968). *To Be a Slave.* Illustrated by T. Feelings. NY: Dial Press.

Mathews, T. (1999). *Always Inventing: A Photobiography of Alexander Graham Bell.* Washington, D.C.: National Geographic Society.

McGill, A. (2000). *In the Hollow of Your Hand: Slave Lullabies.* Paintings by M. Cummings. Boston: Houghton Mifflin.

Meltzer, M. (1999). *Carl Sandburg: A Biography.* Brookfield, CT: Twenty-First Century/Millbrook.

Mollel, T. (1999). *My Rows and Piles of Coins.* Illustrated by E. B. Lewis. NY: Clarion Books.

Morris, A. (1990). *Loving.* Photographs by K. Heyman. NY: Lothrop, Lee & Shepard.

Morris, A. (1989). *Hats, Hats, Hats.* Photographs by K. Heyman. NY: Lothrop, Lee & Shepard.

Myers, W. D. (1999). *At Her Majesty's Request: An African Princess in Victorian England.* NY: Scholastic Press.

Onyefulu, I. (1995). *Emeka's Gift: An African Counting Story.* NY: Cobblehill Books.

Peterson, C. (1999). *Century Farm: One Hundred Years on a Family Farm.* Illustrated with photographs by A. Upitis. Honesdale, PA: Boyds Mill Press.

Rappaport, D. (2000). *Freedom River.* Illustrated by B. Collier. NY: Hyperion.

Siebert, D. (1989). *Heartland.* Paintings by W. Minor. NY: Crowell.

Siebert, D. (1988). *Mojave.* Paintings by W. Minor. NY: Crowell.

Slobodkina, E. (1947). *Caps for Sale.* NY: W R Scott.

Stanley, J. (1992). *Children of the Dust Bowl: The True Story of the School at Weedpatch Camp.* NY: Crown.

Staples, S. F. (1989). *Shabanu: Daughter of the Wind.* NY: Alfred A. Knopf.

Taylor, M. (1976). *Roll of Thunder, Hear My Cry.* NY: Dial Press.

Thomas, J. C. (2000). *Hush Songs: African American Lullabies.* Illustrated by B. Joysmith. NY: Hyperion Books.

Thomas, V. M. (1997). *Lest We Forget: The Passage from Africa to Slavery and Emancipation.* NY: Crown.

Woodson, J. (2000). *Miracle's Boys.* NY: G. P. Putnam & Sons.

Children's Literature Cited for the Homes Unit

Barton, B. (1981). *Building a House.* NY: Greenwillow.

Brooks, N., & Horner, A. (2000). *Town Mouse House.* NY: Walker & Company.

Brooks, N., & Horner, A. (2000). *Country Mouse Cottage.* NY: Walker & Company.

Bruchac, J., & Ross, G. (1995). *The Story of the Milky Way.* Paintings by V.A. Stroud. NY: Dial Books for Young Readers.

Buchanan, K. (1994). *This House Is Made of Mud: Esta Casa Esta Hecha de Lodo.* Illustrated by L. Tracy. Flagstaff, AZ: Northland Publishing.

Bunting, E. (1996). *Going Home.* Illustrated by D. Diaz. NY: HarperCollins.

Bunting, E. (1991). *Fly Away Home.* Illustrated by R. Himler. NY: Clarion Books.

Chin, K. (1995). *Sam and the Lucky Money.* Illustrated by C. Van Wright & Y. H. Hu. NY: Lee & Low Books.

DePaola, T. (1973). *Nana Upstairs and Nana Downstairs.* NY: Putnam Books.

Desimini, L. (1994). *My House.* Illustrated by L. Desimini. New York: Henry Holt.

Dorros, A. (1992). *This Is My House.* NY: Scholastic Inc.

Dragonwagon, C. (1990). *Homeplace.* Illustrated by J. Pinkney. NY: McMillan.

Gibbons, G. (1990). *How a House Is Built.* NY: Holiday House.

Grifalconi, A. (1986). *The Village of Round and Square Houses.* Boston: Little, Brown & Company.

Ho, M. (1996). *Hush!: A Thai Lullaby.* Illustrated by H. Meade. NY: Orchard Books.

Kalman, B. (1994). *Homes around the World.* NY: Crabtree Publishing Company.

MacDonald, M. R., & Jaeger, W. (1999). *The Round Book: Rounds Kids Love to Sing.* Illustrated by Y. L. Davis. New Haven, CT: Linnett.

McDonald, M. (1996). *My House Has Stars.* Paintings by P. Catalanotto. NY: Orchard Books.

McGovern, A. (1997). *The Lady in the Box.* Illustrated by M. Backer. NY: Turtle Books.

Mollel, T. (1997). *Kele's Secret.* Illustrated by C. Stock. NY: Lodestar Books.

Morris, A. (1992). *Houses and Homes.* Photographs by K. Heyman. NY: Lothrop, Lee & Shepard.

Peters, S., & Peters, T. (Eds.). (1999). International Children's Games: 27 pages. *Topics: Online Magazine for Learners of English.* **www.rice.edu/projects/topics/electronic/magazine.**

Saul, C. P. (1995). *Someplace Else.* Illustrated by B. Root. NY: Simon & Schuster.

Shemie, B. (1995). *Houses of Adobe.* Montreal, Canada: Tundra Books.

Shemie, B. (1991). *Houses of Hide and Earth.* Montreal, Canada: Tundra Books.

Shemie, B. (1989). *Houses of Snow, Skin, and Bones.* Montreal, Canada: Tundra Books.

Sibley, A. (1996). *The Someday House.* Illustrated by R. Litzinger. NY: Orchard Books.

Sibley, A. (1995). *Homeplace.* Illustrated by W. A. Halperin. NY: Orchard Books.

Weiss, H. (1988). *Shelters: From Tepee to Igloo.* NY: Crowell.

Wood, T. (1995). *Houses and Homes.* NY: Viking.

Children's Literature Cited for the Community, Culture, and Resistance Unit

Ayres, K. (1998). *North by Night: A Story of the Underground Railroad.* NY: Delacorte Press.

Bial, R. (1997). *The Strength of These Arms.* NY: Houghton Mifflin Company.

Bial, R. (1995). *The Underground Railroad.* NY: Houghton Mifflin Company.

Bryant, A. (1975). *Walk Together Children.* NY: Atheneum.

Carbone, E. (1998). *Stealing Freedom.* NY: Alfred A. Knopf.

Cohen, A. L. (Compiler). (1993). *From Sea to Shining Sea: A Treasury of American Folklore and Folksongs.* Illustrated by 11 Caldecott Medal and 4 Caldecott Honor Book Artists. NY: Scholastic Inc.

Fradin, D. B. (2001). *My Family Shall Be Free: The Life of Peter Still.* NY: HarperCollins.

Fradin, D. B. (2000). *Bound for the North Star: True Stories of Fugitive Slaves.* NY: Clarion Books.

Guccione, L. D. (1995). *Come Morning.* Minneapolis, MN: Carolrhoda Books.

Hamilton, V. (1997). *A Ring of Tricksters.* Illustrated by B. Moser. NY: Scholastic.

Hamilton, V. (1993). *Many Thousand Gone: African Americans from Slavery to Freedom.* Illustrated by L. & D. Dillon. NY: Alfred A. Knopf.

Hamilton, V. (1985). *The People Could Fly.* Illustrated by L. & D. Dillon. NY: Alfred A. Knopf.

Hudson, W., & Hudson, C. (1995). *How Sweet the Sound: African American Songs for Children.* Illustrated by F. Cooper. NY: Scholastic Inc.

Igus, T. (1998). *i see the rhythm.* Paintings by M. Wood. San Francisco, CA: Children's Book Press.

Lawrence, J. (1993). *Harriet and the Promised Land.* NY: Simon & Schuster Books for Young Readers.

Lester, J. (1972). *Long Journey Home.* NY: Dial Press.

Lester, J. (1968). *To Be a Slave.* Illustrated by T. Feelings. NY: Dial Press.

Levine, E. (1991). *If You Traveled on the Underground Railroad.* Illustrated by L. Johnson. NY: Scholastic Inc.

Lewis, J. P. (2000). *Freedom Like Sunlight: Praisesongs for Black Americans.* Paintings by J. Thompson. Mankato, MN: Creative Editions.

Lyons, M. E. (1993). *Stitching the Stars: The Story Quilts of Harriet Powers.* NY: Charles Scribner's Sons.

McCurdy, M. (Ed.). (1994). *Escape from Slavery: The Boyhood of Frederick Douglass in His Own Words.* Illustrated by M. McCurdy. New York: Alfred A. Knopf.

McGill, A. (2000). *In the Hollow of Your Hand: Slave Lullabies.* Paintings by M. Cummings. Boston: Houghton Mifflin.

McKissack, P. C., & McKissack, F. L. (1999). *Black Hands, White Sails.* NY: Scholastic Inc.

McKissack, P. C., & McKissack, F. L. (1996). *Rebels against Slavery: American Slave Revolts.* NY: Scholastic Inc.

McKissack, P. C., & McKissack, F. L. (1994). *Christmas in the Big House, Christmas in the Quarters.* Illustrated by J. Thompson. NY: Scholastic Inc.

McKissack, P. C., & McKissack, F. L. (1992). *Sojourner Truth: Ain't I a Woman?.* NY: Scholastic Inc.

McPherson, S. M. (1999). *Sisters against Slavery: A Story about Sarah and Angelina Grimke.* Illustrated by K. Ritz. Minneapolis, MN: Carolrhoda Books.

Meaderis, A. S. (1991). *Dancing with the Indians.* Illustrated by S. Byrd. NY: Holiday House.

Meltzer, M. (Ed). (1995). *Frederick Douglass: In His Own Words.* San Diego, CA: Harcourt Brace.

Nolen, J. (2000). *Big Jabe.* Illustrated by K. Nelson. NY: Lothrop, Lee & Shepard.

Rappaport, D. (2000). *Freedom River.* Illustrated by B. Collier. NY: Hyperion.

Rappaport, D. (1991). *Escape from Slavery: Five Journeys to Freedom.* Illustrated by C. Lilly. NY: Harper Collins.

Ringgold, F. (1993). *Aunt Harriet's Underground Railroad in the Sky.* NY: Crown.

Ringgold, F. (1991). *Tar Beach.* NY: Crown.

Rochelle, B. (Compiler). (2001). *Words with Wings: A Treasury of African American Poetry and Art.* NY: HarperCollins.

Rockwell, A. (2000). *Only Passing Through: The Story of Sojourner Truth.* Illustrated by R. G. Christie. NY: Alfred A. Knopf.

Rohmer, H. (Ed.). (1999). *Honoring Our Ancestors.* San Francisco, CA: Children's Book Press.

Schroeder, A. (1996). *Minty: A Story of Young Harriet Tubman.* Pictures by J. Pinkney. NY: Dial Books for Young Readers.

Schwartz, V. F. (2000). *Send One Angel Down.* NY: Holiday House.

Siegelson, K. L. (1999). *In the Time of the Drums.* Illustrated by B. Pinkney. NY: Hyperion Books.

Steptoe, M. (Ed.). (1994). *Our Song, Our Toil: The Story of American Slavery as Told by Slaves.* Brookfield, CT: Millbrook Press.

Stowe, C. M. (2000). *The Second Escape of Arthur Cooper.* Tarrytown, NY: Michael Cavendish.

Stowe, H. B. (1852/1996). *Uncle Tom's Cabin.* New York: Modern Library.

Thomas, J. C. (2000). *Hush Songs: African American Lullabies.* Illustrated by B. Joysmith. NY: Hyperion Books.

Thomas, V. M. (1997). *Lest We Forget: The Passage from Africa to Slavery and Emancipation.* NY: Crown.

Williams, S. A. (1992). *Working Cotton.* Illustrated by C. Bayard. New York: Harcourt Brace.

Wilson, S. G. (1999). *African American Quilting: The Warmth of Tradition.* NY: Rosen Publishing Group.

Woodruff, E. (1998). *Dear Austin: Letters from the Underground Railroad.* NY: Alfred A. Knopf.

Recordings for the Homes Unit

Assorted Recording Artists. (1999). *World Playground: A Musical Adventure for Kids.* NY: Putumayo.

Recordings for the Community Culture Unit

Sykes, J. (1998). *Jubilant.* NY: Sony Music Entertainment, Inc.

References

Adler, S. (2000). Honoring the Past, Building the Future. (Keynote Address at the 2000 Annual Conference of the National Council for the Social Studies). San Antonio, TX.

Banks, J. A. (2000). Balancing unity and diversity. Paper presented at the 2000 Annual Conference of the National Council for the Social Studies. San Antonio, TX.

Banks, J. A. (1987). The Social Studies, ethnic diversity, and social change. *The Elementary School Journal, 87*(5), 531–543.

Brophy, J. (2000). Understanding cultural universals. Paper presented at the 2000 Annual Conference of the National Council for the Social Studies. San Antonio, TX.

Dunn., M. A. (2000). Closing the book on Social Studies: Four classroom teachers go beyond the textbook. *The Social Studies, 91*(3), 132-137.

George, M. A., & Stix, A. (2000). Using multilevel young adult literature in middle school American Studies. *The Social Studies, 91*(1), 25–31.

Houser, N. O. (1999) Critical literature for the Social Studies. *Social Education, 63*(4), 212–215.

Huck, C. S., Hepler, S., Hickman, J., & Kiefer, B. Z. (2001). *Children's Literature in the Elementary School* (7th ed.). Boston: McGraw-Hill.

Levstik, L. S., & Barton, K. C. (2001). *Doing History.* Mahwah, NJ: Lawrence Erlbaum Associates Publishers.

Loewen, J. W. (1994). *Lies My Teacher Told Me.* NY: Touchstone: Simon & Schuster.

Maxim, G. W. (1999). *Social Studies and the Elementary School Child.* Upper Saddle River, NJ: Prentice-Hall Inc.

National Council for the Social Studies. (1994). *Expectations of Excellence: Curriculum Standards for the Social Studies.* Washington, DC: National Council for the Social Studies.

Pappas, C. C., Kiefer, B. Z., & Levstik, L. S. (1999). *An Integrated Language Perspective in the Elementary School.* NY: Longman.

Peterson, R., & Eeds, M. (1990). *Grand Conversations: Literature Groups in Action.* NY: Scholastic Inc.

Stix, A. (2000). Mixing it up: A multilevel book room and flexible literature circles. *Social Education, 64*(4), 218–220.

Wasta, S., & Lott, C. C. (2000). Civil War stories: An integrated approach to developing perspective. *The Social Studies, 91*(2), 62–69.

Weinberg, S. (1999). Historical thinking and other unnatural acts. *Phi Delta Kappan, 80*(7), 488–499.

Zarillo, J. J. (2000). *Teaching Elementary Social Studies.* Upper Saddle River, NJ: Prentice-Hall.

APPENDIX

National Standards for the Elementary Classroom

National Standards for Arts Education
- *Dance*
- *Music*
- *Theater*
- *Visual Arts*

National Standards for the English Language Arts

National Standards for School Mathematics
- *Number and Operations*
- *Algebra*
- *Geometry*
- *Measurement*
- *Data Analysis and Probability*
- *Problem Solving*
- *Reasoning and Proof*
- *Communication*
- *Connections*
- *Representation*

National Science Education Standards
- *Content Standard: K-12*
- *Science Content Standards: K-4*
- *Science Content Standards: 5-8*

National Standards for the Social Studies

Each of the professional organizations has published standards for what students are expected to know and be able to do in their respective disciplines. Provided here are the National Standards for children in the elementary grades.

NATIONAL STANDARDS FOR ARTS EDUCATION

The Consortium of National Arts Education Associations. (1994). *Dance, Music, Theatre, Visual Arts: What Every Young American Should Know and Be Able to Do in the Arts. The National Standards for Arts Education.* Reston, VA: Music Educators National Conference.

Dance

1. Content Standard: Identifying and demonstrating movement elements and skills in performing dance

2. Content Standard: Understanding choreographic principles, processes, and structures

3. Content Standard: Understanding dance as a way to create and communicate meaning

4. Content Standard: Applying and demonstrating critical and creative thinking skills in dance

5. Content Standard: Demonstrating and understanding dance in various cultures and historical periods

6. Content Standard: Making connections between dance and healthful living

7. Content Standard: Making connections between dance and other disciplines

Music

1. Content Standard: Singing, alone and with others, a varied repertoire of music

2. Content Standard: Performing on instruments, alone and with others, a varied repertoire of music

3. Content Standard: Improvising melodies, variations, and accompaniments

4. Content Standard: Composing and arranging music within specified guidelines

5. Content Standard: Reading and notating music

6. Content Standard: Listening to, analyzing, and describing music

7. Content Standard: Evaluating music and music performances

8. Content Standard: Understanding relationships between music, the other arts, and disciplines outside the arts

9. Content Standard: Understanding music in relation to history and culture

Theater

1. Content Standard: Script writing by the creation of improvisations and scripted scenes based on personal experience and heritage, imagination, literature, and history

2. Content Standard: Acting by developing basic acting skills to portray characters who interact in improvised and scripted scenes

3. Content Standard: Designing by developing environments for improvised and scripted scenes

4. Content Standard: Directing by organizing rehearsals for improvised and scripted scenes

5. Content Standard: Researching by using cultural and historical information to support improvised and scripted scenes

6. Content Standard: Comparing and incorporating art forms by analyzing methods of presentation and audience response for theater, dramatic media (such as film, television, and electronic media), and other art forms

7. Content Standard: Analyzing, evaluating, and constructing meanings from improvised and scripted scenes and from theater, film, television, and electronic media productions

8. Content Standard: Understanding context by analyzing the role of theater, film, television, and electronic media in the community and in other cultures

Visual Arts

1. Content Standard: Understanding and applying media, techniques, and processes

2. Content Standard: Using knowledge of structures and functions

3. Content Standard: Choosing and evaluating a range of subject matter, symbols, and ideas

4. Content Standard: Understanding the visual arts in relation to history and cultures

5. Content Standard: Reflecting upon and assessing the characteristics and merits of their work and the work of others

6. Content Standard: Making connections between visual arts and other disciplines

From *National Standards for Arts Education*, published by Music Educators National Conference (MENC). Copyright © 1994 by MENC. Used by permission. The complete National Arts Standards and additional materials relating to the Standards are available from MENC—The Ntaional Association for Music Education, 1806 Robert Fulton Drive, Reston, VA 20191 (telephone 800/336-3768).

NATIONAL STANDARDS FOR THE ENGLISH LANGUAGE ARTS

The National Council of Teachers of English and The International Reading Association. (1996). *Standards for the English Language Arts*. Urbana, IL: NCTE.

1. Students read a wide range of print and nonprint texts to build an understanding of texts, of themselves, and of the cultures of the United States and the world; to acquire new information; to respond to the needs and demands of society and the workplace; and for personal fulfillment. Among these texts are fiction and nonfiction, classic and/or contemporary works.

2. Students read a wide range of literature from many periods in many genres to build an understanding of the many dimensions (e.g., philosophical, ethical, aesthetic) of human experience.

3. Students apply a wide range of strategies to comprehend, interpret, evaluate, and appreciate texts. They draw on their prior experience, their interactions with other readers and writers, their knowledge of word meaning and of other texts, their word identification strategies, and their understanding of textual features (e.g., sound-letter correspondence, sentence structure, context, graphics).

4. Students adjust their use of spoken, written, and visual language (e.g., conventions, style, vocabulary) to communicate effectively with a variety of audiences and for different purposes.

5. Students employ a wide range of strategies as they write and use different writing process elements appropriately to communicate with different audiences for a variety of purposes.

6. Students apply knowledge of language structure, language conventions (e.g., spelling and punctuation), media techniques, figurative language, and genre to create, critique, and discuss print and nonprint texts.

7. Students conduct research on issues and interests by generating ideas and questions, and by posing problems. They gather, evaluate, and synthesize data from a variety of sources (e.g., print and nonprint texts, artifacts, people) to communicate their discoveries in ways that suit their purpose and audience.

8. Students use a variety of technological and informational resources (e.g., libraries, databases, computer networks, video) to gather and synthesize information and to create and communicate knowledge.

9. Students develop an understanding of and respect for diversity in language use, patterns,

and dialects across cultures, ethnic groups, geographic regions, and social roles.

10. Students whose first language is not English make use of their first language to develop competency in the English language arts and to develop understanding of content across the curriculum.

11. Students participate as knowledgeable, reflective, creative, and critical members of a variety of literacy communities.

12. Students use spoken, written, and visual language to accomplish their own purposes (e.g., for learning, enjoyment, persuasion, and the exchange of information).

Reprinted by permission.

NATIONAL STANDARDS FOR SCHOOL MATHEMATICS

The National Council of Teachers of Mathematics. (2000). *Principles and Standards for School Mathematics.* Reston, VA: NCTM Inc.

Number and Operations

Instructional programs from prekindergarten through grade 12 should enable all students to—

- Understand numbers, ways of representing numbers, relationships among numbers, and number systems
- Understand meanings of operations and how they relate to one another
- Compute fluently and make reasonable estimates

Algebra

Instructional programs from prekindergarten through grade 12 should enable all students to—

- Understand patterns, relations, and functions
- Represent and analyze mathematical situations and structures using algebraic symbols

- Use mathematical models to represent and understand quantitative relationships
- Analyze change in various contexts

Geometry

Instructional programs from prekindergarten through grade 12 should enable all students to—

- Analyze characteristics and properties of two- and three-dimensional geometric shapes and develop mathematical arguments about geometric relationships
- Specify locations and describe spatial relationships using coordinate geometry and other representational systems
- Apply transformations and use symmetry to analyze mathematical situations
- Use visualization, spatial reasoning, and geometric modeling to solve problems

Measurement

Instructional programs from prekindergarten through grade 12 should enable all students to—

- Understand measurable attributes of objects and the units, systems, and processes of measurement
- Apply appropriate techniques, tools, and formulas to determine measurements

Data Analysis and Probability

Instructional programs from prekindergarten through grade 12 should enable all students to—

- Formulate questions that can be addressed with data and collect, organize, and display relevant data to answer them
- Select and use appropriate statistical methods to analyze data
- Develop and evaluate inferences and predictions that are based on data
- Understand and apply basic concepts of probability

Problem Solving

Instructional programs from prekindergarten through grade 12 should enable all students to—

- Build new mathematical knowledge through problem solving
- Solve problems that arise in mathematics and in other contexts
- Apply and adapt a variety of appropriate strategies to solve problems
- Monitor and reflect on the process of mathematical problem solving

Reasoning and Proof

Instructional programs from prekindergarten through grade 12 should enable all students to—

- Recognize reasoning and proof as fundamental aspects of mathematics
- Make and investigate mathematical conjectures
- Develop and evaluate mathematical arguments and proofs
- Select and use various types of reasoning and methods of proof

Communication

Instructional programs from prekindergarten through grade 12 should enable all students to—

- Organize and consolidate their mathematical thinking through communication
- Communicate their mathematical thinking coherently and clearly to peers, teachers, and others
- Analyze and evaluate the mathematical thinking and strategies of others
- Use the language of mathematics to express mathematical ideas precisely

Connections

Instructional programs from prekindergarten through grade 12 should enable all students to—

- Recognize and use connections among mathematical ideas
- Understand how mathematical ideas interconnect and build on one another to produce a coherent whole
- Recognize and apply mathematics in contexts outside mathematics

Representation

Instructional programs from prekindergarten through grade 12 should enable all students to—

- Create and use representations to organize, record, and communicate mathematical ideas
- Select, apply, and translate among mathematical representations to solve problems
- Use representations to model and interpret physical, social, and mathematical phenomena

Reprinted by permission.

NATIONAL SCIENCE EDUCATION STANDARDS

The National Research Council. (1996). *National Science Education Standards*. Washington, D.C.: National Academy Press.

Content Standard: K–12

Unifying Concepts and Processes

Standard: As a result of activities in grades K–12, all students should develop understanding and abilities aligned with the following concepts and processes:

Systems, order, and organization

Evidence, models, and explanation

Constancy, change, and measurement

Evolution and equilibrium

Form and function

Science Content Standards: K–4

Science as Inquiry

Content Standard A: As a result of activities in grades K–4, all students should develop:

Abilities necessary to do scientific inquiry

Understanding about scientific inquiry

Physical Science

Content Standard B: As a result of the activities in grades K–4, all students should develop an understanding of

Properties of objects and materials

Position and motion of objects

Light, heat, electricity, and magnetism

Life Science

Content Standard C: As a result of the activities in grades K–4, all students should develop an understanding of

The characteristics of organisms

Life cycles of organisms

Organisms and environments

Earth and Space Science

Content Standard D: As a result of the activities in grades K–4, all students should develop an understanding of

Properties of earth materials

Objects in the sky

Changes in earth and sky

Science and Technology

Content Standard E: As a result of the activities in grades K–4, all students should develop an understanding of

Abilities of technological design

Understanding about science and technology

Abilities to distinguish between natural objects and objects made by humans

Science in Personal and Social Perspectives

Content Standard F: As a result of the activities in grades K–4, all students should develop an understanding of

Personal health

Characteristics and changes in populations

Types of resources

Changes in environments

Science and technology in local challenges

History and Nature of Science

Content Standard G: As a result of the activities in grades K–4, all students should develop an understanding of

Science as a human endeavor

Science Content Standards: 5–8

Science as Inquiry

Content Standard A: As a result of activities in grades 5–8, all students should develop an understanding of

Abilities necessary to do scientific inquiry

Understanding about scientific inquiry

Physical Science

Content Standard B: As a result of activities in grades 5–8, all students should develop an understanding of

Properties and changes of properties in matter

Motions and forces

Transfer of energy

Life Science

Content Standard C: As a result of activities in grades 5–8, all students should develop an understanding of

Structure and function in living systems

Reproduction and heredity

Regulation and behavior

Populations and ecosystems

Diversity and adaptations of organisms

Earth and Space Science

Content Standard D: As a result of activities in grades 5–8, all students should develop an understanding of

Structure of the earth system

Earth's history

Earth in the solar system

Science and Technology

Content Standard E: As a result of activities in grades 5–8, all students should develop an understanding of

Abilities of technological design

Understandings about science and technology

Science in Personal and Social Perspectives

Content Standard F: As a result of activities in grades 5–8, all students should develop an understanding of

Personal health

Populations, resources, and environments

Natural hazards

Risks and benefits

Science and technology in society

History and Nature of Science

Content Standard G: As a result of activities in grades 5–8, all students should develop an understanding of

Science as a human endeavor

Nature of science

History of science

Reprinted by permission.

NATIONAL STANDARDS FOR THE SOCIAL STUDIES

The National Council for the Social Studies. (1994). *Curriculum Standards for Social Studies: Expectations of Excellence.* Washington, DC: NCSS.

I Culture

Social studies programs should include experiences that provide for the study of culture and cultural diversity.

II Time, Continuity, & Change

Social studies programs should include experiences that provide for the study of the ways human beings view themselves in and over time.

III People, Places, & Environments

Social studies programs should include experiences that provide for the study of people, places, and environments.

IV Individual Development & Identity

Social studies programs should include experiences that provide for the study of individual development and identity.

V Individuals, Groups, & Institutions

Social studies programs should include experiences that provide for the study of interactions among individuals, groups, and institutions.

VI Power, Authority, & Governance

Social studies programs should include experiences that provide for the study of how people create and change structures of power, authority, and governance.

VII Production, Distribution, & Consumption

Social studies programs should include experiences that provide for the study of how people organize for the production, distribution, and consumption of goods and services.

VIII Science, Technology, & Society

Social studies programs should include experiences that provide for the study of relationships among science, technology, and society.

IX Global Connections

Social studies programs should include experiences that provide for the study of global connections and interdependence.

X Civic Ideals & Practices

Social studies programs should include experiences that provide for the study of the ideals, principles, and practices of citizenship in a democratic republic.

© National Council for the Social Studies. Reprinted by permission.